T0325905

SOCIAL EXPERIMENTS
WITH INFORMATION TECHNOLOGY
AND
THE CHALLENGES OF INNOVATION

This report, prepared for the Commission of the European Communities, Directorate-General for Science, Research and Development, as part of the FAST Programme (Forecasting and Assessment in the Field of Science and Technology), contains a selection of papers from the EEC Conference on Social Experiments with Information Technology, held in Odense, Denmark, on 13–15 January 1986. The Conference was organized by the Telematics Project, Odense University, Denmark, and the Commission of the European Communities, FAST Programme.

SOCIAL EXPERIMENTS WITH INFORMATION TECHNOLOGY AND THE CHALLENGES OF INNOVATION

A selection of Papers from the EEC Conference on
Social Experiments with Information Technology
in Odense, Denmark, January 13-15, 1986

edited by

Lars Qvortrup, Claire Ancelin,
Jim Frawley, Jill Hartley,
François Pichault and Peter Pop

Organized by

Telematics Project, Odense University, Denmark
and
Commission of the European Communities, FAST Programme

D. Reidel Publishing Company

A MEMBER OF THE KLUWER ACADEMIC PUBLISHERS GROUP

Dordrecht / Boston / Lancaster / Tokyo

for the Commission of the European Communities

Library of Congress Cataloging in Publication Data

Social experiments with information technology and the challenges of innovation.

    1.   Electronic data processing—Social aspects. 2.   Technological innova-
tions—Social aspects. I.   Qvortrup, Lars.
QA76.9.C66S6   1987   303.4'834   87–4831
ISBN 90–277–2488–1

Publication arrangements by
Commission of the European Communities
Directorate-General Telecommunications, Information Industries and Innovation, Luxembourg

EUR 11028 EN

© 1987 ECSC, EEC, EAEC, Brussels and Luxembourg

LEGAL NOTICE
Neither the Commission of the European Communities nor any person acting on behalf of the
Commission is responsible for the use which might be made of the following information.

Published by D. Reidel Publishing Company,
P.O. Box 17, 3300 AA Dordrecht, Holland.

Sold and distributed in the U.S.A. and Canada
by Kluwer Academic Publishers,
101 Philip Drive, Assinippi Park, Norwell, MA 02061, U.S.A.

In all other countries, sold and distributed
by Kluwer Academic Publishers Group,
P.O. Box 322, 3300 AH Dordrecht, Holland.

All Rights Reserved
No part of the material protected by this copyright notice may be reproduced or
utilized in any form or by any means, electronic or mechanical,
including photocopying, recording or by any information storage and
retrieval system, without written permission from the copyright owner.
Printed in The Netherlands

PREFACE

There have been many social experiments with information technology in E.E.C. countries (Prestel, Bildschirmtext, Télétel; broadband network and teleconferencing experiments; experiments with I.T. in agriculture, in rural areas, in healthcare, local communities, social services; etc.). However, these social experiments are not well defined, and they have rarely been synthesized and evaluated.

The aim of the conference on Social Experiments with Information Techno-logy at Odense University January 13-15 1986 was to exchange experience about social experiments, to evaluate the experimental strategies used, and to create a synthesis of the experimental activities in all the E.E.C. member countries.

This book contains a selection of the papers presented at the conference. The conference was organized by the Telematics Project, Odense Universi-ty, with the cooperation of the FAST programme of the European Communi-ties. All the papers are summarized in the introductory article, and they have all been published in the "FAST Occasional Papers" Nos. 83-84, April 1986.

The efforts of a number of people contributed to the success of the conference. I am much obliged to my colleagues in the scientific committee, Claire Ancelin, Nicole Dewandre, Jim Frawley, Antonio Guarnery, Jill Hartley, François Pichault, Heiner Treinen and Peter Vervest, and to my editorial colleagues Claire Ancelin, Jim Frawley, Jill Hartley, François Pichault and Peter Pop. I would also like to express my warm appreciation of the role played by Riccardo Petrella, head of the FAST programme. Finally I am indebted to the authors and participants in the conference, to Philip Edmonds for linguistic corrections, to Odense University's typing office, and to the conference and editorial secretary, Kirsten Albjerg.

Lars Qvortrup

Telematics Project

CONTENTS

INTRODUCTION

Lars Qvortrup

The designation "Social Experiments with Information Technology" originated in France in the early 1980s - as "Expérimentation sociale en télématique" - and at that time it referred to such R. and D. activities as the interactive videotex programmes known as Télétel 3V around Paris, CLAIRE in Grenoble, and TELEM-Nantes, as well as to the integrated broadband network project i Biarritz.

At the present time, however, there is urgent need for a more general normative definition of the concept, since it has been employed differently in the various different E.E.C. countries, and since it has been used to designate activities reflecting very different societal interests:

- grass-roots activities involving new information technology, such as Folkedata in Denmark, and the I.T.E.C.s in England, have on occasion been designated social experiments with I.T.;
- governmental initiatives to develop national I.T. services on the basis of specifically delimited local community pilot projects, such as Bildschirmtext in West Germany, have also on occasion been designated social experiments with information technology;
- private firms' strategies for socially-oriented product refinement and/or marketing, such as value added network services based on videotex, have also on occasion been designated social experiments with information technology.

In the concluding article (pp. 271ff) the following proposed, normative definition is presented (see p. 286). This definition was elaborated after the conference and is not, necessarily, shared by all contributions in this volume:

Social experiments with information technology are specific forms of implementation of I.T.

- in which the primary aim is to establish new forms of social organisation using information technology;
- in which the activities and the resulting socio-technical products can be used as models for a more widespread - though necessarily

contextually-modified - implementation of similar I.T. systems;

- and in which, to this latter end, independent researchers describe and evaluate the implementation process concerned and its results.

Social experiments qualify as "participatory workshops" if all the parties involved in, or influenced by, the development of the I.T. system concerned, participate on an equal footing in decision-making with regard to the social organisation and application of the I.T. system in question. If not - that is if the main subject is a hardware or software manufacturer or a third party - the social experiment may more appropriately be designated a "social laboratory".

EVALUATIVE HYPOTHESES

No general evaluation of social experiments with I.T. has as yet been carried out. Based upon a large number of empirical examples, national overviews from most European countries and the analyses and evaluations presented at the conference in Odense it seems, however, justified to present the following three evaluative hypotheses:

Social experimentation can promote socially beneficial ways of utilizing new information technology

As computers and telecommunications facilities become cheaper, more powerful and more widespread, they will become increasingly integrated within our daily lives, within public and private organisations, and within society in general. This implies - in the words of the conclusory FAST report Eurofutures - that "...it is necessary to recognize that the robustness of societies depends not only on their external competitiveness and techno-industrial strength but also on a high degree of societal flexibility, allowing for continuous social innovations and for the adaptation of technological achievements to social and individual needs." (FAST Report, Eurofutures. The Challenges of Innovation, 1984 p. 70).

The conclusion of Eurofutures is that we must "...ensure that the needs of society and of the individual influence directly, and at an early stage, developments in NIT; only in this way can NIT become an indispensable tool in combatting key problems such as energy provision, employment, social communication, education and training, and societal alienation of minorities, etc." (Ibid. p. 71)

Social experimentation is one such instrument, allowing all parties involved in the development of a specific I.T. system to influence its application and utilisation.

The first evaluative hypothesis is therefore that social experiments are processes in which society as a whole (and not just the hardware, software, or marketing companies directly involved) can promote socially beneficial ways of utilizing new information technology.

> *Social Experimentation is a method for the production of high quality information and communication systems and thus an instrument of competitive relevance*

In the ESPRIT report on the human factors involved in the user-system interface, Bruce Christie states that users of new I.T. "...as well as low cost, high capability, reliability, and so on (...) are increasingly demanding high quality in human factors of the user-system interface. It is in this area more than any other that the competition will be waged. No matter what progress Europe may make on the other aspects of information technology, it will lose the race unless it takes steps to meet the human factors criterion as well." (Bruce Christie, Human Factors of the User-System Interface. A Report on an ESPRIT Preparatory Study. 1985). However, the human factors aspect should not be considered as an individual psychological phenomenon only, i.e. as a relation designating a purely personal relationship between an individual human being and an individual machine. The human factors phenomenon cannot be separated from the social context: it is also a sociological phenomenon.

This fact is of not inconsiderable significance within a European context, for one may deduce from it that the production and refinement of socially advanced information systems in no short measure depend on the prior existence of well-functioning social institutions: for example, you cannot establish an advanced electronic library system without already-existing, socially-advanced public libraries, or without well-educated librarians and users. Which, in turn, means that Europe, with its advanced social institutions, has an unusually good opportunity for the development of socially advanced information systems. To profit from this opportunity Europe must, however, focus more intensively on the human and organisational factors aspect instead of missing out on the potentially substantial returns by limiting its efforts to the production of low cost and high capability hardware.

The second - and primarily economic - evaluative hypothesis is that social experimentation is one method - and a rather promising one - for the production, evaluation, and refinement of socially advanced information systems. As such, social experimentation is an instrument of economic relevance for the European production of information systems. The necessary precondition is, however, that social experimentation strategies and methods are further refined. A considerable amount of research is still needed to understand the interaction between I.T. systems and human organisational factors, and to operationalise this knowledge, such that it may be used to provide guidelines for future social experiments.

> *Social experimentation is an instrument for influencing rather than merely predicting the future*

When evaluating social experiments with I.T. it is important not only to specify what one can do with social experiments, but also to state exactly what they are not so good at.

Social experimentation seems not to be so valuable as an instrument for predicting the future, because the social context within social experiments is normally not representative: service prices are very often low in social experiments; the learning environment and support from public or private institutions tend to be above average; etc. For the same reason most social experiments are not good instruments for traditional technology assessment: their contextual specificity makes it quite difficult to generalise from them about the possible consequences of new I.T. in society.

Social experiments are thus not primarily valuable as forecasting instruments; they are, however, extremely valuable as interventions at the micro-level in the relation between social and technological innovation. Being interventions at the micro-level, their influence on longer-term macro-level social or economic trends depends upon the political support for social experiments and upon the will to transform the results of social experiments into political action. Yet it is important to recognise their indirect influence as well: many social experiments have had a significant agenda setting function, and they have constituted important components in the societal learning process concerning new I.T.

Our third evaluative hypothesis is that social experimentation is not primarily a forecasting instrument. It is rather a way of influencing the future by developing new socially advanced I.T. products and services, by demonstrating new forms of social organisation using I.T., and by catalyzing social awareness and generating societal learning processes.

SUMMARY OF THE PROCEEDINGS OF THE ODENSE CONFERENCE JANUARY 13-15 1986

Speakers at the conference came from all over Western Europe and represented a wide variety of backgrounds and disciplines. Papers were presented by academics, by telecommunications authority representatives, and by experimental practitioners. However, a common feature was that all the papers presented research and experience rooted in the practical problems of conducting social experiments with information technology.

The papers were classified under the following major themes:

1. Social and conceptual aspects of social experiments
2. Social experiments from an applicational point of view
3. Social experiments from a technical point of view
4. Strategical aspects of social experiments
5. Methodological aspects of social experiments
6. General conclusions and recommendations

Social and Conceptual Aspects

The opening lecture was given by Robert Jungk. In all his books the recurrent theme has been: how can we build a better future? From the early book - Die Zukunft hat schon begonnen (1952) - right up to the latest book from 1983, Menschenbeben, the approach has been critical, but at the same time hopeful, and I think that critical enthusiasm has been an important common denominator.

But it is also important to note the practical emphasis in Robert Jungk's books: how do we transform critical enthusiasm into social practice? To answer this question, one has to define the concept of a "better future". According to Robert Jungk it is first and foremost a democratic future: the future belongs to all of us, not only to small oligarchic groups of interested parties or "experts". But it will belong only to those who are continually involved in the process of discussing and inventing valuable human goals, of "inventing" and "producing" desirable futures. A tool for such "social inventions" is - in the words of Robert Jungk - the "future workshop" or the "social experiment", expressions that he coined right back in the 1950s. In his lecture, Robert Jungk presented the concepts of social innovation and social experimentation; he emphasized the difficulties, but also the compelling necessity for social experimentation in a time of social, ecological, and technological crisis; and he exemplified the "new tendency" towards collaboration between progressive movements and public institutions which have both realised the urgent necessity for the democratic and non-violent evolution of our industrial civilisation.

After the opening paper from Robert Jungk, papers were presented by Claire Ancelin (DGT-Spes, France), Alain Briole (IDATE, France), and William H. Melody (ESRC, England).

In France, social experimentation with telematics has been part of the official national policy for five years. But according to Claire Ancelin it has never been satisfactorily defined: the concept has been used to designate a vast number of heterogeneous activities. It has been used for practical tests of new information technologies, and for the development of new services based on older technologies; it has been used to cover activities with quite different actors: national and local public institutions, national and local private organisations, etc; the users involved in all these so-called social experiments have played different roles, from "guinea pigs" to active and authoritative participants, and they have represented different social categories: local citizens, specific user groups, professional users, etc.; furthermore, activities going under the name of social experiments have been organised in different ways, and finally, the objectives of field trials labelled as social experiments have been very heterogeneous: some have tested a specific technology, others have mapped potential needs or have tested a new service. This heterogeneity - which represents the situation in other European countries as well - has led to much confusion both in relation to public policy, and with regard to the exchanging of experiences within national and international research fora, and as far as the pooling of experimental qualifications has been concerned, as well.

But even though social experiments have never been satisfactorily defined in France, they have - according to Alain Briole - been important instruments in the fields of social science and social practice reflecting the complicated interrelationship between technical and social innovation. Although the focus in contemporary France has changed from innovation to acceptability problems, social experiments may still be very fruitful social instruments.

On the other hand, social experimentation is, of course, no "magic formula", and, in his presentation, Bill Melody emphasized the limitations of the concept. In the grander scheme of things, we are all involved in a massive social experiment with new I.T., the laboratory being most of the western world, and in these terms most deliberately arranged social experiments are just "snap-shots" which cannot even give us a reliable picture of, let alone influence longer-term trends.

Social Experiments from an Applicational Point of View

The papers presenting social experiments from an applicational point of view were divided into five sections: social experiments with I.T. in agriculture and rural areas; in health-care; in education; in local communities; and in social services.

Agriculture and Rural Areas

It has often been postulated that I.T. may reduce the negative consequences of geographical distance. This belief has been substantiated by the so-called "tele-houses" in Denmark, Norway and Sweden which were represented by Henning Albrechtsen (manager of the telehouse in Härjedalen - "Härjedalens telestuga" - in Sweden). The "telestuga" - or "Electronic Village Hall", as it is called - in the province of Jämtland was established in September 1985 with the aims of giving the local population access to modern telecommunications and data-processing equipment on a shared basis, thereby liberating local tradesmen and citizens from some of the problems created by the distance to the regional economic centres and cultural and educational centres. The idea has spread: a number of "tele-houses" have been (or are being) established in Sweden, Norway and Denmark.

From Dublin, Joseph Mannion examined the necessity for and scope of electronic technology as a tool for information management in agriculture. Based on a research project designed to identify the information needs of potential users of the Irish videotex service - and on experience of computerised information-systems for agricultural advisory/extension services and farmers - Joseph Mannion emphasized the importance of getting access to, and having the ability to handle, information in modern agriculture. However this is not an easy task, and the challenge for those who service the agricultural industry is to develop and implement ways and means of improving the efficiency of information management. A precondition is, however, that you are able to identify professional needs, to define organisational consequences, to contribute to the collaboration between parties involved, and to offer training courses.

Health-care

From the Microelectronics Resource Centre in Dublin, R.H. Allen presented the problems of the use of I.T. by disabled people. The first, and biggest, problem of designing aid systems for disabled people is the fact that there really is no such person as the "typically" disabled person. Thus there are no standard solutions: I.T. design and application in this field depend on a collaboration between engineers, social and medical scientists, and the users themselves. The extent to which I.T. is used will be dependent on the degree to which the information providers take the problems of disabled people into account in the design of their systems, Allen underlined.

Anker Brink Lund and Jytte Møller Christensen (University of Roskilde, Denmark) exemplified a method involving integrated collaboration in the implementation of I.T. and in the evaluation of the needs for I.T.: the so-called "future workshops". Future workshops have been used in the Danish health-care sector on an experimental level as an approach which provides all the parties involved in, or influenced by, the implementation of new I.T. in the health care sector, practical opportunities for the development of imaginative future scenarios.

Finally, Domenico Ranucci (SIP, Italy) presented a number of telematics projects within the Italian national public-health-service sector: telephone transmission of ECGs and other telecommunications services for remote diagnosis, and experiments and analyses aimed at setting up a national health information-system.

Education

In the field of education (and in health care, too) Oluf Danielsen, Jørgen Andreasen and Flemming Nielsen (Telus Project, Denmark) presented a number of experiments in Denmark using I.T. (databases and computer conference systems) in primary and secondary schools and re-training courses. Tage Høyer Hansen (Copenhagen) in his paper introduced a project in Copenhagen - the Education Centre in Technology and Informatics - providing job-training for young unemployed people in the field of informatics.

Local Communities

There are a number of projects in Europe putting I.T. at the service of specific local communities. At the conference, Mafalda Valentini (ENEA, ITALY) presented the plans for using I.T. in the Prato textile area in Italy.

Prato is a monoproduction community in which I.T. is being introduced on the basis of in-depth analyses of communications and relational networks, and as a result of collective decisions. The paper presented the methods for - and the results of - an analysis of a local community's information and communication needs.

Social Services

From London, Paul Ticher gave an overview of the increasing use of computers in voluntary organisations. He emphasized the problems of the technology-led implementation of new I.T.; but he also exemplified the relevance of effective computing power for groups of people organised in the voluntary sector. Gareth Morgan, National Association of Citizens' Advice Bureaux, dealt with the computing of welfare benefits in the U.K. The first - usable - benefits calculation systems on computer began in 1975, and today a considerable number of computer-based welfare calculation and advisory systems are being used in England. Finally, in this section, David Kimpton presented the computer workshop run by the Greater London Council's Central Computer Services, CCS. The computer workshop is the focal point where the knowledge, and experience, of the CCS is intended to meet the needs of ordinary Londoners; its aim is to help voluntary groups in London to function more effectively with the aid of computer techniques and equipment. David Kimpton especially emphasized a programme for disabled people and a welfare benefits programme.

Social Experiments from a Technical Point of View

One of the first I.T. systems which gave rise to social experiments with I.T. was interactive videotex, and in the section on social experiments from a technical point of view experiences from the UK, France, West Germany and Denmark were presented. The section also included papers on computer-conferencing experiments in France and West-Germany and presentations of broadband cable experiments in the Netherlands and in France.

Interactive Videotex

In the UK, British Telecom originally conceived of Prestel, the UK's public videotex service, as a means of encouraging increased residential use of the telephone network at off-peak times. In practice, however, by the beginning of 1982 (three years after the launching of Prestel) only approximately 2,000 out of the 15,000 registered sets were thought to be in private households. One of the consequences was that the Club 403 research project was set up to examine the use of videotex on the residential market. Club 403 was based in Birmingham, and since 1982 it has had a total permanent membership of 1267 households. These households have been offered tele-shopping, educational services, home-booking, a children's database, home-banking, and tele-betting. In his paper, Michel E. Olszewski, RBL (Research International) outlined the techniques used in the research project and some of its major findings.

In France, the national videotex system, <u>Télétel</u>, was launched in 1982. Where in the U.K. an ordinary television set is used as the videotex terminal, in France a small and cheap "Minitel" terminal has been marketed. In September 1985 the number of Minitel terminals exceeded one million, and more than 1500 services were offered (including the "Electronic Directory"). A large number of experiments have been conducted with the general public, and in her paper Claire Ancelin covered the experiments conducted in Vélizy, Strasbourg, Nantes, and Grenoble. The experiment in Strasbourg (in which a daily newspaper's messaging system was "pirated" by citizens in Strasbourg) was reviewed by Raymond-Stone Iwaasa, and the Télétel 3V experiment was presented in the paper by Alain Magnier.

What has been learned from the French videotex experiments? Five years ago expectations were certainly much higher than today: but even though I.T. - and social experiments with I.T. - isn't a magic tool, social experiments with videotex in France have been valuable in the following ways:
- they have stimulated public awareness of I.T;
- they have separated potentially successful service suppliers (those whose use of computerised data processing represents a logical part of their activities) from potentially unsuccessful service suppliers;

- they have elucidated the importance of relevant information (rather than "smart" software etc.) for the success of a videotex service;
- and they have emphasized that the choice of software should depend on the users concerned rather than on abstract considerations as regards keyword vs. tree search structures, etc.

The German version of videotex is called Bildschirmtext. In 1980 two large field experiments were started in Berlin and in Düsseldorf, and since 1984 Bildschirmtext has been introduced step by step in different areas of the Federal Republic of Germany. Peter Gräf (Institut für Wirtschaftsgeographie, Universität München) in his paper analysed the implementation of Bildschirmtext as a socio-geographical issue, and he maintained that the very low dissemination of Bildschirmtext can partly be explained by a failure to take sufficient account of the influence of regional differences; in effect, it has arisen from an unreasoned transfer of research results from the field experiments in Berlin and Düsseldorf. In general, public awareness and acceptance of Bildschirmtext has been low, and, after two years of experience of its general implementation, the current trend is towards an increasing specialisation of Bildschirmtext for business-applications, while the penetration of Bildschirmtext among private subscribers is very low.

The same lesson has been learned in Denmark. The Danish videotex system, Teledata, was reported on by Sigurd Bennike (Consulta, Denmark). He enumerated a number of "internal conflicts" in the interactive videotex system, pointing to the fact that videotex is mostly aimed at professional users with well-defined information demands. Consequently, Teledata will probably not be introduced into private households.

Computer Conference Systems

In the papers by Gaëtan Cambra and Michael Pieper the potentialities of computer conference systems were discussed. In his paper, Gaëtan Cambra (TEN, Paris) presented the capabilities of the French teleconference system TCAO, "téléconférence assistée par ordinateur" (computer-assisted teleconferencing), and he gave an account of the promising results of experiments with TCAO. A profitable dialogue between users and system suppliers has been established allowing for continuous improvements of the system, and a new professional role - the management of a computer-assisted conference system - has been defined. On the assumption that further improvements will be made (integration of different networks, an improved "SOS service" etc.), Gaëtan Cambra foresees that TCAO will become an important tool in the production and circulation of information at a national and a European level as well.

Michael Pieper (Gesellschaft für Mathematik und Datenverarbeitung, FRG) was more sceptical. In this paper, the gap between intention and reality in computer-conferencing was analysed. Originally, computer-conferencing was intended to assist the consensus-oriented discussion of complex problems over a long distance, but, in general, the reality has been disappointing. The reason is that the complex role-playing abilities in natural conversation processes are still restricted in computer-based communications systems.

This fact points to a far more basic and serious dilemma for orgware production. According to Michael Pieper, the capability of social experiments to provide tools for orgware improvements in applied Information Technology seems to be threatened by deeply grounded, and up till now insurmountable incompatibilities between technological and sociological paradigms of organised problem-solving.

Broadband Cable

Finally, Nick Jankowski and Frank Olderaan (Catholic University, Nijmegen, the Netherlands) presented the plans for a two-way broadband cable experiment in Zaltbommel in the Netherlands, and Bernard Marquet (CCETT, France) gave a summary of a French experiment with a télé-vidéothèque. The difficulties of organising and evaluating a field trial within a social and political context which necessitates recurrent changes in the experiment itself is exemplified by the Zaltbommel case. While in France the limitations of a so-called "democratic" choice of programmes (where viewers registered their wishes for the evening's télé-vidéothèque programmes, and the resulting programme was then determined by the demands of the majority) clearly emerged. Bernard Marquet emphasised that large-scale social experimentation is still needed (and is on its way in Biarritz and

Montpellier) in order to create a model in which viewers can satisfactorily participate in the choice of programmes.

Strategical Aspects of Social Experiments

Based upon experience from field trials with telematics in Norway and in other countries, Kjell Olav Mathisen from the Norwegian Telecommunications Administration's Research Establishment posed the question of what can be gained from conducting field trials. Mathisen's answer is that field trials will not give us hard facts about future markets, social effects, or organisational forms. According to Mathisen a field trial (or social experiment) is an active venture that contributes to shaping - or influencing the shape of - the future rather than predicting it. Its strength is to demonstrate the new, thereby putting it on the public agenda and making the users participate in the process of development.

I think that it is fair to say that Ole Nymann and Malthe Jacobsen (from the Danish PTT and from Mentor Informatik) share Mathisen's point of view. But in some respects they go the whole hog in operationalising this philosophy. According to Nymann and Jacobsen, social experiments are tools for all parties interested in the development of advanced I.T. products. The reason is that what once were specific potential user groups, with well-defined and clearly articulated information demands, have been largely superseded by broader and less specific groups of potential users. Consequently, the product-developer today has to find new ways; and one of these is to establish social environments in which the non-professional user is allowed to participate in the creative process of defining new applications. The emphasis within product development moves from the designer's laboratory into the "real world laboratory", formed by the social experiment in which all parties involved participate on an equal footing in decision-making with regard to the social organisation and application of the I.T. system in question. The Danish social experiment INFAA (sometimes called a "social hot-house" for I.T. development) is summarised as an illustration of the ideas expressed by Nymann and Jacobsen.

Similar considerations with regard to the field of I.T. implementation in an office environment were presented by Norbert Alter from DGT/SPES in

Paris. He emphasised that one should not confuse social experimentation with I.T. as a scientific or socio-technical activity with the process of innovation within the specific enterprise. Still, the accumulation of organisational experience in the continuous renewal and development of professional organisations (a process of "permanent re-organisation") can be regarded as an experimental system in itself, and Norbert Alter finished his paper by considering the possibilities of applying experimental methods to the renewal and development of professional organisations.

Also in this session, Hans Mammen, Gitte Marling, and Kresten Storgaard (FIL, Denmark) presented strategies for research applied to social experiments, and Jorge Gaspar (Portugal), Chris Jensen-Butler and Svend Erik Jeppesen (Aarhus University, Denmark) outlined a proposal for the study of the relationship between improvements in telecommunications and regional development in Portugal. Hans Mammen (et al.) gave an account of the methodological and strategical findings of the Danish group of researchers concerned with I.T. in local communities, FIL. And Jorge Gaspar (et al.) discussed the relationship between telecommunications improvements and regional development, both considering the specific Portuguese situation and presenting a theoretical framework for such socio-geographical studies.

Methodological Aspects of Social Experiments

As a social researcher, how do you evaluate social experiments with information technology? This question was answered by Harry Bouwman and George Muskens (from the University of Amsterdam and IVA, Tilburg University, the Netherlands) who considered the role and the methods of a researcher involved in evaluating a specific social experiment. And it was answered by Sylvie Craipeau and Francis Kretz (IDATE and CCETT, France) who evaluated the whole idea of social experimentation in the field of information technology, on the basis of the French experience.

Harry Bouwman's and George Muskens' point of departure for analysing the role and methods of evaluative research related to social experimentation was the Ditzitel experiment: Ditzitel is a hybrid viewdata system using telephone lines to call up information, and a cable network to provide the information. Ditzitel is intended to be offered on Amsterdam's local cable network with 300,000 subscribers.

Most institutions involved in new media experiments are accustomed to making decisions on the basis of traditional market research. In the case of media experiments, or of the introduction of new media, or new services, another approach seems - according to Bouwman and Muskens - to be more relevant. Bouwman and Muskens argue that a common rudimentary feature in such experiments is that an identifiable actor tries to change some audience's behaviour by manipulation or supply factors; which is why media experiments of this kind resemble scientific experiments in which stimulated groups are supposed to change behaviour compared to non-stimulated or control groups. Therefore, Bouwman and Muskens conclude, paradigms from such experimental research might appropriately be applied to media and information technology experiments. In their paper, Bouwman and Muskens present one such paradigm from experimental research; and they elaborate a theory about the specific functions of the Ditzitel medium (and of all interactive media); a theory with particular relevance to information-seeking behaviour.

The paper by Craipeau and Kretz sets out to analyse the methods and the structural parameters in social experiments conducted in France in the field of communications services, with specific reference, however, to experiments with public services used in residential areas or in public places, while experiments with institutional or professional communications services are not considered. The paper's starting point comprises three studies that were carried out at IDATE in 1982-1984. More generally, its empirical basis includes experiments in France which were initiated in 1980-82 (the télétel network accessed from Minitel terminals, offering the electronic directory; the experiments in Vélizy, Versailles and Val de Bievre with advanced, interactive videotex services; and other, local experiments, including CLAIRE, TELEM-Nantes and Gretel), and which were finalised and/or transformed into commercial or normal public service in 1983-85. The time of writing of this paper is therefore eminently suitable for an overall evaluation of the whole idea of social experimentation, such as the concept has been realised in France.

The paper starts with some conceptual considerations; it then presents a number of specific examples of social experiments in France; and it ends up with the presentation of the general structure of social experiments. The final - and major - part of this contribution is, however, a consideration of practical problems in the field of social experimentation.

General Conclusions and Recommendations

In the concluding round of papers, Peter Pop (Rotterdam School of Management), François Pichault (Université de Liège), and Jill Hartley (PREST, University of Manchester), gave a general evaluation of social experiments with information technology from the different points of view of technicians, initiators, and end-users respectively, and Lars Qvortrup (Telematic Project, Odense University) presented some general conclusions and recommendations for future initiatives. Finally, Riccardo Petrella (head of the FAST programme) rounded off the proceedings by specifying the role of social experiments in relation to a broader European context of social and technological innovation.

The Technological Point of View

From a technological point of view it is relevant to choose the design of information-processing systems as a starting point for the evaluation of social experiments. According to Peter Pop the biggest problem in this design process seems to be the problem of communication between social and technical science. Social scientists analyse data-structures and process-flows and define relevant applications, with the results of their analytical activity becoming inputs for the engineers' functional specification of the system to be designed. The problem is that the two system-analytical approaches are very different as to the theories and methods they apply. Consequently, Peter Pop suggests that the interface between the social and technical aspects of information-systems design should be subject to systematic research, since this interface problem is at the core of any orgware design project. Such research is a precondition for the design of socially-advanced information systems in general and for the successful conduct of social experiments in particular.

Furthermore, it is suggested that - in order to emphasize the social aspect of social experiments - only fully reliable technological products should be used; and that one should consider the establishment of a "service compatibility" standard in order to ensure that new I.T. systems providing a particular service are compatible with other infrastructural I.T. systems already in use, providing other kinds of services.

The Initiators' Point of View

From the initiators' point of view the question of public intervention is important. At the present time one can find powerful national telecommunications administrations conducting social experiments (videotex experiments, broadband network experiments, etc.). But Francois Pichault emphasizes that private actors (cable-TV companies, newspaper-organisations, banks, etc.) play a still more important role in the experimental field (videotex applications, telebanking, etc.).

Social experiments are increasingly aimed at professional users, and, in effect, at very limited categories of users. If one wants to retain the primary aim of socially-beneficial and advanced social experiments (and there may even be very sound economic reasons for doing so), the intervention of public authorities, encouraging social initiatives deliberately oriented towards social aims, will require serious reconsideration. Only in this way will public authorities be enabled to define more specific goals for their intervention in this field.

The Role of End-Users

According to Jill Hartley, it is appropriate to consider social experimentation as a mutual learning-process if one wants to evaluate the role of end-users.

It would be misguided to view technological developments as the one and only determinant of new forms of social and economic organisation and behaviour. Rather there is a complex interaction between technological innovation and the response of individual and collective users of the technology. Thus the key to the diffusion process is the mutual learning-process involving supplier and user and their consequent mutual adaptation. The responses of the users provide indications for the development of new technological applications; but these new applications in turn often modify the users' behaviour, thus giving rise to what might aptly be termed "social inventions". In the final instance, the success of technological innovations depends on some form of "social experimentation". Thus it is important to recognise, to encourage, and to promote the crucial role of the end-users, be it only as relatively passive providers of feedback, or, at the other end of the scale, as directly and actively contributing innovators.

Jill Hartley's conclusion is that, although governmental attitudes, particularly in France, are said to reflect a trend towards the rejection of social experimentation or at least a disinclination to commit public funds to these ventures, this is not really a valuable or useful description of ongoing I.T. activities at all levels, even though in purely quantitative terms experimentation may generally be said to be at risk. Firstly, most implementation processes (as has already been emphasized) involve a considerable amount of social and organisational innovation and thus contain crucial elements of learning, even though the implementation activity may not be _perceived_ as one of "experimentation". Secondly, there is evidence of an increasing recognition of the importance of the end-user link and, consequently, of the importance of encouraging the mutual learning process provoked by technological innovations which benefits the end-users as well as improving the quality of information systems. Awareness programmes, I.T. in education, and publicly-funded open-access centres are all examples of this phenomenon. Thirdly, there appears to have been a growth in the number of projects where end-users define for themselves the uses to which I.T. could be put, i.e. where they are recognised as innovators. And finally, the more specific targetting of end-users and the growing range of initiators of social experiments has, in some cases, drawn end-users and initiators together, such that the end-users are also the initiators. In these cases the needs of the end-user can be expected to be paramount.

General Conclusions and Recommendations for Future Initiatives

Finally, a set of general conclusions and recommendations including a proposed normative definition of social experiments with information technology was summarised by Lars Qvortrup. Based upon the above-mentioned evaluative hypothesis that <u>social experiments are socially relevant</u> because social experiments are processes in which society as a whole (and not just the companies directly involved) can promote socially-beneficial ways of utilizing new information technology, and that <u>social experiments are economically relevant</u> because they are rather promising instruments for the production, evaluation, and refinement of socially-advanced information systems, the concluding paper ends up by presenting a number of recommendations for action, which are summarised below:

Social experiments should be organised as mutual learning processes in which the end-users can have an influence on the organisation of new information systems, and in which a close collaboration between social and technological expertise is established.

Such social experiments should be given public support - financial and otherwise - and should be integrated into general public planning concerning the adoption of new information technology.

A precondition for the European production of socially-advanced information systems is that current social experimentation strategies and methods are further refined. A considerable amount of research is still needed to understand the interaction between I.T. systems and human and organisational factors, and to operationalise this knowledge, such that it may be used to provide guidelines for future social experiments. The concept of "orgware architecture" is presented to designate this area of pure and applied research, and it is recommended that a permanent network be established, permitting researchers in Europe to further elaborate the concept of orgware architecture, and to evaluate its social and economic relevance.

As the last speaker, Riccardo Petrella (head of the FAST programme) rounded off the proceedings by specifying the role of social experiments in relation to a broader European context of social and technological innovation.

Riccardo Petrella presented three major contextual trends. Firstly he mentioned the structural change from the public to the private sphere. Secondly, he emphasized the importance of end-users in the innovation process; it is too narrow-minded to consider only scientific laboratories and private factories as innovators, because every day the end-user expresses his demands, specifies his new needs, and - in his priorities and his social practice - evaluates new technology. Here lies an important innovative resource. Thirdly, he pointed out the problem of increasing social disparity and inequality, a tendency which is often reinforced by new I.T. services.

The first tendency may modify the institutional background of future social experiments. The second elucidates the function of social experiments: to give end-users a tool for influencing the innovation process and for utilizing this social resource. And the third specifies one of the important objects of social experiments: to influence the development of new information technology making it more user-friendly and better adapted to social institutions, thus counteracting the tendency towards increasing social inequality.

PART I: CONCEPT AND HISTORY

Robert Jungk is the modern inventor of "Social Experiments" and "Future Workshops", concepts that he coined thirty years ago. In his opening paper Robert Jungk evaluates the necessity for, and the difficulties of, social innovation and experimentation in our present critical age. Then, Claire Ancelin and Alain Briole analyse the definition and the history of social experiments with I.T., which have been an important part of national technology policy in France since 1980. Both papers are critical: social experiments have never been satisfactorily defined; and their importance has certainly been overestimated. Still, they have been fruitful instruments for social intervention in the interrelationship between technical and social innovation.

INTRODUCTION TO ROBERT JUNGK, "SOCIAL INNOVATIONS AND EXPERIMENTS AT A CRITICAL TIME".

Lars Qvortrup, Telematics Project, Odense University, Denmark.

Our modern societies strive for the greatest possible mastery over physical nature; their declared goals are to ensure that their citizens obtain the highest possible prosperity.

Mastery over ourselves and over our fellow human beings is, however, the necessary precondition for the achievement of these goals. For it takes discipline to conquer physical nature, and to ensure steadily growing economic returns. Each and every one of us must exert ourselves to the full, must restrain our own unbridled natures; and the various institutions of our societies must be allowed to function without unnecessary disturbance. A combination of technological engineering and so-called "human engineering" - in accordance with the strict observance of the concept of rationality, motivated by a view to profit-maximization, and guaranteed by a safety-net comprising a necessary minimum of social institutions - is enabling our societies to achieve these goals.

Yet the result is that both physical nature, and anarchic or socially moral individuals alike, are under threat; in striving to serve their citizens, our modern societies not only revoke their freedom, but also destroy their very means of subsistence, their natural environment. The pursuit of omnipotence results in unmitigated impotence.

The exposition above is hardly new, of course, but what is so characteristic of Robert Jungk is that he first confronted us with it right back in 1952, in his well-documented and deservedly famous report from the U.S.A.

Die Zukunft hat schon begonnen his book was called, with the subtitle Amerikas Allmacht und Ohnmacht. It was clearly a statement addressed to the whole world: for the future which the Americans had already embarked upon was soon to become common property all over the globe. And Jungk's method was documental: the dialectic between the enslavement of nature and the enslavement of ourselves, between pulverizing the atom and pulverizing our own civilizations, was no longer an abstract admonition couched in critical theory, but an empirical reality. The future had already begun.

Since then, others have been content to repeat Jungk's exposition with a sometimes almost masochistic attention to detail, or a perverse enjoyment of the beauty of the dialectical paradox. But Robert Jungk himself immediately addressed his attention to the next, and most urgent question: by what means could their citizens change the course of our societies?

Traditional means were clearly ineffectual. Free-market liberalism might - at least in theory - conserve the freedom of the individual; but it could do nothing to prevent environmental destruction. Totalitarianism (in the guise of the socialist state, for instance) might - again at least theoretically - conserve the environment, through carefully balanced and coordinated production targets; but only at the price of the betrayal of individual freedom.

So new methods had to be invented to change our societies' fatal course towards environmental annihilation, without sacrificing the freedom of the individual. And, from the 1950s onwards, Robert Jungk has been "a global social inventor", attempting to discover these so urgently required alternative methods - as chairman of the "mankind 2000" project (since 1974), as a member of the "Foundation pour l'invention sociale" (since 1975), and, above all, as a participant in innumerable "future workshops", the very special kinds of research activity which Jungk himself pioneered in Vienna in the late 'fifties.

The future workshop is essentially a forum in which citizens can together draft desirable future scenarios - (irrespective of how impossible they may at first sight appear) - and subsequently realistically examine the possibilities for realizing such drafts. One of the most important aims of the work done in future workshops is to involve every interested party in decision-making processes - processes which are normally the exclusive province of politicians, experts and professional planners. Local or regional problems most frequently occasion future workshops, but the workshop participants soon discover that their own local or provincial problems are every bit as much conditioned by more comprehensive national or international circumstances; circumstances which they are thus (perhaps for the first time in their lives) strongly motivated to challenge, both critically and constructively.

In his book, Zukunftswerkstätten, Wege zur Wiederbelebung der Demokratie, which Robert Jungk wrote in 1981 together with Norbert R. Müllert, the research process in a typical future workshop is divided up into four distinct stages, or phases: a preparatory phase, and three subsequent phases. The preparatory phase involves the selection and public announcement of the specific theme for the future workshop, and includes practical preparations, such as the provision of conference-rooms, equipment, and relevant literature. The actual workshop itself starts with a critical phase, in which participants express and attempt to structure their dissatisfaction, criticisms and negative experiences with regard to the workshop's chosen theme. This is followed by an imaginative phase, in which the criticisms formulated in the first phase are countered by positive desires, scenarios, and alternative ideas, which, again, are structured and canalized into proposed solutions and amendments. Finally, in the realizational phase, the workshop participants return to the current state of affairs pertaining in their societies, with all their existing power-constellations, laws and regulations. Various possibilities are tried out for realizing the proposals which emerged from the imaginative phase, obstacles are pinpointed, realistic strategies are worked out, appropriate activities and projects are undertaken.

The future workshop is, however, much more than a particular kind of seminar or pedagogical strategy, though as such it is singularly inspiring. The vision at the heart of the future workshop is one in which decision-making is fundamentally democratized, in which the populations of our modern societies participate fully and on an equal footing at all levels of socio-political planning. And, in these terms, the concept of the future workshop is above all a concrete manifestation of a political and moral commitment which the alarmingly critical historical development of modern society - pointed out by Jungk as early as 1952 - has rendered a necessity.

The situation today is hardly less critical. Yet it is some consolation that in 1983 - thirty years after his detailed account of the fatally self-destructive course of modern society - Robert Jungk could publish a no-less-detailed account of ubiquitous popular resistance to this destructive tendency.

Menschenbeben was the title of the book this time, and its subtitle was Der Aufstand gegen das Unerträgliche. A "human earthquake" could be detected all over the planet, Jungk maintained - peace movements and other environmental movements, civil rights movements and future workshops were multiplying and prospering everywhere. "Wenn ich bei allem Wissen um den Ernst der Weltlage trotzdem eine Wendung zum Besseren für möglich halte", he concluded, "Dann grundet sich diese Hoffnung vor allem auf solche Vorgänge menschlicher Veränderung, die mehr und mehr Erschütterte zu Erschütteren, Enttäuschte zu Entwerfern machen".

Bibliographical note:

This introduction is based on a reading of the following (cursory) selection of Robert Jungk's complete works:

Robert Jungk: Die Zukunft hat schon begonnen. Amerikas Allmacht und Ohnmacht. Stuttgart-Hamburg 1952.
Robert Jungk: Heller als tausend Sonnen. 1956.
Robert Jungk: Strahlen aus der Asche. 1959.
Robert Jungk: Der Jahrtausendmensch. Bericht aus den Werkstätten der neuen Gesellschaft. München et al 1973.
Robert Jungk: Der Atom-Staat. München 1977.
Robert Jungk und Norbert R. Müllert: Zukunftswerkstätten, Wege zur Wiederbelebung der Demokratie. Hamburg 1981.
Robert Jungk: Menschenbeben. Der Aufstand gegen das Unerträgliche. München 1983.

In addition to these (and his many other) inspiring works, Robert Jungk has written an abundance of articles on related topics. With particular reference to his future workshop concept, the following should be consulted:

Robert Jungk: "Plädoyer für die soziale Phantasie", in Modelle für eine neue Welt, München 1963.
Robert Jungk: "Imagination and the Future", in International Social Science Journal, no. 4 1969.
Robert Jungk: "Einige Erfahrungen mit Zukunftswerkstätten", in Analysen

und Prognosen no. 25, Berlin 1973.

Robert Jungk: "Die Entwicklung sozialer Phantasie als Aufgabe der Zukunftsforschung", in D. Pforte/Schwencke: Ansichten einer künftigen Futurologie. München 1973.

Robert Jungk: "Statt auf den grossen Tag zu warten...", in Kursbuch 53. Berlin 1978.

SOCIAL INNOVATIONS AND EXPERIMENTS AT A CRITICAL TIME

Robert Jungk

1.

At this conference on possible and desirable social innovations and experiments within the framework of our burgeoning Information Societies, I have been given the chance to talk about something which has long been very dear to my heart: namely the compelling necessity for imaginatively conceived and practically tested experimentation throughout all the multifarious spheres of human social interaction.

Let me start by calling your attention to my own particular physical situation at the outset of this talk. Here am I - the lecturer - standing behind a lectern, or sitting behind a table, staring at you - the Silent Audience - you who are more or less compelled to listen to what I am going to say for the next three quarters of an hour! It is a situation which you can find replicated hour after hour, day after day, in countless classrooms and lecture-theatres, in city halls, county halls, and national assembly halls, in commercial conference rooms - and again, in the evenings, in millions of dimly-lit domestic living-rooms: a situation in which more or less silent audiences and spectators passively consume the words and gestures of some speaker - a situation in which, generally, they are unable to interrupt the speaker with some personal contribution of their own to the topic which he is dealing with.

So the question arises: how can all these people - who, for the most part, have been forced to be passive for far too long - how can all these people get hold of the information and ideas which the various speakers seek to impart to them, in a freer and more active way, in a way which might even be faster and save time? How can one - for example within the framework of an international conference such as this - how can one ensure optimal interaction among the participants, with the possibility of a multiplicity of stimulating conversations in which one not only communicates what one already knows, but in which one gains entirely new insight through creative discussion with one's conversational partner? Such conversations do, of course, take place informally, in the coridors <u>outside</u> the conference rooms, but why should they not, in themselves, constitute the very life-blood of the conference itself?

Isn't there, in other words, a necessity for "desirable social innovations" within the flourishing world of international conferences? A necessity for a conference, for example, where no speakers have been specially invited in advance, where no papers have already been prepared, where no carefully prearranged programme has to be followed? Yet already I can see the indulgent smile on many of your lips at the very idea of such a suggestion - the indulgent smile which expresses a criticism of the naivety of such an idea - if not downright indignation, or that incredibly widespread resignation (which one is tempted to call "normal") which relegates anything unconventional or different to the realm of the impossible.

Were it merely a question of improving conference technology however, nothing at all would be deemed impossible! Voices can be amplified, faces can be "blown up", the registration and subsequent widespread dissemination of all that has been said can be improved, can be done faster, can be done more efficiently. Distances of thousands of miles can be bridged, and words in the most disparate of languages instantaneously translated. But improvised speech, a tell-tale stammer, hesitation, or a brief pause (for thought, or in order to allow one's audience a chance to fully register what one has just said) - things like this go against accepted conventions, so no speaker dares to experiment with this kind of otherwise perfectly natural human behaviour.

Breaking conventions, changing human behaviour, these are far more difficult than modifying technical machinery. Fortunately! For where would we be today if the social, psychological, or biological manipulation of our fellow human beings were already as far perfected as so many of the high priests of efficiency, and so many of the cultural pessimists, have so long looked forward to, or warned us against? Still today - and, I fervently hope, for ever - the thoughtful, forgetful, imaginative and fallible partner in the dialectical collaboration between human beings and technological products is the guarantee of freedom, and that unpredictable element of surprise which distinguishes what is vital and alive from the realm of the dead.

Still, therefore, social innovation is determined by factors which cannot be accurately calculated or planned in advance. If one wanted to render such factors totally predictable, the creation of a totalitarian state would be a necessary precondition - a fully mechanical product of social-engineering, incapable of growth or change, doomed in advance to a speedy death.

2.

Which brings us to the question of whether one is at all able to embark on the difficult and perilous task of trying to solve personal and social problems - through the conscious and intensive exertion of one's imagination - without violating the fundamental human desire for self-determination. For the fact that this right has constantly been violated - both by successions of rulers and by successions of peoples who have opposed them, since time imme-morial - does not establish any precedent which we are forced to abide by. On the contrary, it should make us strive all the more determinedly to devise ways and means to ensure that political and social changes are imagined, planned, and executed with the full knowledge and participation of (if possible) all those whose lives will subsequently be affected.

The alternatives - either a "laisser faire" policy, under which any attempted social planning is dismissed out of hand, or centralized social planning at the hands of some power élite - are unacceptable at our present stage of human development: the former because it would lead to chaos, the latter because it would lead to tyranny. And both policies would presumably lead to our eventual total annihilation, since the offensive technological products which are bound to be used in the conflicts which either policy would almost certainly provoke, have now reached such a high level of destructive perfection as to inflict irremediable damage on ourselves and our planetary environment. In fact it is precisely this enormously improved technical quality of our instruments of destruction - the result of what otherwise could have been an endless stream of impressive technological innovations - which renders any kind of truly democratic social innovation so vitally necessary.

Our first priority, therefore, has to be the invention of non-violent ways to bring about social, political, and economic changes. But the eventual utiliza-tion of such methods presupposes radical changes as regards the present level of public information, and radical rethinking with regard to secondary and adult education. <u>Social institutions</u> would have to be developed <u>which</u> <u>would guarantee full civil rights for all and promote democratic participa-</u> <u>tion by all</u>, and which would hold out the promise to all of <u>job possibilities</u> <u>and working-conditions which could satisfy not just their material,</u> <u>but also</u> <u>their psychological, demands and hopes.</u>

Stated as briefly as this, the above sounds far too ambitious and utopian. How can anyone demand so much? Would it not be more appropriate and promising to content ourselves with more modest proposals for social improvements, such as those which, for example, Nicholas Albery's recently-founded "Institute for Social Inventions" is taking up in London? In December 1985 the list included, for example, the following suggestions:
- a prenatal university for research on all aspects of prenatal embryonic influencing;
- the posting of warning-crosses along streets and roads at all the places where traffic accidents have taken place;
- policemen to be recruited from - and selected and employed by - local populations, rather than by national or urban authorities;
- neighbourhood parties and festivals to encourage communal leisure activities and artistic and cultural initiatives.

Projects such as these are, of course, neither particularly imaginative, nor sufficiently important or radical to constitute an adequate response to the dangers and consequent compulsions which have followed in the wake of our present international crisis. Should we then reject them out of hand? Definitely not. Participants in the "Social Invention Workshops" which Nicholas Albery's Institute has already successfully organized in several London schools, gain courage, self-confidence, and experience in the formulation and realisation of modest social innovations. Possibly, such initiatives may be so unproductive as to amount to no more than plastering the blows which our present societies so unrelentingly administer to their citizens, but such initiatives might equally well prepare the ground for more ambitious and profound social changes. In my opinion, this approach to social change, involving proposals, projects and experiments, is the only viable alternative to the more violent, revolutionary approaches which - only too clearly - become more and more likely as our present social crises wax and become more and more acute. Since, however, the last decade has seen an enormous increase in government investments in qualitative and quantitative defence measures, which may be directed against potential internal - as well as external - threats, I think it is fair to assume that any revolutionary attempt to eliminate the causes of our present troubles would only aggravate rather than eradicate them.

3.

In my study at home, I have a woodcut illustrating an Amerindian myth, retold by the author, B. Traven. The woodcut depicts a man piecing together the sparkling fragments of a shattered sun to form a new shining star. I feel that it illustrates rather well what has been my main activity over the last ten to fifteen years. I collect little sparks of hope wherever they may be found shining on the darkened horizon of our time, in the firm expectation that my efforts to combine all the many disparate attempts to improve the human situation all over the globe will provide enough light to restore courage and hope to those who may already have lost them. In effect, if you only look closely enough, you can find hundreds of social innovations, and social experiments applying them, in dozens of nations in all the continents of the world. Indeed, if the United Nations were to draw up a list of all the social innovations which have already been tried out, just as they have done in exemplary fashion with regard to experiments with alternative energy, our contemporaries would be amazed to discover how much ingenuity - so often coupled with very admirable humane effort - how much ingenuity is already involved in the piece-by-piece transformation of society which daily becomes more and more necessary.

Under the present circumstances I cannot - and will not - burden you with a long list of such sucessful experiments, but I would like to single out one or two of them. But first I hope you will bear with me if I spend a little time reflecting upon less promising matters - upon the reasons for the failure of social experiments, in fact.

It took centuries to introduce such social inventions as money, for instance, which replaced the complicated and impractical exchange of goods. It took centuries to introduce the parliamentary system, which provided all adult citizens with a necessary forum for social debate and guaranteed everyone the right to be heard. Technical innovations, however, have been introduced much faster, not least because their enormous and profound influence on the environment, on human beings, and on their societies, was scarcely understood in the beginning. That the apparently esoteric and extremely academic work done in certain physics research laboratories less than ten years ago should have such a tremendous influence on world politics and on the temper of millions of people's lives, was originally only clear to a very few people. The scientific and technological revolution within almost all social, political and economic fields has got off to a flying start because of the sheer lack of knowledge about its potential social, political and economic consequences. Later on, however - and, in most cases, too late - this ignorance has turned out to have been disastrous. On the other hand, when one is trying to realize social innovations, one can only occasionally assume that nobody is aware of what they will bring with them! Generally, it will immediately be clear to everybody that habitual ideas and power constellations will be challenged, that alternative attitudes will be demanded, together with alternative ways of thinking and - last but not least - alternative distributions of property.

When, for example, we try to find out why one of the present time's most necessary, and conceivably most useful, social innovations - a guaranteed wage for everyone without the necessity to work - cannot be carried out, even though representatives of the most disparate ideological positions (from Roman Catholic social workers to Social Democrats) support it, it seems to a large extent to be due to the fact that unemployment has always been considered people's own fault, even though everybody knows perfectly well that, in our time, it is an inevitable consequence of technological rationalization and the restructuring of industry, which the person concerned is powerless to resist.

Again, if in our present epoch of innovation within the fields of industry and communications, a proposal was made to replace national citizenship by continental or even planetary citizenship, and, accordingly, to introduce new passports for us all, as European or World Citizens, the idea would immediately be dismissed as impossible, or at least as impossible for the time being.

Or we could take yet another example of the difficulties one faces in seeking to realize comprehensive social innovations: in this age of mass society, an urgently necessary task is the discovery of means by which democracy can be improved, because of the enormous growth of our populations in relation to the more or less constant number of our parliamentary representatives, and on account of the only-too-apparent growth in the amount of public problems which demand legal regulation. At present, our members of parliament are so overburdened that they can scarcely find the time to tackle the larger questions about how the future should be shaped. Anticipatory planning of this kind therefore becomes the affair of large-scale businesses, and they, particularly in their initial research phases, tend to exclude the public. Democratic participation has thus degenerated into the sporadic and superficial acclaim of the results of decision-making which, in itself, is difficult for the public to achieve any insight into. Any critical reception by those who are directly affected by such decisions only becomes possible after the ideas have been realized, and any public protest can then be brushed aside as a technically expensive delay going against, for example, the necessity to compete internationally in economic terms, or the "inevitable march of progress". Is not this description correct both as regards the penetration of nuclear technology, and bio-technical technology, within our societies? Haven't the perfectly justified objections and alternative suggestions always come too late as the result of the lack of that democratic modernization which is so urgently required to broaden the basis of our democratic institutions?

4.

In 1973, in a paper published on the occasion of my 60th birthday, I referred to the potential role of information technology for the democratization of our societies in the following words: "How many possibilities for individual participation in democratic decision-making processes may be improved, not least by means of socially-applied electronic techniques, is obvious to anyone who has occupied themselves with problems of information and discussion in this age of national populations totalling over a billion. But we still lack viable practical utopias, not least because those who are informed about these things feel powerless, having understood that neither good ideas, nor the already existing technical capabilities, are sufficient to break down Establishment resistance. In order not to be dismissed as unrealistic, as unserious, as mere fantasists, they are reticent about formulating any of their wishes which might go beyond what people consider possible to realise. But precisely this form of self-censure, this lack of participation on the part of so-called realists (who, in order to be on the safe side, deliberately lower their sights in order to bring their own ambitions into harmony with a reality which, to a greater and greater extent, is unable adequately to cope with increasingly urgent problems, and is thus increasingly unrealistic) - precisely this short-sighted "realism" is one of the main reasons why the social imagination lags far behind the technological imagination".

How, then, can we overcome this anxiety which is shared by rulers and experts alike? To me the answer seems to lie in the suggestion which involves the testing out of social innovations experimentally before they are generally introduced into our societies, in order to reduce, and perhaps even remove completely, the fear of the unknown, by means of the experience gained through such experimentation. However, if such experiments are to be carried out with scientific precision, they will cost a lot of money and time. According to Eleanor Bernert Sheldon, former President of the American Social Science Research Council, social experiments should start with a very careful and detailed assessment of empirical foundations, and time-consuming efforts should be made to select solutions which are perfectly accordant with chosen social contexts. Only thereafter can the actual experiment get under way, and the optimum trial time may run into months, if not years. Subsequent detailed evaluation of the entire experiment should be followed up by a second trial experiment, based on the results of this evaluation. Endless discussions with those involved in the experiments and with local authorities, the selection and establishment of center groups for monitoring the experiments, careful analysis of comparative variations, of negative instances and possible errors - all these are in accordance with the principles of scientific accuracy and detailed self-criticism, but it all takes such a long time that many projects of this kind are dismissed beforehand as lacking in feasibility - and on the grounds that their results would be obsolete long before the trial periods were over. The attempt to force social experiments into the rigid moulds dictated by strictly positivist scientific criteria has thus, for the time being, been abandoned.

5.

Counter-cultural social experiments, often undertaken without any unduly lengthy preparation, have proved much more efficient, in that their results have been widely disseminated under the auspices of the new social movements. In fact it is difficult to find any area of society - private or public - in which new and unconventional ways of realizing oneself have not been tried out. Interpersonal relationships between couples and within families, child-rearing, work, housing, information, health, food, political and economic forms of organization, leisure, and many other fields, have seen experiments in .which they have been radically changed, not only theoretically, but in concrete practical terms. They have become more personally liberating, and/or ethically responsible.

Many - indeed probably most - of these social experiments which have been tried out in practice have undeniably proved to be entirely, or at least partially, mistaken. But the possibility of failure is endemic to the concept of experimentation itself: and, according to many of these self-appointed guinea-pigs, experiments without any real risks are not worth the effort. Yet, even if they don't succeed, radical projects are worthwhile, for they indicate new possibilities which may be able to come into their own under alternative circumstances. For example, experiments with extended families where one can change partners from time to time have - almost without exception - only been successful for short periods of time, but these short periods of time have revealed capacities for love within the participants which would never have been discovered within traditionally exclusive sexual partnerships. The return to conventional life-styles, as far as sexual relationships are concerned, has primarily proved necessary because of demands made on us, by the world around us, to conform. Yet as soon as our current norms need to be changed - (and the taboo-breaking extended families have apparently already exerted a considerable amount of influence in this direction) - then what once was only an experiment may very well be taken up again, as a valuable contribution towards the development of desirable new norms. I think that those people are wrong who maintain that the socially-innovative and experimental counter-culture was only a curious episode in the history of the twentieth century, after which everything could return to normalcy. When, at some later stage, the full scope of all these experiments is investigated, and the full extent of their influence on the increasingly important new social movements of the last two decades becomes clear, this pioneer period of constructive opposition against the technocratic bias of our age will be regarded as the definitive springboard for social developments in entirely new directions; it will be seen to have ushered in inevitable changes in anachronistically conventional behaviour. The Women's Movement, the Ecological Movement, the Peace Movement, and the "New Age" Movement are the successors of the counter-culture, and they have derived enormous profit from it. They have successfully known how to exploit the experiments which were made in the 'sixties and 'seventies, and have incorporated many of their results into the mainstream of our social life. Their supporters' attempts to treat each other, and all those around them, in ways which are very different from those currently obtaining in our patriarchally-influenced, competitive, and growth- and profit-oriented societies in East and West, have already created ripples which - it is becomingly increasingly clear - will in the years to come develop into immensely powerful torrents, threatening to sweep away their most powerful opponents and forcing them to change their traditional modes of behaviour.

6.

Social unrest in the last third of the present century has provoked two prime reactions amongst people of power and influence in our societies: one of them is to ignore what happens, and try to suppress it by means of laws and the legal executive - sending in the police to suppress mass demonstrations, street blockades, occupations of otherwise unoccupied houses, or desperate actions of sabotage.

Others (having learnt from history that, in the long run, the suppression of social movements fighting on a mass scale against what are considered to be unbearable conditions can never succeed) try closely to follow and investigate these protests and objections, so that they can exploit the explosion of public dissatisfaction to their own advantage, without having to give up the reins of power. And, as this E.E.C. conference under the FAST programme so clearly indicates, there are in fact many experiments going on at the moment which enjoy local, regional, state or even international support - experiments which are attempts to do something constructive about people's dissatisfaction, instead of trying to suppress it.

I would like to refer you here to two such examples in Germany, which I myself was instrumental in initiating. In 1977, at a conference for critical scientists in Salzburg, I suggested that we should create a kind of insurance fund for researchers and technicians who, on conscientious grounds, no longer wanted to participate in socially irresponsible projects. My suggested

social innovation was subsequently tried out in practice within the framework of a future-workshop at the Otto Suhr Institute at the Freie Universität, in Berlin. Later on, it was incorporated within a more comprehensive
social experiment: the so-called "Netzwerk Selbsthilfe", the "Self-Help
Network". This is an organization which, out of its own funds, supports such
things as independent research institutes, "Science Shops", alternative
production workshops, critical media and educational experiments. Thus,
within the framework of this institution, critical researchers who have had
to leave Iron Curtain countries branded as dissidents, can find themselves a
permanent niche. Originally, the Network had to manage entirely on its own,
funded by its own members. Later, however, the urban district council in
Berlin became interested in it, and started to provide public funds for it: an
experiment which originally met with a great deal of mistrust both from the
more radical members, who weren't going to allow themselves to be "bought
up", and from more conservative quarters, where the public financing of
"subversive elements" was regarded with considerable suspicion. In actual
fact, neither the radicals' nor the conservatives' worst fears have proved to
be well-founded, and the most important result has been that West Berlin
today, with over a thousand alternative projects, has become a large and
frequently highly successful testing ground for social experiments of all
kinds.

Impressed, amongst other things, by developments such as these, the
government in Nordrhein-Westfalen decided, in 1985, to use part of their
400 million D-mark programme for the modernization of anachronistic
industrial structures to do follow-up research, which was not only to
document and analyse the transformation process, but also, by means of
experiments in connection with this transformation process, to make sure
that the new developments had a socially-acceptable form. Under this grant,
at least 30 future-workshops have been planned, starting in April 1986. They
are to ensure that objections, wishes and expectations amongst employees -
who are to change from traditional industry to highly modern methods of
production - are brought out into the open, and may thus have a determining
influence on the transformation process itself.

Needless to say, democratic participation of this kind right from the initial
planning stage, instead of being only permitted post facto, is likely to run
into a certain amount of opposition from managers and bureaucrats. They

may even manage to stop it altogether. Already the project has been delayed by refusals to sign contracts, even though the latter have been elaborated on the basis of lengthy negotiations between the future-workshop leaders and the relevant ministerial departments.

Yet the above project has, in particular, been inspired by the very successful work done in London by the trades unionist, Mike Cooley, and his colleagues, in establishing decentralized political fora for the reduction of unemployment and for the improvement of living conditions among the underprivileged. According to a Bremen University study of this work, substantial funding - but above all a general mobilization of the will, energies and talents of the local populations concerned - have been the necessary preconditions for some already quite impressive results. Cooperative societies have been founded for (unemployed) employees; local citizens have been involved in decisions affecting their own futures; a collaboration has been established between polytechnics, trades unions and local groups; an institute for alternative production has been founded; a local technological network has been set up; and adult education courses are held on such subjects as alternative modes of production, and ways to realize alternative local political structures. Most importantly, initiatives have been taken such as those called for by the Lucas Aerospace concern - (formerly an armaments factory) - initiatives for the invention of more socially-useful products, such as noiseless vehicles for collective transport, or artificial kidneys, or more user-friendly workshop tools.

7.

Such initial signs of collaboration between public institutions and social movements - collaboration in a common attempt to bring about the non-violent evolution of our industrial societies with the help of social experiments - are indicative of the fact that our societies are on a new course. Critical scientists and civil servants, critically-minded managers and financiers, are joining forces to prevent the destruction of mankind and the environment under the impact of blind progress. They are working together to create a civilisation which respects our environment. And they are doing this in spite of opposition from reactionary forces within our societies, who can no longer sit passively by and wait for them to go away. In London, for example, earlier this year (March 1986), the Greater London Council was dissolved by a decree of the Thatcher administration, with the result that many important cultural innovations were deprived of essential financial support. Yet it has already become clear that these experiments cannot be so easily crushed: alternative funding and organizational help will keep them alive. For, faced as they are by the present economic crisis (which the never-ending spiral of defence investment merely serves to mask cosmetically), those financial and industrial leaders who are aware of the true state of affairs are under new pressure. Nowadays, the need to prevent economic collapse - or at any rate to defer it or temper it for the time being - is frequently a more compelling argument than the traditional lure of competitive profit maximization.

Given the actual distribution of power in our industrial societies at the present time, and given its repressive strength which is bolstered by the fiscal exigencies - and the enhanced policing capabilities - of the armaments industry, successful social change of the classical revolutionary variety, involving a "revolt of the masses", would seem to be virtually impossible. Which renders all the more important the rôle played by far-sighted leaders within the Establishment, who prefer social innovations, born out of our new social movements and realized with the help of intellectuals, to the meaningless suffering of abortive social revolutions. In effect, these critical members of our Establishments are coming out more and more strongly on the side of alternative social innovation. If one considers such a development impossible, and thinks that vested interests, on the one hand, and uncompromising revolutionary urges, on the other, are incompatible, and that these can never be united in an honest and productive collaboration, then one has underestimated the human species' ability, precisely in situations of crisis, to invent ever new and flexible and unexpected solutions to its problems. Resignation, which merely serves to prop up an unacceptable status quo, is no help to us. A spirit of openness and tolerance towards new ideas, coupled with the courage to try out what in the first instance seems impossible, but what tomorrow may become a new reality - those are the only attitudes which can help us to make true advances.

THE DISSEMINATION OF THE NEW INFORMATION AND COMMUNICATION TECHNOLOGIES

Claire Ancelin, DGT-SPES, France

In France, social experimentation with telematics has been part of the official national policy for five years. But the concept has never been satisfactorily defined; it has been used to designate a vast number of heterogeneous activities. This situation has led to much confusion both in relation to public policy, and with regard to the exchanging of experiences within research fora.

The subject of social experimentation in the field of information and communication technologies has met with considerable success in recent years, particularly in France.

But are we all talking about the same thing? When one asks questions on this subject, one cannot fail to be struck by the differences in the answers. For confirmation of this one need only skim through the national reports and the contributions to this symposium - in which some felt it necessary to state exactly what they themselves understood by social experimentation - or look through the programme of the 1982 International IDATE days at Montpellier, which dealt with social experimentation in telematics.

We thus encounter new techniques, or old techniques to which new uses are assigned, various different promotors (the State, local authorities, private-sector promotors, individual initiatives), different users (individuals, citizens within their own cities, professional users, etc.), different modes of organization (giving, lending, providing against payment, providing with a greater or lesser degree of participation, etc.) and, above all, different aims: to try out the technique, to test users' reactions to the technique, to try out services, an organization, etc.

In brief, the term social experimentation is used in all cases where a change is introduced or the data are altered.

In view of this great diversity, some people end up by having doubts and were already telling us about their perplexity during the above-mentioned IDATE days (1):

- tele-working: is it a problem of work organization or of social experimentation? (Norbert Alter)
- Teletel: a social experiment? (Jean Marie Charon)
- telematics at the Office régional d'éducation permanente (National Office for Permanent Education): is this social experimentation? (Hélène Dufau-Montillaud).

. . .

Because, even for a given experiment, the situation can be extremely vague. Thus, even within the Direction Générale des Télécommunications, which is the promoter of the Teletel 3V (T3V) videotex experiment, there was far from being a consensus concerning the status of this experiment (2):

For the head of the Telematics Department it could only be a form of social experimentation. For the manager of the Commercial and Telematics Affairs Department the aim was to enable the suppliers of information to test market conditions. The project team, responsible for running the experiment on the ground, preferred to refer to it as a predevelopment test. Lastly, the suppliers of T3V services themselves were able to pursue various aims: for some the project was just a showcase, for others it was the development of a new activity.

The term "social experimentation", which is easy to use for discussion purposes, thus cannot be easily pinned down. This fact would be less important, except in theoretical analyses, if there were not a danger that a certain conception of social experimentation might obscure other thinking about the spread of the new technologies and the ways in which they are appropriated by their users. For in come cases - and these are perhaps not the most infrequent - what is being done is more in the nature of a test-tube experiment than a social project: the users are confronted with a technique, and what happens is observed and recorded without there being any real participation on their part or any mobilization around a project. In extreme cases these are alibi experiments, when they serve as the a priori justification for the introduction of the techniques.

Nevertheless, if one considers the many French videotex experiments, they have in fact, despite all the vagueness with which they have been surrounded, turned out to be the forerunners of a socialization of technology.

They have definitely served as a test bench both in their technical aspects and in the planning of services (six years ago, who knew what a videotex service was?). They have made possible the birth of new skills and provided the occasion for negotiation, reconciliation and presentation of this technique (see Alain Briole's paper: a moment in the history of the new communication techniques: social experimentation 1980/1985).

A comparison of the various experiments and their execution has also confirmed the importance of the editorial function. The myth of neutral, objective information which has a meaning independently of its author has often been found to be absolutely out of line with the reality of the uses made of it, because the giving of precise information is not in itself sufficient to make it relevant and usable (3).

Certain implications of editorial responsibility have also been demonstrated: there is updating work, of course, but also the need to carry out a specific operation of editing and presentation of information (editing on videotex is not the same as on paper), and possibly a choice to be made between two possible wordings (the weight of words...) and the need to ensure the coexistence of competing suppliers of services.

Furthermore, these experiments have also sometimes made it possible for the users to produce uses - the best guarantee of successful appropriation. The most famous example in France is that of interactive messaging services for the general public, or dialogue messaging services.

These came into being in Strasbourg as a result of a pirate ('hacking') operation carried out by users who found the weak spot in a private messaging system, and who, above all, did not hesitate to tell other users (by videotex) how to use this unexpected service. But this service also developed because its promoter, a regional newspaper, ultimately had no alternative but to accept this pirating and followed its users, confining itself to laying down a few rules of good conduct (4).

This can be seen to be an essential dimension of social experimentation: it is a mutual learning process for the promoter and for the user, an open-ended process in which there are degrees of freedom. And what has been found with regard to experiments for the general public can also be found in other forms in professional areas.

Thus, Norbert Alter notes, concerning the introduction of office automation techniques (5): "We must let people take advantage of the degree of freedom made possible by office automation. I think it is important that businessmen should understand that what they do, in spite of themselves more often than not, namely experimenting by trials, evaluations, correction of errors, starting and restarting, is not negative but, on the contrary, something which they could establish as a principle... We must accept freedom, it is the price of innovation".

And Francis Pavé, who is working on information technologies, says: "A good model is a circumvented model. If people cheat with it, you can be sure that it has acquired the social reality for which it was intended and which it influences. Acceptance of information technologies by the users thus takes place also via acceptance of the deformation of their projects by those who promote them" (6).

The question is thus probably less one of experimentation in the strict sense of the term than of whether the promoters of the new technologies are prepared to accept and manage the deviations which will take place. But it is also a question of identifying the various forms of dissemination, which come into being. Because behind the question of social experimentation there is indeed that of diffusion and appropriation, especially during this period when new technologies are seen by many as a possible strategy for getting out of a crisis, often surrounded by all the myths of a new democracy, of, at last, the accessibility of information for everybody (7).

We have just seen that, in certain circumstances, experience and experimentation can play a part in bringing about this dissemination, but there are also other factors to be taken into account.

First of all, of course, very simply, the time factor. The appropriation of new technologies by a population is a lengthy process; this is a platitude, but do we not sometimes tend to forget it and to try to introduce them too fast?

Then there is the role of men (and women). We have seen the role which could be played by the user in the production and dissemination of new uses in connection with the Strasbourg messaging service.

This role of intermediary, of mediator between the technique and other users, which is played by some of the latter, is no exception in France. A retrospective analysis of technical innovations shows that, in this country, new technique often generate such a system of intermediaries (8), who facilitate their introduction into the economic and social fabric, who popularize their use not only by employing these techniques themselves but also by making a point of bringing them to the attention of potential users around them, of showing them their advantages. The mediator is therefore at one and the same time an expert who has mastered the technique (sometimes at the risk of allowing himself to be fascinated by it), an interpreter able to make the transition between the potentialities of the innovation and the field of applications, and a teacher capable of transmitting his enthusiasm and knowledge, even though, depending on the case in question, one or other of these three components may be predominant (9).

During the 1970s private radio stations (subsequently free radio stations) were the forum for a militant and social mediation (encouragement of social appropriation of technologies in order to stimulate democratic debate), after which they developed, from 1982-83 onwards, towards a situation in which technical expertise and professionalization often took precedence over the initial aims; private local radio stations no longer have much in common with the pirate radio stations (see our national contribution "The new media in France: experimentation, acculturation and economic development"). But, parallel with this, microinformatics generated (especially in users' clubs) a phenomenon of mediation which is perhaps all the more important because there are substantial training requirements in this field and because social mediation derives its strength from working in the transmission of knowledge (10).

It should be pointed out, however, that, while this mediation exists in France as an actual practice and as a subject of research, there is no trace of it in Anglo-Saxon studies. A possible explanation is that mediation - this bridge between the technique and the user - may in these countries be regarded as and included in marketing strategy (11); this is probably a line to be pursued in comparative research.

Finally, the last point I shall mention is the need for leaders to come forward with regard to man-machine communication networks. Leaders entrusted with the task of fostering and putting into perspective this communication, which otherwise quickly becomes lifeless and devoid of meaning beyond the field of mere technical performance. Thus, after the explosion of interactive messaging services, which initially developed in complete freedom, leaders, paid by the suppliers of services, come on the scene with the task, thanks to their own messages, of promoting messaging services, possibly directing their tone, bringing in new subjects of conversation, restimulating discussion... This role is even more explicit in the case of computer-assisted teleconferencing, where the participants are required to work together within the framework of specific conferences (tasks). The function of the leader will be to make up for the physical separation of the participants and the lack of synchronism of communication and to solve the resultant problems. He will have to be capable of creating a context common to all the members, setting aims and a work schedule, and then of keeping communication alive by recalling the work to be done, by assuring the authors of the usefulness and utilization of their contributions, by establishing connecting lines enabling each party to satisfy himself (and become convinced of) the existence of the conference and of the role of each party within it (12).

The sole purpose of these few words on the subject of dissemination is to open up lines to be followed in connection with social experimentation. But there remains one subject which needs to be thought about: - how, beyond the specific features of the experiments described in this symposium, can we take advantage of the experiments of others, avoiding confining ourselves to an enumeration of factual examples?

NOTES

1. See the Proceedings of the International IDATE Days, "Social experimentation in telematics", October 1982, IDATE Bulletin No. 9.

2. See "Vélizy ou les premiers pas le la télématique grand public", Jean Marie Charon and Eddy Cherki, in "Télématique, Promenade dans les usages", under the direction of Marie Marchand and Claire Ancelin, Documentation Française, 1984.

3. For example, an item of information about consumer goods will not have the same meaning depending on whether its author is a consumer association or the local dealer.

4. This type of service is responsible in France for the present success of videotex for the general public in terms of traffic.

5. See "Le Monde de l'informatique" of 27 May 1985.

6. See his article "Technologie acceptée, technologie dévoyée" in "La provocation, hommes et machines en société", CESTA, 1985.

7. These are positive myths which are just as much of a handicap as the fears of Big Brother, because they prevent these technologies from taking their proper place.

8. See "La fonction de médiation dans l'audiovisuel", Bernard Guillou, DGT-SPES, roneoed note, May 1982.

9. See "Informatique, une nouvelle race de médiateurs", Marie Marchand, in La Lettre du SPES (Prospective et Telecom), No. 6, March 1985.

10. See "Les médiateurs dans les nouvelles technologies de communication, leur rôle, leur histoire, leurs motivations", study by Patrick Viveret, carried out for SPES-DGT, December 1985.

11. See "La fonction de médiation dans la diffusion des nouvelles technologies de communication", Marie Marchand, DGT-SPES, roneoed note, October 1985.

12. See "Des services à valeur ajoutée à dimension humaine: la téléconférence assistée par ordinateur, la télévidéothègue" in La Lettre du SPES (Prospective et Telecom), No. 8, January 1986, and the contributions of Gaétan Cambra and Barnard Marquet to this symposium.

A MOMENT IN THE HISTORY OF THE NEW COMMUNICATION TECHNIQUES: SOCIAL EXPERIMENTATION 1980/1985

Alain Briole, IDATE, France

Subsequently to vanish again under something of a cloud, the concept of the social experiment briefly held the forefront of the stage in France at the turn of the present decade, when the nation was confronted by the imperative necessity to develop new techniques of telecommunication. In fact it was under the auspices of this concept - so dear to utopians' hearts, and so ideally suited to the introduction, if not the development, of new information and telecommunications technology - that the latter first made its appearance in France, in the years 1980 to 1982. The effects of this powerful metaphor, both in awakening an imaginative social awareness, and in legitimating a new technological rationality, have forged the concepts and values which today constitute the frame of reference for our present assimilation of I.T. and telematics technology in France. This paper retraces this development, taking as its point of departure one important moment in the early history of the decade when, in October 1982, Montpellier's IDATE held its fourth international conference on social experiments with telematics. In the article, I attempt to summarize the major themes of this seminal conference, so that the reader may better be able to appreciate the ways in which the present frame of reference for the assimilation of new I.T. and telematics technology in France has been formulated, and what constitutes its vital essence.

PREAMBLE

The preparation of a paper for the Odense conference on social experiments induced us to look back to what was indisputably an important moment in the development of the concept of social experimentation applied to New Communication Techniques: the October 1982 Seminar Organized by IDATE (1).

Rather than go through once more the whole history of this concept, which has been the subject of other publications (2), it became increasingly clear to me that it was more relevant to concentrate on what, in the discussions which then took place, was still operative today.

What these discussions bear witness to is in fact the historical process of transformation on which French society was embarking: it is this production of the unified meaning of the development of New Communication Techniques, since then repeated on many occasions, that provided the frame of reference for this movement, which has since expanded.

These discussions are those of social actors who are involved in differing degrees in the development of New Communication Techniques, but whose role is certainly not confined to just talking: members of government departments, technicians, industrialists, they are contributing concretely to the transformation of French society in this field, as is abundantly demonstrated by the list of these speakers.

The underlying meaning of the title of this paper amounts, to our mind, to this: not the specific, concrete development of new services of new uses, but a picking out of the themes of a seminal conference which enabled us to grasp, if not to master, the far-reaching transformation which we are undergoing at present; work relating both to imaginative social awareness and to the legitimation of a new technological way of thinking which has generated the values and concepts of today.

Today, in actual fact, the idea of social experimentation is tending to disappear; it seems to us that the key idea is rather that of acceptability. This is proof that the movement which consisted in reconciling the actors in three decisive social fields, i.e. politics (in the widest sense), technology and the social sciences (each, of course, at different levels), has succeeded.

In an initial version this text covered two of these fields: that of a commentary on extracts of texts from the papers of various contributors to the 4th International Days. While this commentary made the situation abundantly clear, it was so ponderous and long as to greatly exceed the bounds of a contribution to this symposium. We have therefore retained only the second part: comments which summarize the themes of the main discussion on the development of New Communication Techniques, and the relationships between them, with constant reference to a compendium of texts which is assumed to be familiar (3).

This text is dated, in that it refers essentially to telematics; but as it stands, being not an account of the state of one or other technical system but a compilation of fragments of an oral discussion - fragments the meaning of which, interrelated, constituted the social frame of reference for the dissemination of a technical innovation and the transformations which it is bringing about - it is still, I believe, of great current relevance, throwing light on some of the present choices.

SPACES/NETWORKS

Social experimentation in telematics starts with an agreement; it is the place where the conditions for a common interchange between all the protagonists are fulfilled; it entails first of all a statement of the rules of the game and its subject, the stake involved.

This formulation without any real subject is aimed at showing that this process, this so widely shared discussion may seem to have no enunciator and to be a discussion between everybody and open to everybody, somewhat like language itself (4). The fiction of experimentation takes on an autonomous character and comprehends the whole of reality. It becomes for a time - but, erasing this important restriction, it attempts to be for all times, in place of time - the natural place for embracing the social organization. However, the formulation of the stake of social experimentation makes it possible to identify a dominant participant who, not being able to create this discussion, looks after its distribution. The networks (first of all physical, the network which establishes the links between technical devices - telecommunications - and then, by metaphor, the network which codifies social exchanges - communication), the subjects of the experimentation, identify this actor; it is the Telecommunications Administration, which, by its "pre-experimentation" work, its position and its project, lays down the rule and the aim; as an imperative requirement beyond itself, of which it specifies all the forms in detail. As a veritable immediate recording of the experimentation, the notion of network is taken up by all the actors and in all the spaces, which incorporate it in their strategy of alliances or conflicts to the point where in some cases, perhaps, they discover its impossibility.

THE DUAL CONSENSUS

The Technical, Industrial and Economic Stakes

At the end of the 1970s telematics became the spearhead of the redeployment of the telephone industry, borne by the Telecommunications Administration.

There, from the outset, there came into being the first consensus, the one which makes social experimentation possible. A consensus which, despite its futuristic notes - and perhaps precisely because of them - cannot fail to give the impression of being an echo of the movement of technological enthusiasm which, after the Saint-Simonians, pervaded the end of the 19th century (5). While they do not dispel all the fears, these stakes are the subject of a unanimous national discussion which has never been in dispute; whether one is a technician, a politician or a future user, one will find in this first universal representation the absolute limit to all controversy.

Even those who are most vigilant in keeping watch on the plans pursued by the machinery of State cannot do other in this case than confirm the legitimacy of this project. While the means may be a subject to dispute, there is definite agreement on the aims.

Social Communication

This consensus immediately calls for another, which in turn legitimates the step of social experimentation; this consensus did not develop all at once, but, being more complex, by a two-stage movement. It concerns the consequences of these stakes represented by the new communication technologies, and starts from a picture of upheaval.

As far back as 1978 the destabilizing effects of the introduction of new means of communication on entire sectors of activity held the centre of the stage; their effects on everyday life, less perceptible, nevertheless aroused the same - gloomy - forbodings, as did also their effects on the traditional institutions of social communication. While telematics is information technology plus the telephone, it is - precisely - not the telephone.

This coming upheaval was amplified by the press, which was primarily affected by technical innovation. The first national telematics experiments, such as the trials of the electronic telephone directory in Ille-et-Vilaine, appeared for a moment to foreshadow a massive rejection. However, this attitude of rejection of the destabilization of communication networks concealed the reality of the process which had been embarked upon; the networks were already, at some of their points, in the process of breaking up or being recomposed. Four years later, current events bear witness to the fact that this phenomenon definitely preceded its rejection, and to its permanence: today the protagonists of telematics are still concentrating on the network: the aim is to position themselves at the nodal communication points. Communication is no longer an interchange, but a strategy. The fact is that in this field technology goes just as far as does imagination, even further than imagination, because it goes faster and fulfils all the old dreams of going beyond the bounds of time.

Unless, by a reversal, technology is not the cause but merely the confirmation of a profound change originating from further back... Because, fundamentally, is it not the form of technical thinking that constitutes the very meaning of communication? A form which, at one and the same time, creates and controls movement.

For does not technical thinking set its mark on the concept of communication to such an extent that it is no longer possible to distinguish what in it relates to the network from what might relate to other things - exchange?

A few landmarks: the idea of communication made its entry into the human sciences at a late stage; it does not appear, for instance, in the plan of classification of sociology produced by E. Durkheim or M. Mauss (6). However, in his "Essai de linguistique générale", R. Jakobson (7) is fairly clear about the contributions of telecommunications engineering to modern linguistics. It is in fact from this that the basic structure of communication (transmitter/channel/code/receiver) originates.

Technology operates, from two angles, on the very meaning of communication. Just as it embodied all the threats to which communication is exposed, technology is also the factor which activates all its potentialities. Consensus became possible through the concept of breaking up, the idea of communication dispels the menace. The postulate of communication is so definite that there is no longer any need to mention it as the origin; it has dissolved into the equivalence "technical progress/social progress". By successive refinements, communication becomes communications technology and the latter becomes a synonym of the progress of civilization.

Communication is therefore the symbol of unity. But, like any symbol, it is first of all marked by ambivalence, constantly activating the threat which it dispels; it is rather, therefore, the symbol of unification. A sign of the danger with which culture is always threatened, communication is no less than the categorical imperative of modern society. Its rites allow of a certain tolerance, but the dogma, for its part, is untouchable.

Continuing the metaphor, communication has, as can be seen, its devout adherents and its officiating priests; they are perhaps the same persons... Perhaps this discussion of/about communication has no other meaning than to signify this problematic exchange between the - political and technical - machinery of state and civil society.

The debate to which telematics has given rise in any case reflects the remarkable continuity of the process of cultural homogenization by which, in France, the concept of communication is marked (8). Is not the expansion of networks, which is the object pursued via the experiments, less undifferentiated than it appears, being marked by a protagonist with many faces?

Beneath the surface of these discussions there are two forms, two expressions, of the same relationship: between the local and the national or between the centre and the periphery. The most local experimentation always aims at generalization and transparency, the two attributes of ideal communication. Transparency of the medium, transparency of the message, transparency of the participation? That is less certain. Power, the stake of the relationship between the equipment and the territory - the stake of communication - reintroduces opaqueness into the heart of the network. The unanimity of acceptence of the semiological equation; technique = future = progress, falls apart as soon as the question of designating the space in which it is to be deployed arises.

A look into the old books of rhetoric will help us to understand these contradictory-dimensions which make up the concept of communication (9). The essentially antagonistic basis of communication makes it possible to pinpoint the nature of the consensus which it brings about; there is agreement about conflict and the forms which it assumes.

Social experimentation in telematics is overridingly determined by these two major factors of technology and communications; it is their concrete embodiment: a transparent space where everything must be seen and said, a contradictory space in which its divergent interests must be regulated, the space for anticipation of a future which is already here.

It might be thought that we delight in emphasizing the major themes (myths) which form the starting point of social experimentation in telematics; on rereading the texts, on seeing the incantational way in which they appear amid so much discussion - which, incidentally, deals with specific problems, in other terms therefore - we have the feeling that we are in fact barely emphasizing them. The incantation is as far removed as possible from being gratuitous, or frenzied: what these discussions conjure up is the idea of a break which is inherent in social experimentation: an epistemological break, a socio-political break. The counterpart to the innovating operation. Only then can social experimentation tip over into functionality.

When the major themes have been stated, the machinery of social experimentation can be reduced to a simple opposition; here there is a supply (of technology) and there a demand (for communication) - and, between these terms, a mediation has to take place; thus, social experimentation becomes operational.

Its operational nature sometimes gives rise to extremely abstract measures; it is thus possible to imagine perfect configurations of communication networks. In this case the work of designing reduces itself to listing the procedures to be employed, which come down to the question of choosing the points to be linked. Something is lost, however, in this line of action, entirely concentrated, as it is, on positiveness. While the theoretical construction is satisfactory, it must not be allowed to conceal the complexity of the process which it embraces. The use of a system, a network, is not unimportant, either before or after it has been designed.

Here, without abandoning positivity - but as a limit - the action embarked upon takes into account the specific nature of the use - something like the practices -which is too often and too quickly denied not to come back some time or other and ruin the beautiful plans. The emergence of social experimentation in telematics is the answer to this need for integration. But the tangled web of rationalities involved in this process is not easily comprehended; it necessitates abandonment of the plane of representations - the stage - in favour of that of history - the actors.

TELEMATICS/THE ACTORS

The introduction of telematics into French society has been punctuated by two phases, bringing on to the stage different actors and reflecting changes of strategies. The first phase is that when only the national authorities guide the development of new telecommunication techniques; the second sees the growing intervention of the local aspect, at the same time as the appearance of the notion of social experimentation. For it is with the appearance of this new protagonist that a transition will take place from the experimental system which is entirely confined to technicalities to a system which aims at paying attention to the dynamic socio-institutional factors generated by innovation, and to the relationship between the system and its use.

The analysis made by S. Gauthronet (10) of the first developments of telematics in Europe applies perfectly to the French situation. The institutions made responsible for the development of the new telecommunication techniques, in their beginnings, were quickly identified.

Aware of its role, which had become traditional, as the driving force behind the telephone industry, the Direction Générale des Télécommunications (DGT) imposed telematics as one of the major factors in the French economy; putting into concrete form the guidelines stated in the "Nora-Minc" report (11), it decided to develop videotex, and in 1980, at an interval of few months, it launched two pilot operations: the electronic telephone directory at Ille-et-Vilaine and Télétel at Vélizy. Confident of the justification for its choices, the Direction Générale des Télécommunications carried out these two operations with the intention of completely controlling their execution, in order to ensure the irreversibility of the spread of the innovation.

In order to perform its functions the DGT therefore created two project teams; one for the Ille-et-Vilaine electronic directory and the other for Télétel 3V. The first is under the control of CNET/DAI I and the second is subordinate to the DACT. These two teams occupy a specific position within the DGT based on a determination to remove the partitions in the administration, which makes them the spokesmen for all the government departments involved in the development of videotex.

In addition to the development of the application for which they have been made responsible, each of these teams has a special function in relation to the socio-economic partner of the Telecommunications Administration; the "electronic directory" team is more particularly entrusted with relations with the heads of the telephone industry, and the "Télétel" team with relations with the bodies providing data-processing or information services; their function in fact overlaps with the fields for which their parent directorate is responsible. For the execution of the projects on the ground, the project teams work either with decentralized units of their original organization (Rennes CCETT, Lannion CNET for the electronic directory) or with the regional organizations of the Telecommunications Directorate; the latter merely take the place of the central departments, and their powers are confined to dealing with network problems; they can also carry out public relations tasks with the leaders of public opinion at the places where the experiments are carried out. At the same time, at regional level, management units for the telematics campaign are established, to pave the way for the DGT's campaign for the promotion of new products.

The administrative nature of the process of disseminating the technological innovation will be strengthened by the creation of another agency, which will be made responsible for the development of certain applications of videotex, namely CEESI-A (Centre d'Etudes et d'Expérimentation des Systèmes d'Information).

This body has a dual function: on the one hand, to create a department responsible for announcing the use of the system, i.e. for playing more or less the same promoting role within the DGT as that of the DGT in relation to the telephone and data-processing industry; that of working to improve relations between the Administration and those who are subject to its control and, for this purpose, of co-ordinating the action of public departments which have different functions, both horizontally and between central ans external government departments.

In the longer term, the CEESI is responsible for creating the conditions for the take-over of control of telematic systems/services by local authorities.

Despite appearances, we have not here abandoned the problems of social experimentation in making this detour into recent history: this entire movement by the Telecommunications Administration was part of a course of action marked by the concept of experimentation envisaged as an essential main line of a simultaneous reform of government and of society.

In the light of this movement it is perhaps no longer surprising to see the Telecommunications Administration developing a line of action exclusively governed by its own aims, which causes it to miss out entire sections of social reality. This attitude has a name, it indicates a method of organization and of government action: technocracy. It has become customary to use this term to define a type of technological rationalization of the administration of public welfare which more or less skilfully fits in with private interests. Perhaps this is not being quite precise enough; in any case, this judgment must be qualified for this particular government department and viewed as being not so much cynical but rather as representing a certain form of inevitability.

Many contributions to the Fourth International Days of IDATE emphasized this intersection of the technicians' phase with the social phase. The code to this mystery can be deciphered by looking at the analysis made by Mr. Roqueplot of the mark made by technology. The very form of the technical purpose of the Telecommunications Administration obliges it to adopt a line of action which is so often criticized; the very essence of telecommunication is the elimination of space and time, the negation of distance, the equalizing of all points in the territory, speed and uniformity (12). What is implemented in the DGT's experimental action is none other than the effect of this imaginative concept or rather of this symbol of the network: concern for efficiency, neutralization of intermediate factors, a generalizing purpose.

The action of the only body which, apart from the Telecommunications Directorate, was directly responsible for the development of videotex, soon ran up against its limits, despite some notable achievements. Administrative limits first of all; also limits due to an excessively instrumentalist view of a measure of reorganization, which will have the same effects on the DGT's own action.

It can be seen how, in this first phase, the Telecommunications Administration, either directly or by roundabout means, embodies the project for the diffusion of technical innovation: it incorporates on the one hand the industrial and economic objectives underlying telematics and determines the smallest details of the concrete framework for its development. The main effect of this action is the neutralization of all the traditional mediations which normally govern the relations between a central government department and the territory it covers, the social dimension. Telematics was a national matter; the clash was violent: the DGT was proposing to perform all the mediating functions everywhere (13). The excessively marked arbitrariness of this line of action provoked an unexpected - yet foreseeable - reaction. Parliament could not do other than pay attention to the emotion aroused in the traditional media, for several reasons.

By attempting to convince only in terms of efficiency, disregarding the role and importance of the traditional mediators of French society, the DGT, as the executive organ of the State, was checked in its headlong course by the legislative authorities, which demand that a closer check be kept on its decisions and its action. The government's first reaction was to confirm the original guidelines adopted by the DGT. This attitude, which was also indicative of a view of the relationships between the machinery of government and civil society, was to be modified.

At the beginning of 1981 the Commission de suivi des expériences de télématique destinées au public (Committee for following up experiments in telematics intended for the public) was established by the Secretary of State for the PTT. The Committee's activities, while they led to important results such as the creation of a legal framework for experiments in telematics, did not, despite its wishes, fundamentally solve the problem of the respective positions of Parliament and the Government with regard to decisions for which the latter remains solely responsible.

The demand that a check be kept on the Telecommunications Administration was maintained until the time when it changed its own strategy in the summer of 1981.

At that time, the meaning of the experimentation changed from being technico-commercial to technico-social. This transformation reflected a widening of the field - the network - of decision-making; it did not fundamentally change its position in time. Just as, at the level of the uses, an experimental conception proceeding by abstraction is opposed to an approach which takes into account the notion of specific utilizations - in other words, the singular as an aspect of the universal - at the level of action there is perhaps an opposition between a linear, mechanistic vision and a more conscious conception of the complexity of the decision-making process.

In this national debate the experimentation approach for a long time continued to be of a formal nature; thus the Follow-up Committee did not have any power to intervene in the concrete course of the experiments; its action related solely to the general framework of the action undertaken by the Government, without the general aims or - on the opposite side - the procedures employed locally ever being disputed. A different set of problems will appear with the new line of action adopted by the DGT, of seeking to arrive at a consensus with all the social actors involved in the dissemination of the innovation: the Committee becomes the first stage in the dialogue between the Telecommunications Administration and the local participants. The Telecommunications Administration will develop this approach just on the basis of the links between parliamentarians and their constituencies.

Several approaches in the DGT's strategy make allowance, in their very approximation, for a new orientation of telecommunications, in which the repercussions of the conflicts are postponed, appear at unexpected points and are sometimes - inevitably - surprising. We are now at this second phase of telematics where the local factor comes on to the scene, responsible for ensuring the continuity of the development of the new systems. In this new experimentation space we witness first of all a veritable reversal of positions. Those who were desirous of keeping a check on and limiting the experiments now call for them, while those who wanted to impose a system now offer it, henceforth lending a willing ear to all wishes expressed.

The change is not only a matter of words. The change of position of the Telecommunications Administration as time goes on is paralleled by a shift in the institutional and territorial space for which the experimenters are made responsible. At the end of 1981 the Regional Telecommunications Directorates assumed responsibility for the development of the applications of videotex in their territories. The Telecommunications Administration did not so much change strategy as take advantage of a dual status, a dual image; the Regional Telecommunications Director became the first inter-locutor, the privileged agent of the local factor and no longer just the representative of the central administration. This distinction is not unimpor-tant and deserves closer attention.

The Telecommunications Administration and the Territory: a Dual Link

Because its expansion is relatively recent - dating from the 1970s - the Telecommunications Administration is characterized by an original organi-zation and position within the French administrative structure. Unlike other government departments which, like it, have an organizational function, it is not, at regional level, subordinate to the "Etablissement Public Régional", the Prefect. The Regional Telecommunications Directors are directly re-sponsible to the Director-General of Telecommunications; the Telecom-munications budget is autonomous. This separation from the local area was accentuated even further in the period which saw the creation of the Délégations de Zone in 1980, which no longer coincided with the French regional administrative divisions; although there has now been a return to a more traditional level of territorial responsibility for the Administration's external departments, their representative nevertheless has an incomparable degree of freedom of action (14); this "national" status of the representat-ives of the Telecommunications Administration, the relative autonomy of their activity, enables them to stand aside as being above parties. Their very abstraction gives them, more than other bodies, the status of representat-ives of the public interest.

This image of neutrality is coupled with a positivity conferred by the very technology of telecommunications. The plan for the creation of networks (telephone or telematics) cannot be regarded as an infringement of - private or public - individual interests, comparable to a road construction project, which affects land and immediately marks out space.

Here the problems come later; the Telecommunications Directorate first of all contributes something which is additional and does not remove anything: a point which is capable of puzzling even the most well-informed. A further abstraction: the technical mastery of the representatives of the Telecommunications Administration is indisputable. The local authority may rightly dispute the route of a motorway; it is, on the other hand, rather at a loss when it comes to the deployment of telecommunications techniques. If it has requests to make - and, it would seem that this is all it does - it has to rely on the other party. On top of this expert intervention there is an intervention from the political angle, which, paradoxically, is based on an apolitical position. A final abstraction, which is really mortifying: if the tensions on the local plane are too great and there is a stalemate as regards the situation for a telematics project, the regional telecommunications body may refer the matter back to the central administration so that it can withdraw or change its approach. This is perhaps overstating the position somewhat - but only slightly: account must be taken of the forces behind a process the uniqueness of which is too liable to be minimized. There is a big dose of symbolism in these apparently cold operations which is accounted for not only by the technical administration alone but also - and just as much - by the social groups, the territories concerned or those which represent them.

The subject of communication does not only involve, as has been seen, arriving at a consensus at the level of representative bodies; it also covers a whole range of activities which have a direct effect on various sectors of activity and which are first perceived by those who act for the community via its institutions. Hence it is they who first of all - and rightly - appear on the local scene of telematics experimentation. Information is a constant concern for the members of local authorities.

Increasing the efficiency of their action by mastering information, measuring its effects and reporting on their activities are the primary aims of the local authorities with regard to communication. Recognition of the role played by information in the running of public affairs has induced many elected representatives to make it an essential dimension of all policies. The new telecommunication technique have all the necessary attractive features for this approach. It might even be thought that the technical system in itself will go so far as to make up for the lack of communication, or again that technology will only have an existing or depressing effect - in any case no other effect than itself. But the - simplistic - assumption of a desire in political quarters to achieve communication for communication's sake does not hold water. Even though there is indeed an element of delusion, an expectation of extra power in the aim of rationalization of information, there is above all the desire to rationalize the running of the territory, an aim which destroys the delusion aspect. The local authorities are modelling the area for which they are responsible, and this is the task that they assign to telematics.

Echoing the unanimity which, as has been seen, brings together the protagonists of telematics on the national plane, there is at local level a desire for eonomic development, of which telematics can be an instrument. It inspires two hopes: increasing productivity and creating jobs.

This aim, put forward by the politicians, may also be adopted by the regional representatives of the Telecommunications Administration; an echo, and hence also a distortion.

The abstraction of telematics will take on solid shape in the fabric of local interests, and this in two ways: it may become part of a firmly-based policy, and it may become the essential feature of a forward-looking policy, a speculative project; this leads to a convergence of all projects, being at one and the same time a condition of what will be and the thing of the future itself; the dual status of telematics: at the same time a project which combines and the instrument of a project which goes beyond it.

INFORMATION AND PLANNING

An instrument of an economic project in which there is full scope for the rationalization of information, telematics is also, for the municipalities, a tool for the planning of the local space - a space which is both physical and social, within which modes of circulation and interlinking must be established. Videotex is regarded above all as a means of communication.

The concept of network also determines the image of videotex viewed as an information service which strengthens the link between the administration and those who are administered. It is part of the public communication policy, an answer to the crisis of justification which is being experienced by administrations and municipalities, an attempt at reconciliation between the civil society and the world of politics.

THE DEBATE BETWEEN TECHNICIANS AND POLITICIANS

But the reversal of the relationship between the Telecommunications Administration and the local receiving environment which took place in 1981 is perhaps an illusion. While local demand did in fact take over from an "arbitrary and technocratic" policy, the neutrality of technicians and engineers disappears within the very status of experts which the elected representatives allow them. The political project of social communication and decentralization, defended in local quarters, would then be lost in an all-embracing technical project.

THE EQUILIBRIA OF THE LOCAL FACTORS

In 1981 Gabriel Dupuy (15) identified the objectives which are embodied in the creation of urban networks.

The re-questioning of the equilibrium which governs power relationships in local areas manifests itself particularly with regard to telematics experiments, in the relationship between press and local authorities. Incidentally it is in fact the press, we should recall, which, by its policy of rejection, halted the process of dissemination embarked upon by the DGT. It is now a participant in the projects undertaken in the regions - at least the public authorities hope so - and it poses the question of sharing out the respective territories, roles and prerogatives of each party.

At the time when, for the regional daily press, the question of justification arises, the development of telematics is the occasion for a restatement of justification. Assured at national level, the power of the press has to be built up again at local level.

The case of the Courrier Picart (16) is enlightening in this connection. The high degree of co-ordination of this project, the standing of the men by which it is headed, make it the region's most dynamic project. Its effectiveness can be measured by a simple comparison. The videotex electronic mail service planned by the Regional Council, for its part, is having difficulty in gaining acceptance: that is because, here, technical rationality is clashing with contradictory lines of argument put forward by microterritories (why should there be a terminal here and not there, why should this commune have one before this other one, etc.). Paradoxically, it is becoming easier to act with a view to generalizing the electronic telephone directory than to negotiate a terminal location plan with each local representative. All the more so because, the lower one goes in the territorial subdivisions, the more pressing are the questions posed.

This phenomenon is not, as can be seen, confined to Vélizy. It reflects the interference between two projects, or rather between two wishes to control the same initiative: the relationship between the territory and those who run it. Controlling the technical communication networks means only partially controlling the social networks. The social management of communication opens up another series of questions.

In fact it takes a long time to realize that, in this projection period which telematics still represents today, expectations and imaginings go far beyond what is possible.

This movement from enthusiasm to disenchantment is the effect of the return, in the mirage of telematics, of the concrete practices of information. The form of communication based only on the principle of a technology which proposes to solve the problem turns out to be only a form without content.

The requirements of organization give way to the requirements of use.

A reconsideration of telematics in the light of concrete information practices makes it possible to define more precisely the place where it operates: at the interconnection between the two dimensions in the administration/persons administered relationship: it is in fact the question of the nature and purpose of information, of the meeting of two lines of action.

Lines of action of which one links up with the political function of the government administration and the other with the interchanges of which everyday life is made up. Both lines of action are shot through with transparency and opacity. When the government administration justifies the choice of telematics, it is by invoking a transparency which has at last become possible, as is evidenced by the name Claire. A mythical transparency into which the operation of political and institutional factors reintroduces opacity.

The user then runs up against the opacity of information organized according to an administrative structure with which he is unfamiliar. The user is also the agent of this opacity, insofar as his action is foreign and incomprehensible to the administration. The answer he is given is equally alien.

INFORMATION PRACTICES

Dialogue is possible only via a series of mediations, because the complexity of defining information contents is matched by the complexity of the contacts to be established in terms of places and of methods.

Should the place of contact be private or public? This is not another way of saying individual or collective use; it would appear that the answer to this question consists of a mere reformulation: the place will be private or public.

This settles another question of the development of telematics: the establishment of public equipment partly makes up for the gradualness of the equipping of private locations. The equipping of public locations, as has been seen, directly affects the organization of communication networks. It is possible by this means to modulate the dissemination of information. But access to the system is only the first step in use, and the fact that the

Administration and those whom it administers feel each other to be alien leads to the emergence of a new figure, that of the mediator.

Mention has been made several times of these human intermediaries of the system; their role gives rise to a new anxiety with regard to what they will do to the sophisticated apparatus of information. Insidiously, behind this configuration, there looms the absolute disappearance of the system, its annihilation.

Another form of the transparency of technology, in which its desire for negation is expressed; the dialogue between man and machine, the point where contact takes place: that is certainly the capital point where everything is at stake - a risk which the mediators would minimize for us. How is one to reconcile the formalization of processed data and the more erratic search by the average user? The various possible ways of organizing information are all determined in relation to this question.

All these questions, all these alternatives submitted to the wisdom of the specialists are a way of restating the fundamental problem, that of the status of information.

INFORMATION/DECISION-MAKING

What is this information which is provided to us by telematics systems? Or rather, what is its function? Faced with the frustration generated by information which is, all things considered, mediocre, in many experiments carried out in 1981 and 1982 there is an incipient desire for active telematics, an all-powerful servant.

Exploitation of the speed of data processing, a movement towards a decision making sequence in which the moments of obtaining information, deliberation and decision are in a way simultaneous. In other words, the devising of a system in which decision-making is equivalent to information management.

This comes down to a reversal of the usual order of circulation of information; to no longer giving precedence to the transmitter but first of all to the receiver of information. The Administration - since, as can be seen, it is administrative information with which we are concerned - adopts an attitude which is new to it, a pragmatic approach in which the information statement is considered first of all in its implication for the user, and no longer solely in relation to the consistency of the apparatus which provides it. Again a question of speed - the system must be designed in advance. Paradoxially, this is equivalent to a reversal of the positions of the machine and the user: the latter becomes the supplier of information and the machine decides.

This delegation of the decision-making step is reflected concretely in some institutional and technical organization hypotheses of information systems, such as the segmentation of the public or the position of the mediator. Delegation does not fail to give rise to certain misgivings; does it not merely represent a dispossession?

A conception which is entirely devoted to operationality, to the rationalization of interchanges, is again opposed by a representation of everyday life which is intended to stop short of a technological aim; the medical reference ("the body social") calls for no comment. Something akin to life is in fact touched by the meeting of these two systems, the one embodied more clearly in an anthropological representation and the other in a more technological representation.

The opposition referred to just now harks back to a phenomenon which is perceptible in the various experiments in telematics for the general public, which makes it necessary to consider the method of dissemination of innovation. Marginal experiments such as that of TLM do in fact seem to be taking this course. Hence the idea that the substitution of services which underlay the designing of the first telematics systems can be only a temporary orientation, that the new systems must produce new uses.

On the other hand, that does in fact entail a reorganization of communication networks. This loop of the debate on the development of new means of communication in connection with experiments reflects a risk in telematics: that of reproducing, at great expense, something that already exists.

These new uses which are foreshadowed but not identified will result from an essential dimension of telematics systems, namely interactivity.

Just beneath the surface of all the interventions there is a quasi-obsessional evocation of time: this time which is lacking, this distant or already passed time expresses the plan or the wish for a space in which the different social phases would coincide: that of the technicians, that of the decision-makers, that of the users. One could also add that of at least two codes. Consensus, harmony, measure... It can be understood, therefore, that innovation mobilizes investigators from every quarter: responsibility for making the translation into reality comes back to them.

CONCLUSION

The disturbing thing about social experimentation, to the point of making some people deny its existence, is above all its artificial side (its artificiality). And it is true that, although the simulation is in fact said to be what it is, this is always done, despite everything, without mentioning its name. It is therefore necessary, for the development of new means of communication, to abandon this idea, knowing that to state the rule would spoil the game. But we would not be fooled all the same and, in its very seriousness, the historical phenomenon represented by the advent of new forms of communication will always be detectable through these bars, within reach of anyone who is bold enough to grasp it. And why, for that matter, should we not reverse the argument and assert, contrary to those for whom the artificiality of the experiment is synonymous with sterility, that it is in fact the essential feature of the work of the metaphor, the production of an "acting as if" situation, that has constituted the entire effectiveness of social experimentation in the field of new communication techniques, here and now.

NOTES

1. "L'expérimentation sociale en Télématique". Montpellier, October 1982.
2. A. Briole, R. Lauraire, S. Craipeau: Genése de la notion d'Expérimentation Sociale. IDATE. 1983.
3. Proceedings of the October 1982 symposium.
4. Saussure: in his linguistics lectures "pas de propriété dans la langue" ("no ownership in language").
5. P. Ory "Les expositions universelles". 1981.
6. Without mentioning its adoption as a university discipline.
7. R. Jakobson: "Essai de linguistique générale". 1953.
8. A process which was started as far back as the 17th century, especially by the school (Foucault, de Certeau).
9. Fontanier: "Les figures du discours".
10. "Le vidéotex en Europe". D.F. 1982.
11. L'informatisation de la Société. D.F. 1980.
12. Other works have shown the recurrence of these themes in the imaginary conception of telecommunications, see S. Craipeau and A. Tyar "Telecommunications et Science-fiction", IDATE, January 1983.
13. Perhaps this panorama should be qualified; what is described here refers back more to the policy of the development of the electronic directory which was in the foreground; in its shadow, the Télétel project was already exploring other ways, despite a generally identical course.
14. It should be added that the DRTs are often the first investors in their regions; this means that their economic power is considerable.
15. Gabriel Dupuy: "Pour une génétique des réseaux urbains: de l'assainissement à la télématique", Proceedings of the 1981 IDATE Symposium "Des réseaux locaux".
16. J.M. Charon in "Réseaux" No. 15 and IDATE study 1983 (see note 2).

PART II: EXAMPLES

One can find social experiments with I.T. in almost every sector of society: in agriculture, health-care, education, social services, private homes, local communities, public information services, private businesses, grass-roots movements, etc. And these social experiments involve many different kinds of technology: interactive videotex, teletext, broadband networks, interactive video, teleconferencing, etc. In part II, Henning Albrechtsen introduces the "tele-house" experiment in Vemdalen, Sweden, and its Scandinavian context is summarised by Lars Qvortrup. Joseph Mannion reviews a number of experiments with agricultural computerised information systems in Ireland, and Gareth Morgan gives an overview of the development of micro-computer systems designed to calculate individual social security and welfare benefits in the U.K. In the two last papers of this section, Gaëtan Cambra and Michael Pieper discuss the pros and cons of computer-conferencing, and the relevance - and problems - of social experiments for gaining a clearer picture of end-user needs.

THE ELECTRONIC VILLAGE HALL OF VEMDALEN

Henning Albrechtsen, Vemdalen, Sweden

The first fully operational Scandinavian Information and Community Service Centre has been established in Vemdalen, a small village in the middle of rural Sweden. In the centre, local people have access to N.I.T. on a cooperative basis, thus making them independent of the distance to economic, administrative, educational and cultural centres.

In the small village of Vemdalen the visitor can see an unexpected sight. On the first floor of the building containing the local general store, a considerable number of modern computers and high-tech equipment are being used diligently by local people from 8 o'clock in the morning til 10 o'clock in the evening.

The equipment is worth a closer look. PC 'AT's, fifteen personal computers from the US and Japan, word-processors/teletexes from Holland, Telefax, videotex, in short: lots of high-tech equipment in the heart of a sparsely populated, mountainous part of Sweden. And all this equipment is being used by 15 percent of the total population of the village, and all ages are represented: children from their tenth year and pensioners denote the range. And the Electronic Village Hall is not only an educational centre for the village itself, but also for the region of Härjedalen, a municipality the size of the island of Funen - approx. 13000 square kilometers - but with barely 13000 inhabitants, i.e. one person per square kilometer.

The region of Härjedalen is situated in the middle of Sweden - a country 2000 kilometers in length - and borders on Norway. It is part of the administrative province of Jämtland which once was a part of Norway and thus belonged to the Danish crown for approx. four hundred years. During the period of violent altercations between Denmark/Norway and Sweden, the Scandinavians became involved in the Thirty Years' War. The Danish king, Kristian IV, had scant success, whereas Protestant Sweden joined forces with Catholic France and triumphed, even though the Swedes lost their gallant king. On their way back from the European Continent the victorious Swedish generals conquered Denmark, and as a result of the peace-negotiations at the village of Brömsebro in 1645 Denmark was forced to surrender Jämtland/Härjedalen to Sweden.

Even today Härjedalen is a remote part of Sweden. The inhabitants have taken advantage of their mountains and have transformed some villages into skiing-resorts, and as Jämtland/Härjedalen is one of the few mountain-regions of Sweden, lots of tourists flock around in the high season, the months of February, March and April. The region abounds in large forests of pine, fir and spruce, and on the moors peat is found which ensures work for a number of people. But tourism is stagnating. There is no pulp-industry, and the old craftsmen are a dying breed. The young people of Härjedalen, although loving their beautiful country, are forced to leave their mountain-home and take up work in the industrialized parts of Sweden around the cities of Stockholm, Gothenburg and Malmö.

The northern parts of Sweden have lost a large number of inhabitants in the course of the last decades. The furniture vans on their way from the sparsely populated areas in the northern and western parts of Sweden have been a frequent sight on their way towards the southern and eastern regions of the country. The Swedish governments have for a good many years tried to halt the stream of people seeking the cities, but the efforts have largely been in vain. The County Government Board of Jämtland saw clearly that more efficient measures were needed, and the socialist government of Sweden allocated the sum of 10 million Swedish kronor to propagate the diffusion of new technology in the province.

The Jämtland County Government Board and the University College of Östersund in close cooperation with the Nordic Council of Ministers in April 1985 arranged a seminar with participants from the Scandinavian countries. The seminar was held at Östersund, the main town of the province. One of the speakers at the seminar was Mr. Jan Michel from the village of Fjaltring in Denmark. In an inspiring speech he told about his idea of establishing "Tele-huse" in sparsely populated parts of Denmark. His thoughts were eagerly taken up by some Swedish participants, and a committee consisting of high-ranking officials of the county Government Board and the University College plus myself commenced discussing a Swedish model. The Swedish Televerket, being responsible for all telecommunications in the country, saw the vast possibilities and its local director joined the committee, and it was decided to start up "Härjedalens Telestuga", the Electronic Village Hall of Härjedalen, as soon as possible. A document, taking lots of ideas from the Danes, established the aims of the Electronic Village Hall as follows:

1 To give the local population the chance of using modern technological equipment, thus removing their fear of the computer and their resistance to it.

2 To help local tradesmen to buy the right kind of equipment, suited to their needs.

3 To educate a large number of people in the use of modern computers, thus making them independent of the distance to the cultural centres and facilitating their access to the information-age.

4 To further local democracy.

5 To increase international cooperation.

The local politicians in the community were quite sceptical about the project in its first phases. The committee had drawn up a budget of SEK 700.000 (corresponding roughly to the same amount in French francs) for the first six months, but the local politicians showed no inclination to contribute. As the local papers, the local radio and local entrepreneurs praised the project, the mayor and his colleagues however, had second thoughts. The budget was extended to one million Swedish kronor, and the community council unanimously voted for allocating 400.000 SEK to the Telestuga. In the end the local politicians did not want to leave all initiative with the County Government Board, and to the Televerket who paid SEK 300.000 chiefly in the form of equipment (Teletex, Telefax, Videotex, and some personal computers).

From the very start the idea of the Electronic Village Hall was met with considerable interest inside and outside Sweden, and when the Telestuga was officially opened on September 13, 1985, we were happy to receive delegations from Denmark, USA, Norway, Italy, France and the U.K. among our guests. A delegation from the OECD, including former British Cabinet Minister, Mrs. Shirley Williams, MP, attended, and from the EEC Mr. Lars Qvortrup honoured us with his presence. A seminar was held and the papers of Härjedalen wrote profusely on the opening. It is estimated that considerably more than fifty percent of the total population attended the official opening of the Telestuga by professor, Inez Sperr Brisfjord of Long Island University.

No idea is right, unless it appears at the right moment, says Alvin Toffler. The idea of the Electronic Village Hall was indeed introduced to the people of Härjedalen at the right moment. A civil servant from a neighbouring village expressed the general feeling in the following terms: "Some ten or fifteen years ago I heard a tiny noise behind me; the computer was said to be of importance for everybody in the future. Today I have the feeling that the noise has increased and has overtaken me. I risk being left behind if I do not catch the train at the very last moment."

In the week following the opening we held informative meetings in the Telestuga for interested persons from the region. Lots of people came to see us, and today more than a hundred persons from Vemdalen follow 10-12 different courses. The participants in the courses come from all walks of life: small-scale entrepreneurs and/or their wives, shop assistants, farmers, craftsmen and children. We started an "Open House" arrangement on Friday afternoons for the children, in the pious hope that, after having tried a number of computer-games for some months, they would express a desire to get a proper computer education. They started asking for courses after six weeks, and when we gave the pupils in the 4th, 5th, 6th forms of the village school the offer of two lessons a week sixteen out of a total of 21 children joined the course. When their elder brothers and sisters heard about it, we were forced to start courses for them as well.

The aim of the present general education is to create a demand for specialized courses in book-keeping, planning, calculation, word-processing, communications, computer-aided design and many other subjects. The Telestuga today employs five persons, and it is to be expected that this number will be increased shortly. It is the intention to establish in connection with the Telestuga a number of jobs where people sit at home working each with their own computer, which again is connected to the main computer in the Telestuga. This kind of work has been viewed with distrust by the unions, if it means that single individuals are doing some kind of low-paid homework for large corporations, as such workers are easily exploited in their isolation. In the framework of the Telestuga they are ensured fair wages, and they will become members of the Telestuga staff. We have not yet created one single job of this kind, but two married couples have energetically embarked on getting a proper education which means that they can remain in the contryside instead of being forced to work in the big city. The Telestuga maintains close contact with the trade unions, one of which, the TCO, has formally signed an agreement on joint education with "Härjedalens Telestuga".

The Electronic Village Hall of Vemdalen is equipped with a combined television/videotex set. A rather large room has been cosily furnished with locally manufactured furniture and a large TV-set. In this room all villagers are welcome to watch TV-programmes received from satellites, with programmes in English, German, and French, and plans for more satellites are on their way. Between the television programmes the videotex gives relevant information on subjects of local interest: the agenda from the last meeting in the community council, information from the Country Government Board, information on vacant situations in the district, etc. Many small villages today have no natural meeting-place for the villagers. Pubs are rare in rural Sweden. In the village of Vemdalen the drawing room of the Telestuga is used every day by a considerable number of people.

Another advantage for the locals in having the Telestuga so near is the fact that they are welcome to use the computers in a separate room, either for training - many people drop in when they have finished shopping in the grocery store, while other persons use their lunch-break for retraining last night's lessons - or for doing their book-keeping. In the drawing room they find technological papers and magazines - and people with whom they can discuss the implications of the information age for their community and themselves. During these discussions numerous new ideas are launched, some of them to disappear again, others to be converted into real-life undertakings.

The Telestuga also offers service to enterprises, small and large, of the region. Letters, offers, drawings etc. are sent by telefax according to instructions given by phone. The Telestuga offers help in translating business offers and letters into a number of foreign languages, and the letters reach the intended addresses in a few seconds by Teletex. In this way smaller enterprises can exploit the advantages of the new technology without having to invest in costly equipment, and many firms, clubs and associations already use the services of "Härjedalens Telestuga".

The initial investment in the Telestuga was one million Swedish kronor. From the outset it was expected that the project would have further funds at the beginning of 1986. From the first day, however, the Telestuga was entrusted with the task of making computer/plotter programmes for a large project aiming to utilize some of the numerous moors of Härjedalen for the production of peat. By referendum it has been decided that the nuclear plants of Sweden are to be closed down by 2010, and the hunt for domestic fuel has already begun. As a result of the work on the peat-project, performed in the Telestuga, a new task has been given to us. The Swedish government's Third world aid-organization, SIDA, has launched a well-analyzing project in India, and the computer-programmes for this project are being run in the village of Vemdalen. Our world has really become smaller in this day and age! These two projects, plus the educational activities - 90 lessons a week - and the service to local firms have ensured us a monthly income of approx. SEK 150.000. There is good reason to believe that further grants will not be needed.

"Härjedalens Telestuga" has created new life and a spirit of optimism in the region of Härjedalen. Each month we have several study-groups from other parts of Sweden visiting us, and many of these groups have told us that they will return to their homes to create their own Electronic Village Halls. The Norwegian Television spent a day in the Telestuga, filming the activities and interviewing a number of people, and the resulting programme was shown on "Norsk Rikskringskasting" on a Sunday evening in December. The very next day a group of people from a village outside Bergen telephoned to establish contact, and a new Norwegian Telestuga project is on its way. The project in Vemdalen is followed closely by several countries within the EEC and from overseas.

Jan Michel's idea is spreading. In the province of Jämtland two new Electronic Village Halls were started in November and December, and the Danish project is well on its way. The cooperation between the Lemvig-projekt in Denmark and the Telestuga in Sweden is close, and our contacts with Mr. Lars Qvortrup and the FAST-project of the EEC are excellent. It is my considered opinion that there ought to be lots of Electronic Village Halls all over Europe if we are to maintain our independence vis-à-vis the super-powers in the present Information Era. Let us face it: the Americans and the Russians have beaten us in various technological fields, but we can still catch up if we try hard enough. It is my hope that the Electronic Village Hall will mark the beginning of a new spirit of optimism and entrepreneurship on our old continent.

INFORMATION AND COMMUNITY SERVICE CENTRES IN SCANDINAVIA: A GENERAL OVERVIEW

Lars Qvortrup, Telematics Project, Odense University, Denmark

The aim of this 'postcript' to Henning Albrechtsen's presentation of the Electronic Village Hall of Vemdalen is to introduce the reader more generally to this Scandinavian orgware invention, officially known as the Information and Community Service Centre, a new kind of institution which illustrates well the general nature of social invention. For the invention of the telehouse has been the result of close collaboration between social and technological innovators; it has been based upon the practical expertise of actual end-users; and its further refinement depends on the mutual exchange of experience across boarders in Scandinavia.

THE INFORMATION AND COMMUNITY SERVICE CENTRE - STRUCTURE AND FUNCTIONS

In Sweden, Norway and Denmark a number of so-called Information and Community Service Centres (ICSCs) have been (or are being) established. The main aim of the ICSCs is to provide isolated village communities with access to telecommunications services. Instead of linking individual households onto a network, the working-parties on these projects have chosen to concentrate I.T. facilities within specially designed 'tele-houses', containing video and E.D.P. equipment which are thus at the disposal of the entire local communities involved. The facilities are intended as much for private as for commercial use, with satellite T.V. reception, teleshopping, interactive Citizens Advice services, etc.

The public provision of I.T. facilities is obviously partly designed to supply smaller rural communities and isolated businesses with an informational infrastructure which would be far too costly for them to invest in individually. But it is also partly designed to strengthen these local communities technologically, so as to help them to avoid the twin threats of economic stagnation (as the otherwise inevitable result of commercial and administrative centralisation) and cultural impoverishment (as the result of cultural centralisation and the replacement of local cultural activities by the isolated consumption of passive T.V. entertainment).

A Working Definition of the ICSC Concept

The ICSC was invented in Denmark, the concept evolving out of a so-called "teleproject" in the rural district of Lemvig. The blue-print for the first ICSC project was drawn up in December 1984. Inspiration for this first project was, however, derived from projects informed by similar ideas in many other parts of the world. Experiments had, for example, been made with so-called "Community Information Centers" in the U.S.A. in the 'seventies (cf. Manfred Kochen and Joseph C. Donohue, eds., Information for the Community, Chicago, 1976).

An ICSC may be defined as a centre where N.I.T. apparatus is placed at the disposal of the citizens of a specific local community with a characteristically marginal geographical location, so that communal use may be made of the facilities available. The purpose of the ICSC is to counteract some geographically determined disadvantages which the local community involved has been forced to suffer under, whether they have been of an economic, educational or cultural nature, or have concerned employment, services, or other infrastructural facilities.

Within the limits of a definition of this kind the various ICSCs are of course organised very differently. But it is generally the case that all (or most) of the following basic services are provided in the "tele-houses", as they are colloquially named:

- an information service is available to the local population, with access to municipal information, business information, library catalogues, and other national and international databases;
- the day-to-day management of the ICSC is undertaken by an N.I.T. consultant who helps local businesses and organisations to get the most out of the equipment available;
- facilities are provided for distance working, where the ICSC's provision of a number of work stations in close proximity to each other enables workers to retain a sense of work-place fellowship;
- educational courses are offered in I.T. (introductory computer courses,

for example) <u>and educational courses are provided by means of I.T.</u> (C.A.L., C.A.T. and "Open University"-type online tutorials, for instance);

- <u>telecommunications facilities are provided</u>, enabling local citizens to communicate with the rest of the world within or beyond their national borders, using teletex ot telefax terminals, for instance;

- <u>the ICSC plays a rôle in the political and cultural life of its community</u>, primarily by providing rooms and facilities for meetings, but also by supplying municipal and county information, and by permitting local citizens to watch national and international T.V. programmes together, etc., etc.

ICSCs in the Scandinavian Countries: an Overview

At the time of writing, ICSCs have been planned and are being established in three rural districts in <u>Denmark</u>: in Lemvig (three are under construction); in Egvad (five have been planned); and on the small island of Fejø in the rural district of Ravnsborg (one ICSC). Recently, the Danish Government authorised a grant of 11 million Dkr towards the cost of these experiments. In <u>Norway</u> ICSCs have been planned in Vardø and Hamarøy (in the northern part of Norway) and in Gjesdal, near Stavanger. In <u>Sweden</u> the first fully equipped ICSC to open in the whole of Scandinavia was the one in Vemdalen, a small village in the rural district of Härjedalen, and three more ICSCs in the same municipality have been planned in the small villages of Sveg, Hede and Funäsdalen.

Denmark

As I mentioned earlier, the actual idea of the ICSC originally crystallised in the rural district of Lemvig in Northwest Jutland, towards the end of 1984, as the bearing element within a project intended to support the overall cultural, social and economic development of the area. There are plans to open three so-called "tele-houses"; one in Fjaltring, a village near the West coast of Denmark with a total of 150 households within the village itself and its outlying districts; one in Nørre Nissum, a local educational centre 20 kilometers North-east of Fjaltring and 10 kilometers East of Lemvig, with a number of educational institutions and some 1,400 inhabitants; and one in Lemvig itself, the provincial capital with over 7,000 inhabitants. At the time of writing, these three ICSCs are being fully equipped and are just about to become operational. Their relative proximity facilitates close technical collaboration, which means that - while all three have the same basic equipment - each of them in turn can house its own particular specialised equipment as well, to the benefit of all three of them. At the same time, their individual social settings are sufficiently different - (the remote village, the small town, the provincial capital) - to ensure that the full potential of the ICSC concept is explored.

Still in Jutland, and approximately 75 kilometers south of Lemvig, we find the rural district of Egvad - again, sparsely populated by Danish standards, predominantly agricultural, and with above-average unemployment. Here five ICSCs have been planned, and they are - amongst other things - to undertake experiments with regard to information supplies and services, including a library information service, in connection with existing library facilities. Other experiments are to be made with the provision of a business consultancy service with relation to the local manufacturing, agricultural, and service industries; and distance working has also been envisaged. Local authorities in the rural district are interested in improving their services to citizens in the more outlying areas by using the ICSCs as "decentralized municipal offices", and, with the help of the ICSCs, they hope to be able to provide more efficient educational facilities for adults and children alike. Amongst other things, extension and retraining courses have been planned, together with open computer workshops. And finally, the ICSCs in the rural district of Egvad are to provide frameworks for preventive, and improved on-the-spot health-care projects by facilitating close collaboration between doctors, district nurses, home-helps and social workers, who will have immediate access to hospitals, medical consultants' surgeries, and welfare offices.

Finally, in Denmark, an ICSC project has left the drawing-board and is getting under way on a little island called Fejø, to the south of Zealand. 700 people live on Fejø, but, over the last 20 or 30 years or so, there has been a noticeable decline in the number of islanders who have been locally employed in trades necessary for the regular maintenance of a reasonable standard of living on the island. Publicly-funded institutions, such as the school, old people's home, post-office, and local medical practice, still exist intact, but their continued existence is threatened by the fact that the size of their clientele is so limited. The ICSC experiment on Fejø is thus intended as an attempt to reduce or remedy the problems of geographical isolation which are faced by the inhabitants of many of the 483 islands which - together with the penninsular of Jutland - make up the Danish nation. Agricultural and commercial consultant services have been planned, together with educational extension services, and other N.I.T.-mediated public services.

Norway

In Norway too, as I mentioned earlier, three ICSC projects are at present on the drawing-board. Two of them are to be opened in the northernmost parts of the country, well within the Arctic Circle - one in Vardø, on the north-eastern tip of Norway, 50-100 kilometers north of the Finnish and Soviet borders; and one on Hamarøy between the Lofoten Islands and the Norwegi-an mainland. Vardø has a total of some 3,300 inhabitants, and Hamarøy has over 2,000, but the populations of both regions are dwindling on account of their geographical isolation, and because of their lack of technically-qualified workers. Yet, in spite of the fact that many of the younger inhabitants have left the regions in order to find work further south, they still have a high level of unemployment, which can at present only be remedied by publicly-funded alternative employment projects. The two ICSCs in northern Norway are thus primarily intended as experimental distance-working centres, with work-stations for data- and word-processing. They are, however, also expected to fulfil a number of public service functions.

The third ICSC experiment in Norway is scheduled to take place at the other end of the country - down in the south-western region - in Gjesdal, a rural district bordering on Stavanger. There are both agricultural and manufactu-ring industries in Gjesdal, but the ICSC here is primarily intended to offer distance-working facilities to former Stavanger commuters.

Sweden

The first fully equipped ICSC to open in Scandinavia was the one in Vemdalen: 'Härjedalens Telestuga', which was described in detail in the preceding article by Henning Albrechtsen.

As Albrechtsen mentioned, the "tele-house" at Härjedalen is supposed to provide the village community with five basic services:

1. Information retrieval.
2. A Consultancy Service.
3. Distance working.
4. Training and education.
5. Electronic village hall facilities.

THE SCANDINAVIAN ICSCs: THE DIALECTICS OF REACTIVE AND PROACTIVE SOCIAL INNOVATION

A general tendency towards the centralisation and the concentration of capital is the economic background against which the ICSC initiatives in Denmark, Norway and Sweden have emerged. In the rural district of Lemvig, for example, this economic problem is especially felt by the agricultural sector, reflecting the general trend in Denmark. In 1950, 465,900 people were employed in the agricultural sector in the whole of Denmark, but in 1980 the figure was only 162,880. And if the existing trends continue unmodified, there will only be some 30,000 full-time farms left in 1990. With so few farms spread over the total rural area in Denmark, many traditional but vitally necessary services in the small villages (local shops, craftsmen, schools, public libraries, post offices etc.) will disappear.

A similar tendency may be detected in Sweden. Here the dominant economic sector in rural areas has been forestry. But structural changes and increases in productivity in the forestry business generally have caused unemployment figures to rise far beyond the national average. A further consequence is the loss of the small village's cultural identity, since the tourist industry has now become the most important source of income for a number of mid-Swedish rural districts. The social network, with its households, and with its formal and informal commercial, social and cultural institutions, is falling apart.

Thus the professed aims of the ICSCs in Scandinavia are to counteract, or at any rate mitigate, some of the negative consequences of these seemingly irreversible socio-economic tendencies. Through the provision of services intended to support local businesses - (consultant and information services and improved telecommunications) - and through the provision of distance-working facilities, it is hoped that the ICSCs will be able to alleviate some of the economic and employment problems facing geographically marginal and increasingly depopulated regions within the Scandinavian nations. Through the provision of improved educational facilities (both by means of N.I.T., and with regard to the study of N.I.T. itself), and by rendering more immediately accessible information of public interest from centres of regional and national government, the ICSCs are intended to redress some of the educational and political disadvantages faced by socio-geographically marginal populations. And by supplying library-services and satellite television reception - and by providing meeting and conference facilities - the ICSCs are intended to mitigate some of the cultural disadvantages attendant on remote habitation.

Insofar as the Scandinavian ICSC is, however, only an attempt to put the clock back; or insofar as it is a more or less deliberate attempt to solve urban overcrowding problems by converting former villages into dormitory suburbs at very little cost to the tax-payer; or, thirdly, insofar as the ICSC is an experiment conducted over the heads of the populations concerned by interested outsiders, for either of the above reasons or for some other reason - we will not be able to escape the conclusion that the Scandinavian ICSCs qualify only as "social laboratories". As a social laboratory, the ICSC is a re-active institution, intended only to reduce or alleviate the negative consequences of socio-economic trends, but not intended to produce any qualitative alternative to these tendencies.

If however, the Scandinavian ICSC is to earn the title of a "future (or participatory) workshop" it cannot be purely re-active. It must do more than obstinately cling onto the status quo - irrespective of whether it is the status quo prevailing within the isolated village, or within the modern industrialised nation as a whole. It must, in other words, be socially proactive, or, as futurologists would say, genuinely "anticipative".

It is a sine qua non for the socially anticipative effect of an ICSC that the social experimenters have a positive attitude towards qualitative changes in the prevailing status quo. By providing communal workshop facilities together with work-stations for distance working, the ICSC might be able to question the traditional distinction between paid and unpaid productive work. Similarly, the ICSC might be able radically to redress the socio-political and cultural imbalances which have hitherto prevailed between centre and periphery in modern industrialised nations, since ICSCs could become popular instruments for challenging informational monopolies previously held by the metropolis. And, finally, there can be no doubt about the fact that the ICSC will alter traditional thinking about I.T., in the sense that I.T. apparatus has hitherto come to be regarded strictly as private property, and its successful utilization has to a great extent been dependent on expensive expert guidance, or on the purchase of ready-made standard programme packages.

It is, of course, the more far-reaching perspectives of this kind which make the Scandinavian ICSC potentially enriching, in anticipative terms. But it is no less important to realise that these proactive perspectives may be able to coexist beside - if they do not actually emerge out of - the more reactive visions which prompted the social experiments in the first place. Indeed, in our most promisingly innovative social experiments with ICSCs in Scandinavia, a sober reactive realism goes hand in hand with an anticipatory enthusiasm. For it is, of course, fallacious exclusively and damningly to evaluate the ICSC in terms of some specific social tendency prevalent at the time of its conception. It would be abortive if one were to dismiss the ICSC out of hand merely on the ground that it was originally conceived of as a tool for traditional economic and political interest groups - and that, as such, it forms part of its existing society's ongoing formal economy. For, at one and the same time, the Scandinavian ICSC represents a new social movement's vision of the autonomous organisation of small-scale community life - a vision which cuts across traditional party-lines and the ongoing socio-economic and cultural schisms which they represent. The logical consequence of the full realisation of the anticipative potential of the Scandinavian Information and Community Service Centre is that it will become a vital organisational centre for the qualitative renewal of the social and political economy of the local community and the wider society within which it has been created.

THE USE OF COMPUTERISED INFORMATION SYSTEMS IN AGRICULTURE

Joseph Mannion, Department of Agricultural Extension, University College Dublin

In this paper the necessity for and scope of electronic technology as an aid to information management in agriculture is examined. The results of a research project designed to identify the information needs of potential users of the videotex service in Ireland are also presented. Finally, the implications of computerised information systems for agricultural advisory /extension services and farmers is discussed.

INTRODUCTION

In most developed and developing countries the impact of new technology and the effect of government policies have been powerful instruments of change in the field of agriculture, particularly during the last 50 years. The results include a more efficient and more productive agriculture, a plentiful food supply for consumers and, more recently, overproduction of some commodities in Europe and North America. In terms of the workforce engaged in agriculture the consequences are: (i) a large number of low output farmers some of whom combine their farming with another occupation; and (ii) a smaller number of more efficient high output farmers who make the major contribution to national agricultural output.

All the indicators are that those who are likely to survive in farming will be those who continue to improve technical efficiency through adoption of appropriate modern technologies. Increasingly, however, they must make their management decisions on the basis of more rigorous cost/benefit assessments including the facility to respond directly to market forces. Thus, the successful farmer will not only be up to date on modern production methods but will also be skilled in making production/business management decisions and well briefed on market prospects and requirements. In other words he needs considerable abilities to handle information. This is not an easy task and the challenge for those who service the agricultural industry is to develop and implement ways and means of improving the efficiency and effectiveness of information management at farm level.

Electronic Technology

Electronic technology, in the form of computer based information storage, analysis, retrieval and delivery systems, now represent a means of dealing with the information management problem. Bell et al. (1985, p.11) note that such systems offer not only the opportunity for much more efficient data storage and retrieval by agricultural advisory service personnel but of giving farmers and others in the industry direct access to data bases. Agar (1985, pp.55-61), based on an analysis of the information-using activities of advisers in the U.K., suggests a useful framework for examining the scope of computers as information managers in the work of advisory services with farm audiences. This is shown in Appendix 1. She describes the proliferation in the use of computerised information systems, both within and outside advisory services and gives examples of interactive programmes for decision making in agriculture available in the U.K. (Appendix 2). In the United States the Electronic Technology Task Force Report (Pennsylvania State University, 1985) sponsored by the Extension Service USDA, recommended that:

> The cooperative Extension Service must embrace the philosophy that the adoption of emerging electronic technology will enhance its program delivery capability.

In order to provide a frame of reference for the application of electronic technologies the Task Force divided extension work into three functional groupings: information delivery; educational delivery; and problem solving. The relationship of media technologies to these three functions were examined in order to help extension staff determine the relative advantage of different means of extension delivery. The summary relationship suggested are shown in Appendix 3.

At the Sixth European Seminar on Extension Education the question of how computerised information systems can help extension was raised. In answering this question it was agreed that these systems can help if: they improve the quality of decision making of both extension's clients and extension workers; and they focus on the decisions that are most critical to the economic condition of users (Mannion, 1984, pp.206-211). Aspects of extension work that could be enhanced include: advisory/education target audience identification (categorised by enterprise and other characteristics for extension programmes and activities)(1); priority setting; use of resources; upward and downward flows of information; speedier access of technical and other kinds of information for extension staffs; and overall better information management.

In relation to client decision making it was suggested that computerised information systems have to be integrated into our extension model with the focus on their utility in helping the client in decision making situations (Mannion, 1984, p.210).

This has been the challenge facing the agricultural extension and research organisations in Ireland in developing a computer based information system - videotex - for Irish farmers.

POTENTIAL VIDEOTEX USER STUDY

This section of the paper draws on the results of a research project (Shanahan, 1985) at the Departement of Agricultural Extension, University College Dublin, the purpose of which was to identify: the critical decisions that farmers make; how they currently use information sources in making decisions; and the types of farm decisions on which a computerised information service, such as videotex, could provide useful help for farmers.

In Ireland, two public organisations involved in agricultural research and extension (An Foras Taluntais - the agricultural research organisation, and ACOT - the agricultural education and advisory organisation) are currently involved in initiating a trial videotex service for agricultural interests in two areas of the country. The trial is partially funded by the Commission of the European Community and is operational since October, 1985 (see Appendix 4).

The aim of the trial is to establish the key elements of a good quality service that can form the foundation of a future public service. As part of the preparation for the trial it was recommended that a preliminary study of users' requirements should be undertaken (Aregon, 1983, p.27). The Department of Agricultural Extension research project is part of the preliminary study. It was designed to assist information providers in having relevant and time-critical information available for users when the Irish videotex service, called AgriLine, was launched.

Source of Data

The population for the study was 1,055 dairy farmers living in one of the areas selected for the experimental videotex project (the County Cork 021-subscriber trunk dialling area). The study sample was 137 farmers randomly selected from the study population who met the criteria of having a telephone and a dairy herd of at least 30 cows.

Interviews

In July 1984 a total of 125 interview schedules were completed in the study area.

The Results

1. A High Level of Interest in Videotex

Having been given verbal, written and pictorial description of the proposed videotex service, just over 70 per cent of the farmers interviewed stated they were interested in taking part in the videotex trial.

2. Ability to Use, Cost and the Quality/Relevance of the Service were Key Factors in Intention to Use the Service.

With regard to factors that would influence farmers' decisions to use videotex:

- 65 per cent mentioned factors directly or indirectly related to the training they would need to operate the system;

- 50 per cent cited factors related to the cost of operating the system;

- 38 per cent mentioned factors related to the quality and relevance of the information and services available through the system.

3. <u>High Users of Media, Agricultural Information Sources, Information Available from Farm Management Aids and Management Information Systems were most Interested in Videotex.</u>

- those who owned farm home and office facilities and equipment such as television, filing cabinet, video recorder, home computer, typewriter and a farm office were also more interested in becoming videotex users.

- a higher proportion of those with expertise in the household to operate calculators, typewriters and home computers (than those without this expertise) were interested in the service.

4. While the scale of the farm operation (farm size and enterprise size) were positively associated with intention to use videotex, the level of farm performance was not. However, farmers that were implementing modern farm practices were more interested in videotex than those who were not implementing such practices.

5. <u>The information Needs and Interactive Service Requirements of Potential Videotex Users</u>

In determining the information needs and interactive service requirements of potential videotex users three methods were used in the study:

(i)   the critical decisions that farmers made (or were about to make) in relation to their farming operations and the information used (needed) in deciding on particular courses of action were identified;

(ii)   the gaps between desirable and actual performance of critical farm management practices on the farms of potential videotex users were identified;

(iii) the expressed interests of potential videotex users for information and interactive service (computer programmes) through the system.

Based on an analysis of the results obtained through these three methods, 26 broad subject matter areas, with detailed topics (content) for each subject were identified. In addition, subjects/topics for which interactive farm management analysis package/programmes were needed were outlined.

The 26 broad subject matter areas on which information is needed by potential videotex users are shown in Appendix 2. An example of the detailed topics (content) identified for one subject area together with the possible information source/provider and the time of year when it is needed by farmers using the system, is shown in Appendix 3. The subjects/topics for which users would need interactive farm management analysis packages/programmes are shown in Appendix 4.

It should be noted that the listing of subjects and the topics/content included under each was derived from a "priority of need" ranking. This was based on: the frequency with which farmers mentioned making decisions or taking action on a particular subject/topic/practice; the percentage of farmers whose actual performance on key management practices fell short of the desired/recommended level; and the frequency with which farmers expressed an interest in getting information on a particular subject/topic through videotex.

This approach to identifying the information needs and interactive service requirement of potential videotex users is based on the view that an effective service is one which not only reflects the views of specialist information providers, but also the particular considerations and needs of the farmers. Blokker (1984, p. 231) makes the point that too often those who design information systems allow themselves to be guided by the level of sophistication and the potential of their equipment. One might also add that agricultural research workers who become information providers for such systems, often wish to provide information that answers problems from the perspective of their research interests. In many instances the problems which farmers face in making decisions are quite different.

The study findings in relation to the information needs of potential videotex users highlighted the fact that there was a strong demand for local (as well as national) information on topics related to markets and prices. Users required practical information on the livestock and crop husbandry problems they faced in their farming operations. There was an exceptionally strong demand for information/services requiring access to computer programmes. The highest demand was for programmes that were relatively simple to develop and operate such as: calculating winter feed requirements for livestock; balanced and economic levels of meal feeding; monitoring the level of fertiliser use and requirements; recording and analysing animal performance/production information; and cash income projections for specific enterprises.

IMPLICATIONS FOR THE ESTABLISHMENT OF VIDEOTEX

1. Based on the level of interest of farmers interviewed in the study it is concluded that there is potentially a sizeable market for a videotex information service on commercial farms. In Ireland, it is estimated that about 17,000 or up to 10 per cent of all farmers will be potential users of this equipment within the next five years. The size of the market will depend on the quality of the service developed during the initial trial period and its perceived value for money once a fully commercial service is introduced.

2. The procedures used in this study of identifying: the problems which potential users have in making decisions; the subjects/topics where lack of time-critical information is a problem in implementing recommended practices; and the expressed interests of farmers for information and interactive services; give clear direction to service operators and information providers in developing the database for agricultural videotex users. The findings from this study are being used to guide the development of the Irish videotex service - AgriLine.

3. Potential users of the service, including extension staffs involved, will require training in how to use the equipment. This should include such topics as: setting up the system; terminal start up and close down; system log on and log off; terminal use; system use and commands; application walk through; how to get help; the use of printed or

electronic directories; fault reporting; and understanding and using two-way/interactive farm management analysis packages.

4. Given the requirement for local, as well as national information, "local" information providers will be needed to ensure that the service meets the information/service requirements of different categories to help the local information provider in identifying information needs. These groups would also facilitate user training and ensure that information from the service is indeed used by farmers in decision making.

5. The information/service needs of potential videotex users are of three types. Firstly, there is encyclopaedic information which is updated once or twice a year and is of the reference type dealing with such topics as grants/aids, services, general husbandry recommendations, careers and agricultural education courses. This type of information can be provided mainly at central or national level.

The second type consists of up-to-date, time critical information on prices, markets, interest rates, animal and crop disease forecasts and recommendations, etc. This is updated as often as necessary and can be provided for videotex at local or national level. Findings from the "Green Thumb" study (Clearfield, et al., 1984) show that the success of videotex is very dependent on the frequency of information updating.

The third component of the database is a range of two-way on-line computing services providing users with access to a range of farm management analyses packages. As already mentioned there is need for relatively more simple programmes that enable users to quickly analyse on-farm and off-farm information as an aid to better decision making. The importance of developing this aspect of the database is most essential for the success of videotex.

Implications for Extension Services and their Clientele

1. Extension Cannot Ignore Information Technology

The computer is part of the Information Age in which we now live. Worden (1985, p.7) contends that as more and more farm families purchase their own home computers, Extension must change its methods of delivering programmes to clientele. Information technology, whether it is in the form of videotex or some other system, will be an important communications medium in the future for extension services. Its potential is not just in complementing conventional methods of information dissemination and analysis for farmers but also as an important and immediate source of updating professional extension staff.

Information technology has the added advantage of enabling extension workers to give better advice to farmers (who are videotex users) taking management decisions because of easier access to accurate, vital management information. In the form of videotex it has the potential to deliver information rapidly to a large number of people. However, it cannot substitute for interpersonal/personal communications methods particularly in on-farm situations where lack of information is not the only, or the major, constraint on development.

In designing and developing videotex services it is useful to recall the cautions of Cary et al. (1984) and Peters et al. (1983) that "... information itself does not make decisions and, in excess, may hinder decision making... individuals selectively shed information in order to make choices more manageable". Nevertheless, information technology, used intelligently in conjunction with other extension methods, can considerably improve the quality and efficiency of extension services and, thus, have better informed farmers, making better decisions.

2. Large Scale/Commercial Farmers Most Likely to Benefit from Information Technology

The conclusion of the Sixth European Seminar on Extension Education on the issue of "who benefits?" was that information technology will further widen the gap between "better" farmers and the non-commercial farming sector (Mannion, 1984, p.208). It is worth repeating again the factors, identified at the Seminar, which, it was suggested, were likely to influence the "widening gap hypothesis". These were:

-   The "better" farmers are better educated and have more skills to take advantage of these systems. They look to these systems earlier as aids to decision making.

-   These systems have built-in costs for users and consequently the more commercial farmers can afford to buy them.

- The internal reward systems and policies of extension organisations, the scientific community and the computer industry favour the development of sophisticated systems which better fit the continuous change orientation of advanced farmers.

Findings from the potential videotex users' study reported on in this paper, as well as current proposals for the AgriLine videotex service in Ireland, clearly indicate that, in the early stages at least, large scale/commercial farmers are most likely to benefit from information technology. In view of the adoption pattern of other technologies in agriculture this is not a surprising conclusion.

While it is necessary to critically assess the consequences and equity of this reality (particularly the large amount of extension and other agency resources involved in developing a videotex service) I feel it is more useful to propose how we think those farmers, who are not likely to be the immediate benefactors, might benefit indirectly from the introduction of information technology.

A number of factors/realities can be identified which, I feel, warrant the development of such proposals. These include:

- The growing awareness in some extension services that scarce public funds need to be more clearly focused and directed towards specific target audiences, particularly those who need to, can, and are interested in farm development. In Ireland this is currently the operational policy of ACOT - the agricultural extension service.

- There is an appreciation, at least, that information technology, particularly videotex, can be used to disseminate and retrieve information to and from the commercial sector. Such technology if used in conjunction with management information systems and collective as well as media information methods would mean that more time is available for work with the less developed farming sector.

- Videotex can help extension services to develop a comprehensive database and thereby improve the quality of extension programmes not just for commercial farmers but also for those who have the potential for development. It can also be argued that some of the information in a database, developed primarily to meet the needs of the commercial sector, will also be useful for other categories of farmers.

Arising out of realities such as these there is need to develop creative proposals and policies that will enable the maximum number of farmers to benefit directly and indirectly from the introduction of information technology. This is a task for extension services and extension training centres.

Finally, with regard to extension clientele, it must be noted that marginal farmers are likely to benefit least from computerised systems such as videotex. These are farmers who for a variety of reasons have little realistic prospects for a secure future in farming with their present resources, current farm development policies and market realities. In Ireland the proportion of the farm population in this category is at least 20 per cent (Mannion, 1985).

DEVELOPMENT OF COMPUTERISED INFORMATION SYSTEMS: A COLLABORATIVE PROCESS

If we start from the assumption that computerised information systems have the purpose of helping farmers to make better decisions it is obvious that we need to be very clear on the decisions users are making which would benefit from such systems. Extension personnel, potential users and extension research organisations all have an important contribution to make in identifying the key subject matter areas/topics that should be included in the database.

A variety of information providers including extension personnel, research workers, commercial organisations, agricultural co-operatives and government agencies at national and local level are needed as information providers.

Extension services and extension training centres/universities have important tasks to perform in the collaborative process. In this regard the tasks identified at the Sixth European Seminar on Extension Education are still relevant. These were:

- To identify opportunities for applying these systems

- To determine priority areas in extension work for computerisation

- To define organisation consequences (for tasks, roles, etc.) arising from the introduction of these systems

- To carry out applied research on the decision making processes of users and the extent to which computerised information systems are helping or could help

- To contribute to collaboration between representatives of farmers, local extension workers, agricultural scientists and computer technologists on appropriate systems.

- To train extension workers on how to help farmers/users to make proper use of these systems. Special attention needs to be given to accurate data collection and input. Users also need training and guidance in understanding/interpreting (output) produced by these systems.

The policy issues and recommendations of the ES USDA (Penn. State University 1985, pp.vii-viii) provide useful guidelines against which to assess the establishment of computerised information systems for agriculture.

Finally, I would concur with the comments of Pederson (1985, p.6) where he states that:

... automated data processing is a fine tool for farmers, who are already competent managers. But the challenge for advisory services is first to help farmers acquire the understanding and techniques of systematic management, secondly to construct the EDP (Electronic Data Processing) tools that are as simple as possible and directly geared to the farmers' decision making.

In keeping with the aim of this conference to evaluate the experience to date with information technology it seems appropriate to consider not alone the extent to which CIS systems can improve the quality and programme delivery methods of the organisations who use them, but also the costs/benefits incurred. These should include economic, social and equity criteria particularly where publicly funded agencies are investing in electronic technologies.

NOTE

1. ACOT, the agricultural advisory and education service in the Republic of Ireland currently provides such a computerised system for its farm enterprise advisers as an aid to target audience identification for extension programmes and activities.

REFERENCES

Agar, J., 1985

"Computers as Information Managers", Agricultural Progress, 60, Summer 1985.

Aregon, 1983

Videoimplement, Implementation of Videotex Pilot Experiments in Ireland and Italy. Final Report Aregon International Ltd., London.

Bell, R.L. and F.M.G. Bunney, 1985

"New Challenges for Agricultural Advisory Services", paper presented at Ninth Working Conference of Directors of Agricultural Advisory Services, Paris, Nov 4-8, 1985.

Blokker, K. 1984

"Computer-Aided Extension: What can we learn from EPIPRE and other Automatized information systems in agricultural extension?", Proceedings of the Sixth European Seminar on Extension Education, Lucca Italy, September, pp.227-232.

Cary, J.W. and B.P. Trendall, 1984

"Identifying Implicit Educational Approaches as a Basis for Extension

Training and Development Programmes", Proceedings of the Sixth European Seminar on Extension Education, Lucca, Italy, Dept. pp. 106-131.

Clearfield, F. and P.D. Warner, 1984

"An Agricultural Videotex System: The Green Thumb Pilot Study", Rural Sociology, 49(2), p.284-297.

ES-USDA, 1985

"Electronic Technology: Impact on Extension Delivery Systems", Electronic Technology Task Force Report, Extension Committee on Organisation and Policy and Extension Service, US Department of Agriculture, Pennsylvania, Penn. State University.

Mannion, J., 1985

"Prospects for the Marginal Farmer in Ireland", paper presented at the Irish Farmers' Association Seminar on "What Does the Future Hold for Marginal Farmers in the West of Ireland", Athlone, March.

Mannion, J., 1984

"Group Report: How will developments in information processing influence the role of extension officers?" Proceedings of the Sixth European Seminar on Extension Education, Lucca, Italy, September.

Pedersen, H.H., 1985

"Farm Management Programmes and the Use of Micro-Electronics on Farms", paper presented at Ninth Working Conference of Directors of Agricultural Advisory Services, Paris, Nov 4-8, 1985.

Peters, T.J. and Waterman, R.H., 1983

In Search of Excellence, Harper and Row, New York.

Shanahan, T., 1985

"A study of the factors related to interest in and intention to use a computerised information service on dairy farms in County Cork", unpublished M.Agr.Sc. thesis, Dept. of Agr. Extension, University College Dublin.

Worden, P.E., 1985

"More Computer Application Ideas", Journal of Extension, Spring, pp. 7-10.

APPENDIX 1

Summary

The following diagram shows the relationship of media technologies to the three functions of Extension and to audience size and type. It can help staff determine the relative advantage of different means of Extension delivery.

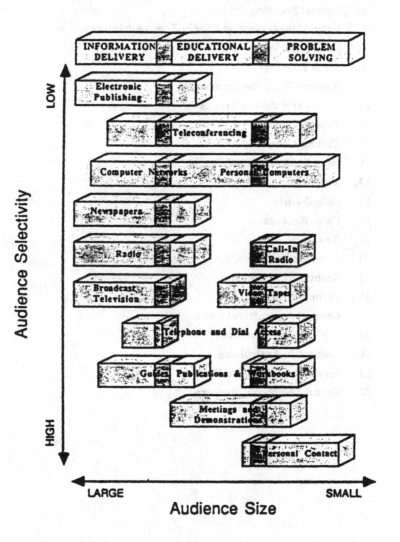

APPENDIX 2

LIST OF SUBJECTS ON WHICH INFORMATION IS NEEDED
BY POTENTIAL VIDEOTEX USERS

1. Fertilisers
2. Meal Feeding Livestock
3. Grassland Management
4. Winter Feed
5. Animal Health and Diseases
6. Animal Breeding
7. Farm Management and Socio-Economic Information
8. Enterprise Mix
9. Farm Buildings
10. Rearing Dairy Replacements
11. Prices and Market Trends
12. Tillage Crops
13. Culling Cows
14. Herd Expansion/Contraction
15. Milk Yild
16. Milk Quality
17. Farm Records
18. Weather
19. Farm Income
20. Grants, Aids, Supports
21. Farm Machinery
22. General Agricultural News
23. Agricultural Education
24. Careers in Agriculture
25. Services Available to Farmers
26. Useful Telephone Numbers

APPENDIX 3

RECOMMENDED INFORMATION/SERVICES TO BE PROVIDED THROUGH VIDEOTEX

Subject	Topics	Possible Source	Time Autumn Calving (Liquid)	Spring Herd (Creamery)
4. Winter Feed	1. Winter feed requirements (C.P.), area to fence off	ACOT/AFT/UCD	Mar-Aug	Mar-Aug
	2. Factors influencing the quality and quantity of silage and hay	ACOT/AFT/UCD	Mar-Aug	Mar-Aug
	3. Silage feed systems - buildings & equipment, prices, availability	ACOT/AFT/Dept. of Agric/machinery dealers	All year	All year
	4. Silage additives, types, rates, prices, methods of application	ACOT/AFT/Co-ops/ merchants	Mar-Aug	Mar-Aug
	5. Winter feeding of dairy cattle	ACOT/AFT	Oct-Apl	Oct-Apl
	6. Reactions between trace elements and additives	ACOT/AFT	All year	All year
	7. List of agr. contractors cutting silage, particularly those with good additive applicators - charges	ACOT/Agricultural Contractors Assoc.	Mar-Aug	Mar-Aug
	8. Growing and feeding of kale and rape	ACOT/AFT/Dept of Agriculture	May-Mar	May-Mar
	9. Alternative feeds, value balancing the diet (C.P.)	ACOT/AFT	May-Mar	May-Mar
	10. Management of grassland for winter feed production- weed control, obstacle removal, etc.	ACOT/AFT	Nov-Jly	Nov-Jly
	11. Eliminating winter fodder scarcities	ACOT/AFT	Mar-Jly	Mar-Jly
	12. Economic benefits from having sufficient good quality winter feed	ACOT/AFT	Mar-Jly	Mar-Jly
	13. Proper storage of winter fodder - pit capacities (C.P.)	ACOT/AFT	Mar-Jly	Mar-Jly

APPENDIX 4

RECOMMENDED SUBJECTS WHERE COMPUTER PROGRAMMES SHOULD BE PROVIDED THROUGH VIDEOTEX

Subject	Topics
1. Fertilisers	1. Monitoring the level of fertiliser use
2. Meal Feeding	1. Type and level of meals to feed 2. Economics of meal feeding 3. Balancing rations 4. Monitoring the level of meals fed
3. Grassland Management	1. Matching stock to grass growth
4. Winter Feed	1. Winter feed requirements and area to fence off 2. Winter feed available 3. Alternative feed, value, balancing the diet 4. Economic benefits from having sufficient feed
5. Animal Health/ Diseases	1. Recording health and infertility of individual cows
6. Breeding	1. Breeding records
7. Farm Management	1. Farm planning 2. Farm records 3. Farm accounts 4. Monitoring farm inputs/out puts 5. Monitoring cash flow 6. Cash income projections 7. Household budgeting 8. Returns on financial investment on the farm 9. Gross margins and the factors influencing them for various enterprises
15. Milk Yield/ Milk Recording	1. Storing and analysing milk yield records

WELFARE BENEFITS COMPUTING IN THE U.K.

Gareth Morgan, National Association of Citizens Advice Bureaux

An overview of the development of micro-computer systems designed to calculate individual entitlement to social security and welfare benefits in the United Kingdom. The paper sets out the history of these systems, the current situation and future developments. It describes the different types of systems that can be used and looks at the issues raised by the use of these programs.

THE BENEFIT SYSTEM

The existence of any non-universal form of income support leads inevitably to the necessity of testing potential recipients for entitlement. These tests may range from the simple to the very complex, as in the case of many means tested benefits. Around these tests have grown an industry of advice and assessment and, as in most industries, this has created a demand for more efficient tools with which to do the job.

In the U.K., where the benefit system has 'just growed', and the system has been patched and amended to try to meet new needs or initiatives and to eliminate anomalies or loopholes the tests can be horrifying. Given the plethora of often vaguely targeted benefits available from both central and local government it is not hard to understand why awareness of entitlement, and thus take up, is often low.

Indeed until comparatively recently even when the existence of a benefit was known entitlement was difficult to calculate because of the degree of discretion used in the award.

Social security is seen as a complex field by advisors, DHSS staff and claimants alike and many claimants feel that they do not receive sufficient explanation of their entitlement.

The gradual move of U.K. benefits from the late 1960s on towards a more rule based system allowed more certainty in calculation and made it possible for advisers to speak of entitlement rather than possibilities. It also allowed for the first time the use of computers.

HISTORY

The first usable benefits calculation system on computer was 'The Invercly-de Project' which began in 1975. The system was developed by M Adler and D du Feu at Edinburgh university from their experience of a feasibility study in Midlothian in 1972. The system covered 27 benefits and made use of a mainframe computer into which punched cards were fed containing information from forms filled by, or on behalf of, clients. The forms were complex and poorly designed and caused initial problems.

The resulting calculations were then posted back to the client in a letter with an accompanying statement both entirely in upper case. The system appeared successful in the way it calculated and identified benefits for clients, and to be reaching people who had not been receiving advice previously.

Unfortunately the time taken in processing the calculation and the rather remote way in which the information was passed back caused problems in follow up and poor take up of the benefits.

> 'Computationally, this system was a success. It fell down in terms of usability. Difficulties experienced with multi-benefit forms, lack of immediacy of advice, illegibility of output and possibly 'remoteness' of the system (from the claimants themselves) led Adler and du Feu to recommend the development of an interactive system.' (1)

At the time the cost of mainframe computing time and terminals made an interactive system, which allowed a dialogue with the user and immediate calculation, prohibitively expensive but in 1980 two developments changed this. Firstly micro-computers with useful amounts of memory, disk storage and processing power became available at a price within the reach of some agencies and departments and the introduction of major changes to supplementary benefit almost entirely eliminated discretion from the calculation of weekly benefit. This acted as a spur to development of small interactive systems. Indeed one of the widely voiced suspicions about the major changes to Supplementary Benefit, the major income support benefit, introduced in 1980 was that the change had been designed in such a way that it would make computerisation of calculations and administration easier.

Two systems appeared almost simultaneously in late 1980 but with very different approaches. The Citizens Advice Bureaux in Cardiff produced a system for use by voluntary Advisors in the CABx, while the University of Surrey produced a program designed to be used by claimants themselves which was installed in Brighton social services department. Descendants of these two systems form the most widely used systems in use to-day.

The interest aroused by these systems caused a flurry of development of systems by advisers and commercial companies. The initial attractiveness of such systems to advisers is easy to understand.

'-   it could ensure that advice workers don't forget about a possible benefit.
  -    the computer can probably do the sums far quicker than anyone with a calculator.
  -    in some ways the computer system can be updated far more easily and quickly than paper files.
  -    where the system is operated by the claimants themselves, they often prefer giving sensitive personal details to an anonymous computer, rather than to a DHSS official or social worker.' (2)

Developers may have seen the growth in advice agencies and services and providing a ready, and possibly somewhat overeager, market.

'In practice, however, anyone wanting to develop a welfare benefits computer program has to wrestle with serious problems:
  -    as advice workers know only too well, the benefit system is very complex, and each benefit can interact with others to add to the confusion.
  -    although entitlement is supposed to be based largely on mandatory

criteria, in fact it is not always so easy to decide whether someone fits a given category or not. Computers are not suitable for making such judgements.

- local differences in housing and other benefits are particularly hard to incorporate into a program for general use.

- above all, perhaps, the welfare benefits system is a "moving target". Rates and other details change frequently, and a major change like Housing Benefit can throw everyone into chaos!' (2)

Many of the attempts at development fell at the first hurdle when faced with the complexity of information and calculation required but the failure of most developers to realise that Welfare Benefits Systems, by the nature of the tasks they perform, require an unusually large amount of maintenance and amendment caused the life of many programs to be comparatively short. Some changes are regular, such as increases in benefit rates, but other changes caused by amendments to the Benefit Rules themselves can be irregular and often, in the case where a loophole is being closed, introduced at very short notice. The introduction of new benefits and withdrawal of old ones is a regular problem faced by developers.

Successful maintenance of programs depends upon the ability to commit long term and considerable resources to the project, this is normally not possible for individuals or small agencies and the rate of return makes it questionable for commercial companies.

Nonetheless there are several different systems in use to-day or under development and I shall describe the basis of their operations.

CURRENT SITUATION

Benefit Systems fall into two main categories:

a) 'Calculation Systems' where the user inputs figures in a formlike fashion, which are then used to calculate amounts payable. With this kind of system the user has to make judgements and apply rules from his own knowledge or from material outside the program. In some cases they also need to make some calculations outside the program to produce the required figures.

b) 'Advisory Systems' where the user is guided through an entire interview and the program is designed to obtain all the data needed for informed choices.

The systems can also be divided into Holistic and Non-Holistic types. In the former several benefits are examined at the same time making use, where possible, of common data, while in the latter only one benefit at a time is looked at.

'Advisory Systems' are generally more thorough and accurate whilst 'Calculation Systems' can be quicker to use.

SYSTEMS IN USE

1. WRAP. - National Association of Citizens Advice Bureaux.

WRAP is an advisory, holistic system covering over 30 benefits. Work is currently in progress on a replacement for this package. See Claims.

2. WIBIS. - Departement of Health and Social Security.

Designed to be used directly by the client. It is a holistic, advisory system.

3. 'Behind the counter' system. - DHSS.

This system is for DHSS staff use in their offices where it carries out the calculations.

4. WRCS. - Southend CAB and Bowertrace Computing.

A non-holistic, calculation package.

5. 'The Lisson Grove system'. - Dr. B. Jarman. Lisson Grove Health Centre.

A non-holistic, calculation system covering contributory as well as non-contributory benefits.

6. Bytelog WB system.

A recently developed holistic, calculation system.

7. Greater London Council domiciliary system.

Developed for very portable battery powered Husky computers. The system is designed for operation by domiciliary workers.

8. 'The Birmingham Hand-held'. - Alick Munden ex Birmingham CAB.

This calculation system runs on tiny Sharp computers/programmable calculators.

IN DEVELOPMENT

Although many developers are waiting to see the effect of the governments' social security reviews before committing resources into development, there are some projects underway.

1. GLC. - Calculation System.

Intended to run on a lap-held portable computer it will be a non-holistic, advisory system covering the three main non-contributory benefits.

2. CLAIMS. - National Association of Citizens Advice Bureaux.

This system will offer the choice of holistic or non-holistic advisory modes of operation. It will cover non-contributory and contributory benefits together with student grants and legal aid calculations. There will be different paths through the system for 'experts' and 'advisors'.

3. DHSS Demonstrator. - Alvey Programme.

This government funded fifth generation research project is not expected to produce a system which will be put into use but to demonstrate possible techniques and approaches to

> '... provide a higher quality of service and a higher degree of flexibility of response to individual special cases and to general policy changes, ... '(3)

NON-CALCULATION SYSTEMS

Information systems that do not carry out calculations may also be considered as welfare benefit systems. For many experienced advisors, particularly in specialist units, the need may be greater for information than for calculations. Much use is made of regulations, commissioners decisions and tactical information. Online databases, such as Lexis, that can be accessed using a telephone and a modem are able to offer rapid access to recent case law and to much full text of statute law but are prohibitively expensive for most advice agencies.

Some work is being carried out in this field, Birmingham CABx and HMSO are looking at mounting the 'Law relating to Supplementary Benefit and Family Income Supplement' (The Yellow Book) onto a micro-computer in a fully indexed form. Similar work is being carried out by Southend CAB using Commissioners Decisions. Prestel is a viewdata system operated by British Telecom and carries much general and new technology information. Lawtel is a legal information summary system on this which is now beginning to be used on a trial basis by advice agencies.

ISSUES

The initial introduction of benefits package into the advice field was greeted with enthusiasm and what was, in retrospect, an understandably over optimistic expectation of their effect. This was not helped by the considerable amount of favourable publicity in the media, both general and specialist.

Experience has demonstrated the importance of careful planning in the introduction of any computer system into advice agencies. Staff need the opportunity to be informed and consulted about the effect of the introduction and its timetabling. Initial awareness training about computers in general and the health and safety implications needs to precede the arrival of the systems as does planning for placement and operation. Training on the system installed and on the programs being used is crucial to the success of the introduction.

RESOURCES

Computer systems are expensive. The reduction in prices of microcomputers that has taken place and will probably continue has not been accompanied by a similar reduction in the cost of software. Indeed where 5 years ago the software formed only a small part of the total package cost, it is not unlikely that it may now form almost half of the total. With cut backs and reductions in grant aid it may seem difficult to justify this kind of expenditure but we should consider some points.

Funding may be available for a computer system and nothing else. It is a sad but nonetheless real fact that many local authorities and other funding bodies will refuse revenue applications but award capital especially for something as seductive as a computer.

If the computer frees advisors for other advice giving tasks this may make the agency more cost effective.

> 'The fact that a computer can do work which might otherwise be done by people is not, of course, an unmixed advantage: it may mean there are fewer jobs for people (whether this is true for the economy as a whole or not, it is clearly true for particular types of work). In the case of public information services, however, the present situation is that the demand far exceeds the capacity of the information-givers. If the staff of advice centres had to spend less of their time working out benefit entitlements, they would be able to spend more of it doing other equally useful advice work.' (4)

Once a computer is available it can also be used for administrative tasks, word processing and record keeping.

STAFF CONCERNS

We must recognise that most discussion about non-client use systems centres on their effect on the agency and its' workers rather than the effect on the client. Advisors are in the unenviable position of working under pressure and with a waiting list of clients. This often leads to unattractive compromises of time vs. thoroughness having to be made and computer systems are assessed from this perspective. Few advisors would deny that holistic assessment can offer a more thorough calculation than any manual assessment in the same time. The issue is whether that amount of time can be given to one client.

Perhaps it is fair to divide the professional users into two groups. Those who are welfare benefits advisors and those who give occasional advice as a part of their normal work. The first group tend understandably to be the more critical of these systems. Their level of expertise is high, their knowledge of the system, of tactics and often of the individuals concerned good. These are the people who might be expected to have the least need for such a system and possibly to feel the most threatened.

More appreciation is felt by those occasional or non-specialist advisors. As a CAB organiser wrote.

> 'My own feeling is that the program is probably less useful to welfare rights specialists than to people who find it difficult to get grips with calculations or who are perhaps part-time workers, as are the majority of CAB volunteers. One of the spin offs of this system has been that volunteers who have used it have been made more aware of the possible questions that can be asked. This is of course subjective, but I would say that the standard of advice giving on welfare benefits without the use of the computer (inevitably the vast majority of our benefits work) has improved as a consequence.'
> (5)

Social workers who do not have a specialist interest in benefits will often fall into the occasional and sometimes even uninterested category.

The relationship between advisor and client is stressed by many advisors. An enormous effort may have been made to integrate the agency into the community. Advisors might feel that computers may jeopardise this special relationship that they have worked so hard to create. Yet is this true? There is evidence that clients do not clearly see agencies in this light.

> 'A recent report by the Community Information Project (CIP) stated, 'Many users prefer a neighbourhood-based advice centre to statutory agencies ... because they can identify with it'. This is a common conviction held by advice workers, particularly those attached to neighbourhood-based centres: that people trust/prefer neighbourhood and voluntary organisations more than the advice of authorities. From the evidence, however, it is doubtful if many people can even distinguish between an authority and a voluntary service, much less prefer one over the other.' (6)

It is also open to doubt whether busy agencies actually have the time to develop the relationships with their clients that they, perhaps, like to feel they do. Advisors who question the use of computers in any advice sessions may have an idealised view of the process.

> 'Claims of "inhumanity" made against such systems should be evaluated in the contexts in which they are used. In G.P.'s surgeries and advice agencies members of the public may see the human expert for as little as four minutes, never make eye contact, not be questioned as thoroughly as they should, and simply not realise what information should be supplied as relevant. In such circumstances, computers may seem far less threatening than the busy human.' (7)

SPEED

It is commonly believed that computer systems take longer to carry out a calculation than an experienced advice worker. The main assertion is that computers ask unnecessary questions. It would be more accurate to say that many advice workers feel confident in their ability to identify areas of benefit rules which will not apply to a client, or that the advisor is able to feel confident about conditions which might take several detailed questions on a machine. This might well be true for expert advisors who deal frequently with benefit problems but I doubt that it applies to the majority of people who offer advice in this field. It is true that where a system covers more than one benefit questions may not apply to the benefit of specific interest to the advisor.

THE CLIENT VIEW

There is little record of clients views of advisor operated systems but the record of increased entitlement assessment, from those users who have produced figures, might lead one to suppose it to be satisfactory from a viewpoint of effectiveness if not operation. The experience with the WIBIS system however seems to show that all sorts of people tried it and found it very satisfactory.

Those users who had previously received or sought information and were able to compare methods were clear in their judgement.

> 'People who used the computer preferred that way of getting information to any other way they had tried.' (8)

The length of time on the computer, about half an hour, did not deter users at all.

> 'The second thing to note about the length of the programme is that hardly any members of the public complained it took too much time. In fact, just the opposite - again and again people told us how much faster it was - than DHSS, UBO, Social Services, even CAB to some extent. What the professionals do not appreciate is that people do not object to long periods of receiving service and attention; what they do object to is long periods of <u>waiting</u> for service and attention.' (8)

Doubts about this, and other client use systems, centred on the ability of a range of clients to use the machines and on the need for additional advice and information apart from calculations. The first point would seem to have been answered, at least where well designed systems are in use.

THE FUTURE IN THE U.K.

The recently published white paper on the reform of social security makes it plain that the government intend to reverse the recent movement towards more rule based assessment with a move back to a more discretionary system.

Should this return to a less rule based, more discretionary system continue we may see the field of welfare benefits computing having to take a leading role in the introduction of 5th generation languages and artificial intelligence systems in order to forecast likely awards of benefit. If systems can be developed that mirror accurately the processes used within the DHSS to award benefits when discretion is the basis, they may be have to be programs that concentrate on tactics and presentation rather than the calculations based systems in use to-day.

REFERENCES

1. Pennie Ottley. Review of Literature on Computerized Advice and Information Services. MRC Applied Psychology Unit, Cambridge, 1981.
2. Community Information Project. Computer Factsheet - Welfare Benefits Programs. CIP, London, 1985.
3. DHSS. The DHSS Demonstrator. DHSS, London, 1985.
4. Tony Lynes. The Use of Computers to inform Social Security Claimants of their Entitlements. LSE, London, 1985.
5. Steve Scully. Computanews No. 1. CIP, London, Jan. 1984.
6. Joyce Epstein. Advice and Information Services. Research Institute of Consumer Affairs, London, 1981.
7. Gillian Bull. Expert Systems and the Voluntary Sector. London Busir...:s School, London, 1984.
8. Joyce Epstein. New Technology - New Entitlement. Research Insti+· for Consumer Affairs, London, 1984.

THE IMPLEMENTATION OF A FRENCH TEXTUAL TELECONFERENCING PROTOTYPE AND EXPERIMENTS IN ITS USES

Gaëtan Cambra, Consultant, TEN, Paris

The capabilities of the French TCAO, "téléconférence assistée par ordina-teurs", and the promising results of experiments with this computer-assisted teleconferencing system are presented. A profitable dialogue between users and system suppliers has been established, allowing for continuous improve-ments of the system, and a new professional role - the manager of a computer-assisted conference system - has been defined. On the assumption that further improvements will be made, TCAO may become an important tool in the production and circulation of information at a national and an international level.

THE CONTEXT

We have recently been witnessing the growth in the use of electronic messaging services in professional communities other than just the service, business and industrial sectors in which these communication products initially appeared.

We thus see university groups, associations federated with each other or operating in networks, working in the sectors of education, the job creation for young people, local development, country planning, architectural consul-tancy or information concerning housing, seeking to obtain electronic communication tools with a view to increasing their productivity, improving the methods of disseminating information, exchanging and capitalizing experience and know-how or the remote setting-up of multi-partner pro-jects.

These few examples of the uses which it is hoped to extend or of the demands requiring to be satisfied are nowadays, in France, coming up against a fairly pronounced shortage in the supply of tools which are available on the market and which meet the requirements as regards ergonomics, simplicity of use and cost which characterize these various populations.

In fact, while "traditional" electronic messaging services are now available on the market in large numbers at levels of quality, performance and reliability or cost which differ widely, they have the common feature of being so-called "point-to-point" messaging services designed to meet two-way communication needs or, at best, to provide communication from one transmitting party to a list of addressees (distribution lists).

Consequently they are not suitable for the setting up of "tele-meetings" in which, concerning a given subject, a group (usually a closed group) of participants decides to devote an "electronic space" (a thematic letter box) to the sending of messages or texts accessible at all times to all the conference subscribers.

Furthermore, the messaging services on the market rarely offer good storage capacities and, above all, good facilities for the retrieval of filed texts other than via the date of issue, the name of the sender or addressee or, again, the subject of the message.

While these entries are sufficient in the great majority of cases, where the messages circulating are brief, factual and quickly become obsolete, that is not the case when the messages are actual texts, which may be of the size of an article, a detailed note or a complex argument which require both complete stability of the content and the possibility of being retrieved by means of relatively sophisticated searching devices akin to or actually of the type employed for document searching.

In addition, the very meaning of "teleconference" is that it enables a number of users to have access simultaneously to the same electronic space. Assignment of a letter box of any messaging service to shared use usually entails the risk of the letter box being engaged if there are a number of calls simultaneously, and this risk increases with the number of potential callers.

Another characteristic of the text conference or "computer-assisted tele-conferencing system" (French abbreviation: TCAO) is the fact that its users can edit and consult an on-line journal or a network bulletin or "letter" for which the methods of production and consultation are different from those of the messages in a conference.

Without dwelling on the functional characteristics of text teleconferencing and how they differ from those of messaging services, emphasis should be laid on the uses which can be developed with the aid of this communication tool.

Rather curiously, although the term "computer-assisted teleconferencing" came into use in France several years ago (1), there is still no software available on the French market which properly meets the known requirements of this system.

The main promoters of the idea are usually guided by the systems developed in the United States, some quite a long time ago - like E.I.E.S., La Source or "Participate", in California - or in Europe: "KOM", developed in Sweden, of which "EUROKOM" is the version made available to the EEC's "ESPRIT" programme (the service centre - host computer - being installed on the premises of University College, Dublin).

These systems are usually highly sophisticated, very expensive and largely used by the university community or by public or industrial research workers (2).

TCAO PROGRAMME OF "CARREFOUR INTERNATIONAL DE LA COMMUNICATION"

Having made an extensive "inventory of the situation", Carrefour International de la Communication decided that the promotion of the applications of TCAO among new strata of users would entail the employment of appropriate software which, while it could not disregard the experience gained with the above-mentioned systems, would in particular have to meet requirements as regards ergonomics and cost which would enable less well-of groups to familiarize themselves with it and to explore methods of communication, transfer and capitalization of information or know-how consistent with their organizational patterns and the structure of the network interconnecting them.

Linking on to those among these already familiar groups of messaging services which are "drawn" towards a use approaching teleconferencing, Carrefour consulted French industrialists and software consultants who, on the basis of a set of specifications of which the contents were for the most part approved by the main promoters of TCAO, were likely to be able to give a technical, industrial and commercial response which would satisfy most of the parameters adopted.

Apart from the emphasis laid on the search for a less expensive arrangement than those which we have mentioned, there was great stress on the problems of transparency of the cost of the services offered by TCAO (messaging service, teleconferencing, storage, search, journal, etc.) and of the scale of charges.

For it is important, from the very conception of the system, to be able to work out various network economy hypotheses for users of the teleconferencing facility. In this connection Carrefour is concerned that the tool which it is advocating to the various networks which have approached it shall not, as soon as it is implemented, run up against difficulties - which often prove insurmountable - connected with meeting the operating costs.

The natural tendency of these new strata of users is usually to approach their politico-administrative sponsor and enter into negotiations with the latter in order to make the use which they wish to make of TCAO affordable.

It can easily be seen that such a "posture" will quickly run up against its limits and that it is of primary importance to design a tool whose economic budget will probably have to be balanced in several ways: by public or quasi-public aid (or private sponsorship) for its operation, a proportional contribution from each user or user group, "space buying" by institutional information producers, sale of editorial products produced by multi-partner conferences, sale by subscription of summary conference notes accessible "on-line", or even advertising revenue.

The ambition of this programme is, as has been seen, to bring about the emergence in France of a type of know-how which is as yet not widespread in circles which do not at present consume much in the way of sophisticated communication products and which, at the same time, are very desirous of "acculturation" on this subject.

This program therefore needs to be accompanied by a system of training of users, activation of the networks employed and follow-up of the first months of experimenting.

This system, which it is important not to minimize, although it will not entail any cumbersome or expensive logistics, will furthermore have the function of establishing - during the period of the experiment conducted by Carrefour - a permanent relationship between the various user networks and the TCAO software development team.

In this connection the strategy adopted consists of making available to potential users a prototype which will enable them, as they learn and their know-how increases, to occupy a position as co-prescribers of the product.

This special position, negotiated with the industrialist who is developing the prototype, is reflected in flexibility and adaptability of the software, the definitive configuration of which is not a priori completely known from the start of the programme.

It is emphasized that this operation, although its aim is to promote and popularize TCAO in France, does not form part of a narrowly national logic and seeks to generate transnational communication networks.

For this reason the specifications call for the implementation of a system accessible according to both the videotex standard and the "ASCII" standard.

Furthermore, the development of national networks of the Transpac type in most European countries and of capacities for interconnection of these networks should make it possible to fulfil this objective of international openness in the best possible way as regards reliability and cost.

To sum up, Carrefour International de la Communication wishes to contribute, by this program, to an advance on three fronts:

- the offering of industrial computer-assisted teleconferencing products,

- the promotion of the <u>uses</u> of TCAO in new population strata, and the conceptualization of the effects of these uses on the "traditional" organizations and on the emergence of new modes of organization,
- thinking on the <u>economics</u> of textual teleconferencing networks.

In the subsequent phases this programme will endeavour to explore the integration of this communication tool with those close or related to it, such as audio- or video-conferencing and tele-writing, still from the point of view of the contribution to be made by these tools to increasing intellectual productivity - or to the emergence of new forms of productivity.

INITIAL STOCKTAKING OF THE TCAO PROGRAM (JANUARY 1986)

More than four months after it started (six months for the first user networks), a number of lessons can already be learnt from this program.

- Participation by users in defining functional changes and improvements to the software was particularly active in most cases.

The most dynamic networks very quickly took the program's aims to heart and adopted a demanding stance towards the industrialist as regards the time limits for making the proposed functional facilities available, the quality of the services offered (ergonomics of the system, presentation of the videotex screens, response times and speed of display, convenience of circulation or "navigation" within the services) and as regards the questions of methods of invoicing (as the TCAO program is not at present operating by the "kiosk" system, the invoicing method is one based on connection time proposed by French Telecom).

- The present configuration of the TCAO service is the product of an interaction between the facilities offered by the industrialist responsible for developing the tool and the demands from users, promoted both by an analysis of the development of their communication needs and by a survey made of the products available on the videotex market in France and on the TCAO services offered abroad (mainly in the United States).

- There is gradually emerging a "<u>communication model</u>" in which a balance is struck between the <u>communication</u> functions in the strict sense of the term (inter-personal messaging service, subject messaging service, shared files, subscriber directories and, shortly, conferences) and the <u>information</u> functions (compilation of telematics journals, intra-network information notes, documentation cards).

- Various scenarios are appearing with regard to the <u>economics of the networks</u>: a subscription by each user for all the services combined, a subscription by each user for each service, single invoicing of all services combined in terms of connection time ("kiosk"), differentiation of costs depending on the services, sale of information products by subscription or by connection time, upstream financing of information products (sponsoring, publicity, manufacturing of "tailor-made" information products for partners other than the network subscribers).

- The <u>training</u> of users and <u>accompaniment</u> (by a substantial operation of "on line" promotion) of the establishment of services were found to be of capital importance for the acceptance of the tool.

- The function of "SOS users" (automatic, via the on-line guide, and human, via consultants entrusted with this task) constitutes a heavier burden than had been envisaged in the initial definition of the program.

- The establishment of communication "bridges" between the subscribers belonging to different networks but having partly overlapping areas of interest calls, in certain cases, for functional modifications of the software, which had at first been inadequately programmed and were consequently sometimes incompatible with the requirements of users, who wish the tool to be as transparent as possible.

- The "life" of a TCAO network require a veritable <u>management</u> (technical, promotional, supervisory, financial, editing, drafting, political), the importance of which the networks - moving on from a phase of relative amateurism to one in which they are endeavouring to achieve genuine professionalism - are gradually discovering.

- This management function is giving rise to new skills, which are gradually being codified as a new <u>profession</u>, remuneration for which must be provided for in the economics of the networks.

- The growth in the volume of uses and the stabilization of the tool at a level of satisfactory functional capabilities are beginning to shape the professional practices of users, without it being possible as yet to identify clearly the changes in working behaviour brought by this tool.

The detail evaluation of this program, which will very shortly have to be undertaken, will make it possible to formulate this point more precisely and produce new knowledge on this question.

- The information disseminated concerning this experimental program and the very rapid spread of telematics in France (over a million Minitel terminals had been distributed by the end of 1985) is having a substantial multiplier effect, even though the use of tools of this type in professional quarters is still very confidential.

- TCAO is a communication tool which is probably better suited to groups or organizations which already have a network structure; its relevance appears to be low in circles which operate on the basis of more hierarchical or Taylorized work organization patterns.

- TCAO is a tool capable of generating added value to the production, processing and circulation of information. Good use is therefore made of it only by groups in which access to and production of information is of strategic importance.

- The logic of network operation and the growing transparency of communication tools at international level are beginning to create prospects of the opening up of trans-frontier networks (especially in Europe) in the case of some of the networks involved in this program.

These prospects have advanced furthest in the sectors of local development, social innovation or training in new technologies.

NOTES

1. See in particular the texts, articles and papers by Annie Bloch, Jacky Akoka or Jean-Sylvain Boutel, for instance.
2. See Robert Mahl: "Les réseaux de la recherche".

COMPUTER-ASSISTED TELECONFERENCING

USER NETWORKS

- La Nouvelle Encyclopédia (Fondation Diderot)
- Local job-creation schemes for young people
- Commission Nationale pour le Développement Social des Quartiers
- Groupe Permanent de lutte contre l'illétrisme
- Union Régionale des entreprises intermédiaires (Rhône-Alpes)
- Local development agencies (DATAR, Ministries of Town and Country Planning and Housing, and of Agriculture)*
- Association Nationale pour le Développement local et les pays*
- Conseil d'architecture, d'urbanisme et d'environnement (CAUE)
- Agences Départementales d'Information sur le Logement (ADIL)
- Cadres de l'Economie Sociale
- Formathèque (La Villette)
- Scientific and technical clubs (La Villette)
- Pilot centres for the training of young people in new technologies
- Fédération des parcs naturels de France*
- Association amicale des ingénieurs de l'Ecole Nationale Supérieure des Télécommunications de Bretagne
- Centre d'information sur les innovations sociales
- Partner operations (Secrétariat d'Etat à l'Economie sociale)*

---

* in "TELEDEV" (Télématique et Développement local)

COMPUTER CONFERENCING: THE GAP BETWEEN INTENTION AND REALITY

Michael Pieper, Research Group for Man-Machine Communication, GMD, FRG.

From Oct. 1980 until Dec. 1981 sociologists from the GMD's former 'Research Group on Social Technology Assessment' have analyzed communication among a group of locally decentralized pilot-users, using the Computer Conferencing System KOMEX. Empirical results of this first KOMEX field-trial indicated a prevailing lack of originally intended computer assistance for group problem-solving and decision-making processes. Concerning these deficiencies, the hypothesis will be advanced that in systems' design certain principles of 'Interpersonal Relations' or 'Human Interaction' - known as the rules of 'role taking' - have only insufficiently been taken into consideration. It will be shown to what extent empirically evaluated sociological assumptions can possibly be transformed into certain orgware demands making for an improved and intentionally more adequate systems design.

THE OBJECTIVES OF COMPUTER CONFERENCING

Aggravating economic competition, and accelerating technological development, forces industrial management as well as public administration to process an expanding complexity of background information, if they are adequately to preserve the economic welfare and social stability of modern societies. Strategic decision-making in industrial and public administration means selecting, combining and evaluating information from ever more different sources. In fact, these activities require an increasing amount of office hours, and for certain reasons one can assume the evaluation activity to be the most time-consuming (cf. Uhlig et al. 1979, 3-12).

Mostly, there is no common understanding of difficult problems and hence no commonly accepted criterion for evaluating suggestions for problem-solving. Problem-oriented insights are rather preformed by the personal

convictions and/or professional responsibilities of managers, clerks or officials partici pating in planning processes. Potentially there will be as many
different suggestions and evaluation patterns as there are different professional responsibilities and corresponding problem-solving demands. However,
the more different personal intentions, professional responsibilities and
problem-solving demands have to be taken into consideration, the more
conflictual and therefore time-consuming it will be, to negotiate commonly
accepted decisions.

The demand to structure informational complexity for reaching most
comprehensive and hence less conflictual decisions can be assumed to
extend the cognitive capabilities of negotiators. Important background
information is often simply neglected by selective perception. So far, wrong
or at least less effective decisions can be regarded to be the result of either
an insufficient or an unprocessable amount of background information.

Naturally, the idea arose to exploit the data processing capabilities of
computers to moderate these deficiencies in discursive negotiations in
planning processes. The essential impulse for this intention came in 1966
from Olaf Helmer, who - at the 'Rand Corporation' - developed a formalized
communication procedure with problem-oriented expert-ratings, called the
DELPHI-method. In 1970, it was Murray Turoff at the 'New Jersey Institute
of Technology', who conducted the first experiments on computer-assistance
for such rating and decision-making processes.

Computer Conferencing was expected to overcome the so-called 'Era of
Forced Choice', that is to say of forcing unacceptable decisions upon
negotiators dealing with a complex problem (cf. Linstone et al. 1975, 479-
516). The data processing capabilities of computers were to be utilized to
facilitate the process of reaching unanimous decisions by storing problem-
solving suggestions into a commonly accessible computer file. The enriched
information base and heightened interconnection of information in this
computer file was assumed to ...

- increase the chance of receiving unexpected and interesting
  messages;
- provide a wider range of strategies for communicants to interrupt
  and augment each others contributions;

- raise the probability of discovering latent consensus.

Computer Conferencing should thus allow a more competent and finally more consensus-oriented discussion of complex problems which cannot be solved by formalisms. In addition, Computer Conferencing technology was expected to mediate discussion processes in decentralised remote problem-solving or planning groups.

These origins of Computer Conferencing induced the GMD's former 'Institute for Planning and Decision-Support Systems' to develop the Computer Conferencing System KOMEX with the special purpose of evaluating the expected consequences of computerbased negotiations.

THE GENERAL OBJECTIVES OF THE KOMEX FIELD-TRIAL

By December 1981 the first practical test of the KOMEX system had been terminated. This test had extended over a period of almost 18 months. A group of social scientists, from five different universities in the Federal Republic of Germany, participated in the field-trial as pilot-users. They carried out a long-term research project on 'Social Network Analysis' supported by the 'German National Science Foundation (DFG)'. In accordance with the original intentions of 'Computer Conferencing', pilot-users expected that KOMEX would be able to support inter-group discussions of research-problems, thus enhancing scientific contacts among the decentralised subgroups of the project's network.

Since October 1980, sociologists of the GMD's former 'Research Group on Social Technology Assessment' have analyzed the communication among these five subgroups. Gathering appropriate empirical data was for the most part guided by analytical interest focussing upon five questions: the first can be summarized as an inquiry into what kind of communication a Computer Conferencing System like KOMEX would be used for. With regard to the remaining four questions we were interested in how far computer-assisted communication among the pilot-users would differ in amount and structure, but also in content and style from conventional modes of mediated communication, e.g. telephone and mailing.

Mainly in the United States, extensive socio-psychological investigations have yielded first indications about certain impacts of Computer Conferencing technology on user dispositions (cf. Pieper 1982, 654). Nevertheless, within the European Community, these research activities have significantly been stimulated by previous investigations of the former 'Communications Studies Group' in London, which - sponsored by the British PTT - compared normal face-to-face communication with different modes of technically-mediated communication, e.g. telephone, video-conferencing and the like (cf. Short et al. 1976). However, computer-assisted communication was not dealt with, and all these investigations were mainly based on experimental small-group research.

RESEARCH DESIGN

Since our research group wanted an analysis of these changes, and being as practice-oriented as possible, we chose a research design differentiating the so-called 'field experiment' from the overall design of a so-called 'field study'. In empirical social research the term 'field investigation' is used in contrast to so-called laboratory experiments if the behaviour of individuals is analysed under the conditions of their natural environment, e.g. in their working environment. The differentiation of the mentioned research designs originates from French: in 'field-experiments' the researcher modifies certain environmental components in order to explain possibly resulting changes in the behavioural patterns of individuals causally in terms of the (modified) components of their environment. In a 'field-study' the researcher selects certain individuals and describes the correlation of certain behavioural characteristics assuming constant field or environmental conditions (cf. French 1953). Concerning our KOMEX field-experiment this led us

-   to manipulate the conditions of communication in the field-setting by introducing KOMEX as an additional device for communication at a certain stage of investigation
-   to maintain optimum surveillance or control of the other exogenous factors defining the working environment of the pilot-users.

Especially the very careful control of exogenous factors defining the working environment involved considerable methodological difficulties.

To get to grips with these problems, we relied on a counterbalanced mixed-method approach. This approach centered upon a method allowing us to content-analyse all 365 messages distributed via KOMEX. Underlying this method was a basic description scheme, allowing as comprehensive and selective as possible a description of the communicated records. The analytical categories of this description scheme, which were ultimately quantified into numerical codes to be analysed by means of the 'Statistical Package of the Social Sciences' application programme, can at best be understood as a controlled cross-tabulation, covering the three most important aspects of our research questions. Content of communication should be imagined as the column, kind of communication as the row vector of this factorial design. Both these dimensions were controlled by a third one, which we designated style of communication.

To date, social experiments in the Teleconferencing area have scarcely focussed upon empirical indications concerning content, kind, and style of interpersonal communication. Maybe these dimensions have been considered to involve too many peculiarities to enable us to observe and ascribe generalizable attributes. Indeed, we found that 'content of communication' was most difficult to classify in a valid and comparable way, because it was determined by the peculiarities of the tasks of each of our five pilot-user subgroups. Nevertheless, despite their peculiarities, all the subgroup-tasks aimed at a common scientific purpose within the whole project network.

We discovered that 'content of communication' could therefore best be classified by the degree of immediacy in which this general objective was met. We distinguished five degrees of immediacy to classify this first dimension:

- instructive and private communication (e.g. questions concerning the handling of the system and 'getting to know each other')
- avocational or secondary communication (e.g. announcements of conventionally mailed information)
- administrative communication (related to procurement, accountancy etc.)
- supportive communication for scientific task accomplishment (e.g. communicating about official journeys, conferences, new books as well as about the management of the scientific data-bases of the pilot-users' project network)

- scientific communication most closely related to the generation of scientific results (e.g. 'writing research reports')

Analysing the messages distributed via KOMEX, we found out that 'kind of communication' could most exhaustively be described by four basic categories of organized problem-solving. These four categories made up our second dimension for content-analytical attribute assignment:

- task-definition (i.e. discussing or deciding what to do)
- task-coordination (i.e. arranging what to do in what order)
- task-documentation (i.e. informing about the state-of-the-art of task accomplishment)
- task-evaluation (i.e. discussing the quality of task accomplishment)

These two factorial crosstab designs were controlled by a third dimension, 'style of communication', which was operationalised in accordance with R.F. Bales' well-known methodological approach of 'Interaction Process Analysis (IPA)'. Some slight but inevitable modifications of this approach were made, in that the IPA was originally an observational methodology. Finally, we devised a category scheme divided into 8 variables, which differentiated between certain styles of information-delivering and information-requesting:

- 'communicating agreement' or 'disagreement' with respect to certain information received from others;
- 'making suggestions' to induce others to accomplish certain tasks or 'requesting suggestions' whether and how to accomplish tasks;
- 'delivering personal opinions' or 'requesting personal opinions', i.e. exchanging value judgements on certain facts being typical of the task to be accomplished;
- 'delivering hints' or 'requesting hints', i.e. exchanging neutral task-oriented information.

With regard to the experimental design of our field-trial, two problems arose in applying this content-analytical category scheme for attribute assignment. First, we had to face the fact that resulting usage patterns could run out of significance, in that they might be uncontrollably effected by certain circumstances in the working environment of the pilot-users. We counterbalanced this problem by observational methods. 'Participatory Observation' by a single observer, delegated temporarily to workshops and conference meetings of the pilot-users, for instance, was a quite efficient method which enabled us to be continuously informed about ongoing overall working activities in the whole project network. Actual working requirements in the decentralised, remote pilot-user subgroups were more difficult to control. Here, we had to resort to 'Self Observation' by the pilot-users themselves. One member of each of the five subgroups was assigned the function of a rapporteur. At certain intervals, this rapporteur had to deliver brief reports on changes or invariable tendencies in workload, manpower and actual task-accomplishment of his own subgroup.

The second problem was that, generally, any content-analytical approach involves problems of validity because of interpretive degrees of freedom in assigning content-analytical attributes. If the encoder cannot gain insight into the contextual and situational origins of a message, his interpretation of its connotative significance has to rely on more or less subjective judgements. To minimize these speculative liberties, we counterbalanced the scientific conclusions of our sociologists investigating technology utilization, with the experiences of the pilot-users applying Computer Conferencing Technology, by means of concluding interviews. In the latter, we followed the principle of a guideline-oriented, narrative interview technique. Beginning with more general questions, we asked more and more specific questions, thus directing the answers of the pilot-users towards a validation of our conclusions.

RESULTS

Whereas at best the total amount, but not the relative distribution among the subgroups, differed between KOMEX-use and conventional types of communication (e.g. telephone and mailing) in amount and structure of pilot-user communication ('who communicated with whom and how often'), we obtained some quite interesting but nevertheless provoking results from our content-analysis. "The more immediate communication focusses upon the scientific purpose of the pilot-users", was our hypothesis, "the more complex and contradictory are the problems to be resolved for task accomplishment".

Indeed nearly 70% of KOMEX communication most immediately referred to problems arising from scientific task accomplishment of the pilot-users (see Table 1). However, the ratio of less pretentious problem-solving activities, i.e. 'task-documentation' and '-coordination', to the most pretentious 'evaluation-' and 'task-definition' activities was 64% to 28% (see Table 2). Most obviously, in 71% of all cases, scientific problems have only been articulated by simple indications and statements ('giving and asking for <u>orientation</u>'); they have hardly ever been discussed argumentatively in the form of interpersonal negotiations (see Table 3).

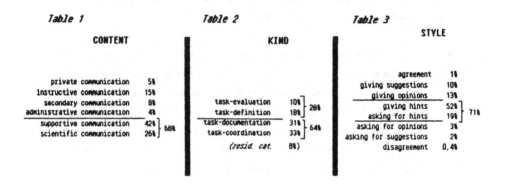

Table 1

CONTENT

private communication	5%
instructive communication	15%
secondary communication	8%
administrative communication	4%
supportive communication	42% ⎫ 68%
scientific communication	26% ⎭

Table 2

KIND

task-evaluation	10% ⎫ 28%
task-definition	18% ⎭
task-documentation	31% ⎫ 64%
task-coordination	33% ⎭
(resid. cat.	8%)

Table 3

STYLE

agreement	1%
giving suggestions	10%
giving opinions	13%
giving hints	52% ⎫ 71%
asking for hints	19% ⎭
asking for opinions	3%
asking for suggestions	2%
disagreement	0.4%

Interviewing the pilot-users revealed that mainly <u>difficulties of conversational context reconstruction</u>, (i.e. difficulties in reconstructing argumentative references among different points of view) must be held responsible for this obvious gap between intention and reality of Computer Conferencing (see insert).

Excerpts from concluding Pilot-User Interviews   (translated from German)

QUESTION: Do you think, that in cases of conflictual negotiations, using KOMEX or another Computer Conferencing System facilitates or complicates the process of reaching consensus ?

pilot-user "x":   If I prophesy any future for the system at all as regards Computer Conferencing, I do so only on the following premises: first of all, what is happening within the system has to be made more visible. Contributions from other participants have to be made more evident. Most of all, the history of the various communication processes has to be clarified, i.e. one has to illustrate, what has happened to certain messages in what way and what has not happened. Thus, indications about who has already recognized a message transmitted by me could, for instance, be reported back. Beyond that, certain comments on my own statements should more easily be referred to. I could also imagine, that it would help if it is indicated, whether these comments basically agree or disagree with my original statement. Otherwise, 'no comment' would also be a reaction which ought to be indicated. Basically, one has to say, that the traces the system-participants left upon disseminated messages need to be evaluated. The system has to know what messages refer to which persons and which other messages !

pilot-user "y":   In Conferencing Systems, I would only rely on one single Conferencing data-base. In this data-base most different indications would be accessible via pointer-functions; e.g. who has written referring comments etc.. All these and other conceivable indications could then be evaluated by the originator of a disseminated staement.

pilot-user "z":   It's a difficult thing ! What would possibly be of advantage: one has a protocol of the communication-process and is able to trace back all sequences. Compared with traditional negotiations, this ensures better control and reliability. All this is possibly comparable with traditional mailing-correspondance, however under those cirumstances there is no intrinsic traceability, i.e. no indication that this information refers to that, that to another, and so on. That's surely an issue, which could unbias and facilitate the process of decision-making. However, these things are certainly not optimally resolved within the KOMEX system.

DISCUSSION

'Social Experiments with Information Technology' are amongst other things intended to instigate technological improvements for more suitable orgware production. With that aim in view, our conclusion that the intended application of Computer Conferencing Systems suffers from difficulties of conversational context reconstruction, needs further theoretical comment.

Industrial as well as political planning is generally redevilled by the lack of a clear and common understanding of the measures to be taken, and of the objectives to be met when solving a given problem. In effect, the main precondition for successful planning and decision-making is to get an adequate understanding of problem oriented suggestions of others. And arguably, it is the interactive process of gaining mutual understanding which has deficiently been taken into consideration when designing Computer Conferencing Systems to enhance the capacity of information processing for group problem-solving. This process of gaining mutual understanding can briefly be described in terms of a conceptual framework from the social sciences, which may be termed 'Symbolic Interactionism' (cf. Mead 1934, Blumer 1969).

According to this conception, partners in a conversation mutually face each other in the social roles of 'communicators' and 'recipients'. In communicating with recipients for planning purposes, communicators follow 'personal intentions' deriving from 'personal insights' into the problem. Recipients for their part assign a certain 'meaning', deriving from their 'personal insight' into the problem, to the information received. Essentially the problem of gaining mutual understanding suffers from the subjectivity of the assignment of informational meaning. Hence recipients' insights into a problem normally differ from those of communicators. Their intentions can only be understood by recipients when the latter are able to reestablish for themselves the generalisable 'Symbolism' of the uttered statements. This is done by referring to other utterances, which then can be checked to see whether they are altogether compatible or incompatible with presupposed prejudices. Social psychology refers to this as it were empathical ability of 'slipping into the shoes of the other', by the term 'role-taking'.

It is the 'role-taking' abilities which are still restricted by computer-based communication systems. There is no doubt that Computer Conferencing Systems support the generation and structured distribution of information, but there is hardly any technological assistance for evaluative or interpretive information processing by recipients. If indeed there is any at all, they can only - rather clumsily - check the conference data-bases for consistent or inconsistent argumentative references, to find evidence of agreement or possible misunderstandings.

The conclusion that empathical 'role-taking abilities' have only insufficiently been taken into Computer Conferencing Systems' design considerations, points to a far more basic and serious dilemma in orgware production: for the suitability of social experiments to provide tools for orgware improvements in applied information technology seems to be undermined by deeply grounded, and up to now insuperable incompatibilities between the technological and sociological paradigms of organized problem-solving.

As is the case in the design of Teleconferencing Systems, the design of information technology has always to conform to 'technological functionalism'. Less well defined organizational problem-solving is, however, much more subserviant to what sociologists call 'sociological interpretivism'. Whereas in the latter paradigm a process-oriented view of problem-solving is prevalent, the first conforms to a static view. In 'technological functionalism' a solution structure exists prior to problem-solving. 'Sociological interpretivism', on the other hand, follows the view of solving problems by structuring solutions. 'Role-taking' with conversational context reconstruction illustrates an important aspect of organized problem-solving dictated by 'sociological interpretivism'. The perhaps well-known idea of designing so-called 'Management Information Systems (MIS)', by relying on orgware derived from 'Applied Systems Analysis', illustrates an approach to orgware production which is dictated by 'technological functionalism'.

Most generally, 'Applied Systems Analysis' describes the whole structure of organizational task-accomplishment in terms of an orderly network of sequential single-operations. Every single-operation is formalized in terms of input- and output-variables, a well-defined activation impulse, and a sequence of elementary processing-units. Whenever all input-variables are determined by output-values of precedent operations, and processing-units are formalized by certain algorithms, the result will be a formal chart of integrated single-operations which will reflect the whole structure of organizational task-accomplishment. Such a chart is then taken as the design-basis for programming corresponding MIS.

Based on these assumptions, decision-support by MIS-technology is at best restricted to tracing back the prestructured consequences of changed parameter-values. However, organizational problem-solving is, at least in its strategic aspects, much more characterized by unexpected exceptions than by its being restrictable to predetermined solution-algorithms. Nowadays, these circumstances are considered to be the main reason why the wide-spread application of MIS has failed.

But what about the intentions of Computer Conferencing to support groups in resolving less well-defined, exceptional problems? Are there any possibili-ties at all of overcoming the socio-technological dilemma created by the fact that computers are deterministic machines, preprogrammed in their functionality, whereas organizational problem-solving is to a large extent voluntaristically shaped by the personal convictions and interpretations of interacting decision-makers?

Orgware-improvements to overcome the socio-technological dilemma of Computer Conferencing may be achievable if we take the assumption of Talcott Parsons - a well-known theorist of functionalism - for granted, that 'the pattern aspect of organizational systems is shaped by the exigencies of actual communication' (cf Parsons 1965, 977). It is this assumption which may have led Linda Putnam to conclude that 'technological functionalism' and 'sociological interpretivism' are not incompatible at all but in a certain sense 'depend on one another for their existence' (cf. Putnam 1983, 53). "Communication", she argues, "is not simply another organizational activity; it creates and recreates the social structures that form the crux of organizing."

CONCLUSIONS FOR ORGWARE IMPROVEMENTS

Given this background, the interactive process of 'Role-taking' or gaining mutual understanding can possibly be taken into Computer Conferencing Systems' design considerations by studying the way in which interpretive problem-solving processes merge into structured solutions. This might be possible, because the degree of structural commitment in voluntaristic problem-solving can be measured by preprogrammable orgware-algorithms.

'Symbolic Interactionism' refers to the process of gaining mutual understanding in accordance with the principle of the so-called 'Triadic Nature of Meaning'. In accordance with this already mentioned theoretical framework, recipients of a certain piece of 'Information', e.g. a problem-solving suggestion, would assign a certain 'Meaning' to this suggestion, by reestablishing for themselves the context of any other information which they think is referred to by the information received. In other words, received information would be understood as a problemoriented 'Message' by referring to the problem-solving suggestions of others.

These interrelations can be illustrated by means of a formalized, graph-theoretical model of interpersonal negotiations. The basic structure of this model consists of a 'Person', who utters a problem-solving statement and an 'Other' person, who perceives this statement. The way 'Other' perceives this statement against the background of personal insights into the problem, resulting from references to other suggestions from the same 'Person', establishes a certain relationship between 'Person' and 'Other', as regards the uttered statement (see Fig. 1).

This relationship follows the mathematical principle of Transitivity in the case of 'agreement' and 'disagreement' between 'Person' and 'Other'. As everyone knows, transitivity prescribes the rule that, when two things are equal to a third one, they are equal one with another; - or vice versa, when one of two things is unequal with a third one, these two things are unequal one with another.

The latter is the case in the situation of 'disagreement'. When 'Person' agrees and 'Other' disagrees with a certain problem-solving statement, the relationship between 'Person' and 'Other' is 'disagreement' (see Fig. 2).

The former is the case in the situation of 'agreement'. When both 'Person' and 'Other' agree with a certain problem-solving statement, the relationship between 'Person' and 'Other' is 'agreement' (see Fig. 3)

In both cases, a formal transitivity underlies the situation.

However, generally a third situation can be identified, in which the formal structure of interpersonal problem-solving becomes intransitive or at least undetermined. That is when 'Person' and 'Other' agree with one problem-solving statement, but 'Person' agrees and 'Other' disagrees with a second statement. In this case there is neither total 'agreement' nor 'disagreement' concerning the solution of the whole problem which the two problem-solving statements refer to. One can say, that 'Person' and 'Other' have to deal with interpersonal 'misunderstanding' (see Fig. 4).

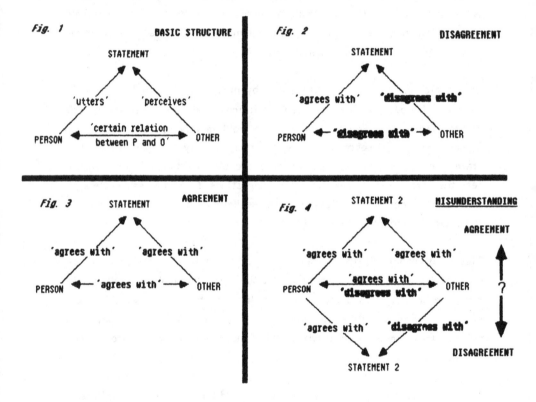

In order to resolve the problem, 'Person' and 'Other' first of all have to identify and then clarify mutual misunderstandings. However, there is evidence for the assumption that the greater the number of individuals involved, and the greater the number of statements uttered in problem-oriented negotiations, the more the negotiators are overtaxed in identifying 'misunderstandings'. 'Role-taking' processes for gaining mutual understanding should therefore be supported by orgware-algorithms checking for ambivalent relations between P and O, which could be deduced from corresponding reference structures in the common Conferencing data-base of the problem-solving groups. The general precondition for such an intransitivity check is that an argumentative reference structure can technologically be established and processed by assigning additional indications to each statement being expressed. At least three types of additional indications would have to be assigned:

- the originator or sender of a statement, the formalized 'Person'
- the receiver of a statement, the formalized 'Other'
- possible references to other statements, marked as at least general 'agreement' or 'disagreement'.

The simplest solution would be to allow conferencing participants to be asked for these indications in corresponding system-driven form-filling dialogues.

To summarise briefly one can say that Computer Conferencing Systems at present mainly provide facilities for structuring the information-flow, that is to say the distribution of information. Therefore, in most of the known cases, the original idea of Computer Conferencing has been withdrawn in favour of the less pretentious conception of Electronic Mailing. Nevertheless, to avoid disappointments and wastage, the gap between the original intention and actual application of Computer Conferencing Systems might be bridged by providing orgware facilities supporting the structured perception of the disseminated problem-solving statements. The empirical suitability of such orgware improvements still needs to be validated by further social experimentation.

BIBLIOGRAPHY

Bales, R.F. (1950): 'Interaction Process Analysis: A method for the Study of Small Groups', Reading (Mass.)

French, J.R.P. (1953): 'Experiments in Field-Settings', in: Festinger/Katz (eds.) 'Research Methods in the Behavioral sciences', New York

Helmer, O. (1966): 'Social Technology. Report on Long-Range Forecasting Study', New York

Linstone, H.A. and M. Turoff (eds.) (1975): 'The Delphi Method. Techniques and Applications', Reading (Mas.)

Parsons, T. et al. (eds.) (1965): 'Theories of Society', New York

Pieper, M. (1982): 'Computer Conferencing and Human Interaction' in: Williams (ed.) 'Pathways to the Information Society', Amsterdam - New York - Oxford

Pieper, M. (1985): 'Methodological Problems of Human Factors Research in Long-Termed CBMS Field-Trials' in: Shackel (ed.) 'Human-Computer Interaction', Amsterdam - New York - Oxford

Putnam, L. and Pacanowsky, M.E. (1983): 'Communication and Organizations. An Interpretive Approach', London

Short et al. (1976): 'The Social Psychology of Telecommunications', London

Turoff, M. (1971): 'Delphi-Conferencing. Technological Memorandum TM-125', Executive Office of the President, Office of Emergency Preparedness, Washington

Turoff, M. (1972): 'PARTY LINE and DISCUSSION. Computerized Conference Systems', in: Winkler (ed.) 'The first International Conference on Computer Communications', Washington D.C. (pp. 161-171)

Uhlig, R. et al (1979): 'The Office of the Future', Amsterdam - New York - Oxford

PART III: STRATEGIES

Social experimentation has catalyzed many strategical discussions about the relationship between social and technological innovation and political attitudes towards the challenge of innovation. One example is the debate in France about "expérimentation sociale" since 1980. Another example concerns the German "Feldversuche" with the videotex system "Bildschirmtext" and with cable-television. In this section, however, experience from Norway and Denmark is presented. Kjell Olav Mathisen from the Norwegian Telecommunications Administration specifies what social experiments - or field trials, as he prefers it - are good at and what they are not good at: their strength is to influence the future rather than to predict it. Ole Nymann and Malthe Jacobsen go one step further: they present social experimentation as an instrument for the development of socially-advanced I.T. products.

FIELD TRIALS: WHAT'S THE USE?

Kjell Olav Mathisen, Norwegian Telecommunications
Administration Research Establishment

Based on experience from field trials (or "social experiments") with telematics, in Norway and abroad, the question posed and analyzed in this article is: what can we possibly gain by doing field trials?

Today, intentions and results in field trials usually mismatch. To fulfil the potential of the field trial, and to secure continued political and commercial support, it is important to recognize its special characteristics. The field trial is low in predictive value on markets or social consequences. Rather, it is an active venture, setting the new technology on the public agenda, spurring innovation and participation.

Some of us, myself included, have spent years of our professional lives doing field trials, or "social experiments", with new information technology. In the process we have also used some millions, in any currency, of public money. There is every reason that we should ask if the results are worth the effort. I think they are, but maybe for other reasons than those usually advocated. Maybe we are doing something else than we say that we are doing, and maybe the results are others than intended. If so, the total rationality of our enterprise - the relation between reasons, actions and results - is at stake.

THE USUAL REASONS FOR DOING FIELD TRIALS

So, why are we doing field trials? A very general answer may be this: it seems intuitively a good way to grapple with the questions of new technology in society. Social surveys, case studies etc - the usual routines in the social researchers repertoire - seem inadequate to meet this new challenge. An alternative is to introduce the new technology on a limited scale to a sample of users, and evaluate the results. This is a practical and spectacular approach that appeals to common sense.

New technology creates social options, and this, in its turn, creates uncertainty about how to act and react. For the sake of argument, I will identify three kinds of practical questions that are articulated in this situation, and label them. The commercial question concerns the economic viability of the new technology. The social worker question concerns what social consequences the new technology will have (social consequences in this context usually imply negative consequences). The political question is about how one could organize and control the new technology, or make it work according to defined social objectives.

The social scientist himself may be motivated by curiosity, academic ambitions, or by political idealism. In any case, he will need money to carry out his research. So, he will have to look for sponsors, and convince them that he will also cater to their needs. To do this, he will have to rephrase his own questions. This may be a matter of words, and no sell-out. However, the researcher will easily come to promise more than he can deliver, or rather, something else than he can deliver. He may also blur his own perspective in the process. The total outcome too often seems to be that the posed problems, the method, and the results drift apart.

I see no easy way around this. The researcher will have to - and indeed should - relate to interest-groups of various kinds. This is part of his own dialogue with society that forms his perspective and makes his work socially relevant.

Anyway, as a result of this process, most "social experiments" in the realm of information technology will articulate one or more of these questions:

- What are the markets for the new technology?
- What will its social impact be?
- What kind of organization will it take to control it?

These may be important questions, but the problem is, can the "social experiment" give the appropriate answers? I don't think so. It may give some clues, but its real strength lies somewhere else. After examining the limits of the "social experiment", and giving some examples of its real results, I will return to its possibilities.

My examples will mainly draw on three projects conducted by the Norwegian Telecommunications Administration (NTA):

-   interactive videotex (100 users, from businesses all over Norway, over $2\frac{1}{2}$ years)
-   broadband services (up to 800 users, in a local community called Jevnaker, proposed duration 5 years)
-   "smart cards" for electronic funds transfer (5000 users, in a town called Lillestrøm, over $1\frac{1}{2}$ years)

A SOCIAL CONTEXT MAKES REAL EXPERIMENTS IMPOSSIBLE

"Social experiment" - My use of quotation marks is not accidental. It indicates that I do not like the terminology. The reason is the word "experiment". This may be defined in different ways, but it always carries along its connotations of natural science, and the idea of a situation where the researcher can manipulate his chosen variables at his will, and be in control.

There may be examples of social research that approximate this ideal of control - most notably in social psychology and its small group experiments - but even there, the idea of a "social experiment" is highly suspicious. In a real social setting, this terminology seems even more inappropriate to me.

What, then, are the alternatives? "Experiments" in health and schooling are regularly named "evaluation research"; this implies a rather passive researcher, evaluating the results of politically induced, systematic changes and measures in these institutions. "Open planning", and "action research", suggest a more active and participating researcher. I guess that "action research" would cover most of the "social experiments". This term has a confused history of its own, however. I would therefore prefer the more neutral "field trial". This term and concept has an established tradition, meaning precisely "social experiments" with new information technology.

"Field Trial" indicates that you introduce something new in a real life setting and see what happens; compare the expression "trial and error". I think this is actually what is done in a "social experiment". The researcher may plan it, and even induce the changes himself, but once started, he has got only slight control of events. The project takes on a life of its own, heading in unexpected directions. This is due both to the participants, and to external changes in the wider social context.

One example from the Norwegian field trials with interactive videotex may illustrate this. To get participants for the field trials seemed easy enough. Many business enterprises, institutions and individuals volunteered. This introduced a problem of representativity and self-selection.

Originally, the field trial was focused on the needs of small businesses. It turned out that small businesses had neither the interest, nor the resources, to participate. To get the project going, we had to let big business in on it. Maybe we could have stuck to our original plan, given more resources for equipment and training. I am not sure. Anyway, this was the real world.

However, another problem turned out to be the continuity of participation. Some people were eager videotex-users from the start, until the novelty wore off. Others were "sitting on the fence", waiting for the real fun to start.

So, the field trial became like an open shop, with people coming and going. In some ways this was advantageous, giving us fresh ideas and new inputs. But it was disastrous for the systematics of the videotex trial, and for any notion of a "before-after" design.

The concept of active participation may make us redefine the problem of control. The participants themselves could be in charge, with the researcher just monitoring events or giving advice.

In the small community of Jevnaker, the NTA has initiated a field trial with a broadband network and various new telecommunications services (cable television and videophone, among others). Here we have tried to realize an ideal of participatory control. In addition to our direct contact with the individual users, and with the local authorities, there is a local liaison group. This group discusses new ideas, makes proposals, and has the right to veto any proposal from the NTA. To some extent, this model has worked. But the liaison group, being an ad hoc representative body, has no more absolute control than the researcher would have had.

The local community is also part of a wider social context. Here, national politics play a part. Both the local community and the NTA wanted to distribute satellite-TV at Jevnaker as part of the cable television service. Due to disagreements between the Ministry of Science and Culture (which handles questions on satellite-TV) and the Ministry of Communications (which governs the NTA) this was not allowed. After a formal complaint, concession to distribute the French TV5 was given, but the British Sky Channel is still not allowed in this particular cable network. This reduced the value of this part of the field trial.

IN THE REAL WORLD, MOST THINGS CHANGE

The relations between a research project like this, the local community, and the wider social context, also highlight the problem of time. With the passage of time, the context of the project will change - sometimes very dramatically. To the researcher, this makes interpretation of data difficult; to others, the total relevance of the field trial may be at stake.

During the Jevnaker project, we have experienced at least two important changes of context, one politically and one technologically induced. To use a cable television (CATV) network for two-way communication services, as in Jevnaker, it has to be upgraded technically and hence becomes more costly. For some time, the convergence of such networks and the ordinary telecommunications network was envisaged by planners and politicians alike. Parallel to this, however, ran the discussion on the telecommunications monopoly (as in most western societies). The political outcome, as it materialized in new regulations and a new government body, was a half-hearted attempt to combine competition in CATV-development with an upgraded technical standard. The practical result was new CATV-networks which are not suited for telecommunications purposes. Competition forces everybody in this business, the NTA included, to develop as cheap networks as possible.

Adding to the waning relevance of CATV-networks were technical developments, like the emergence of SMATV (small cable networks with cheap satellite antennae, serving only some tens or hundreds of subscribers), and the new ISDN network (Integrated Services Digital Network).

In the Jevnaker project, the answer to these contextual changes has been to stress the importance of services, as opposed to technical solutions, and to shift the focus to broadband services, in particular. The design of the field trial allowed for this, but readjusting the course has had its price all the same, including frustrated expectations among some of the users.

As time goes by, things change, and so does the status of knowledge: will the results from the field trial be valid after the end of the trial, when the context has changed? How can you even define the results in those circumstances?

A PROBLEM OF SCALE

A similar problem of inference applies to scale. At best, you may only generalize from Jevnaker to other small communities. You may scarcely draw conclusions about communications in a city. Even more important: communication activity is exponentially related to the number of people involved. A field trial, which both by definition and necessity involves a limited number of participants, may only give a vague picture of real communication patterns. Even when you manage to engage most people in an organization or a community in the field trial, communication with the outside world becomes an important missing link.

FROM LIMITATIONS TO POSSIBILITIES

There are other snags, but by now I hope that I have made my point as to the limitations of field trials (or "social experiments", if you insist). As most tools of social scientists, I think they have small predictive value. They may provide some indications about future markets, social consequences, and organizational forms, but they are at best no more than clues.

What then, are the actual results of field trials, and what are their special merits? As before, I will adduce on some examples from my own experience.

THE AGENDA SETTING FUNCTION

A field trial that at first glance seems to contradict my main thesis - i.e. concerning the limits of field trials - has been conducted with the joint cooperation of banks, commerce, the postal administration and the NTA. Started in the autumn of 1984, and still in progress, it has the explicit objective of investigating the future market for electronic funds transfer. 5000 volunteers in the small town of Lillestrøm have been given "smart cards" (after the French fashion) that may be used for payment instead of cash or cheques. The smart card activates a sales point terminal that communicates with the customer's bank. In the card itself a chip keeps track of all transactions. For the customer, this is a less cumbersome process than using a cheque, and the trial service has become very popular. The cards have been in frequent use, and there have been few technical problems.

May we then make specific conclusions about the market for this kind of service? No, not necessarily. The reason is simple: the price of the service. While some cheques carry a fee, all card transactions have been for free.

The price to the customer in a real service, in its turn, will depend upon a number of factors. One of the most decisive will be how the service is organized. Herein lies, I think, the real importance of our field trial at Lillestrøm: it has put the future organization of electronic funds transfer in Norway on the public agenda. The implementation of the trial system has shed light on the conflict of interests in this area. It has also made it possible for the interested parties to discuss future forms of organization, on the basis of their own experience.

This agenda-setting function may be used more intentionally: The project at Jevnaker may be seen as part of the NTA's push to get into the CATV-market, marking out its territory and displaying its ambitions (cf. the marketing examples below).

Doing a field trial is a spectacular form of research. It catches the attention of the media, and the imagination of the public, by demonstrating the new. The journalist gets the opportunity to visualize, to put the new technology into a social context, and generally to put a human touch to his high-tech story. To the politician, a general problem is the fuzzy possibilities of the future. By materializing and demonstrating some of these possibilities, the field trial sharpens his focus and provokes reactions. Thus, there are good reasons why field trials have an effective agenda setting function.

THE PEDAGOGICAL FUNCTION

Putting something on the agenda also means having an opportunity to get across a message, or pieces of information. For those participating in the field trial, this can be synonymous with an active process of learning by doing.

This process may be more or less systematically used for specific purposes. An example of the former is the use of the Jevnaker-project for internal education in the NTA. Among those working with CATV, technicians and market planners alike have been informed of the experiences from Jevnaker, or have been there on excursions, and some of them have for a period of time participated in the development themselves.

A less purposive kind of learning took place during the Norwegian videotex trial. The newspapers, for some time, participated rather heavily in this trial - until they realized that this new medium neither represented an easy outlet for their surplus information, nor was it a competitive threat to their traditional product. So, for the time being, they lost interest in videotex. However, during their participation they had formed working groups, been on study tours, analyzed the market for new information products, and made policy-decisions about how to handle the new opportunities. This infrastructure of knowledge and knowledgeable people gave the newspapers a head start when, with a change of government in 1980, other new media suddenly gained importance (notably local broadcasting and satellite-TV).

Learning from a field trial may be intra-organizational, as in the case of the NTA and the newspapers, or it may involve the general public, locally or nationally. An informed public is important for any political process. But people are not only employees and citizens, they are also consumers. Marketing represents a specific kind of learning. To know and to articulate our needs, we have to know about the means to satisfy them.

Here we have an important, but seldom explicit motive of many field trials:

to demonstrate the products of industry. A field trial is a very powerful way of spreading information about high-tech products. To recognize this motive is, I think, important for an understanding of many of the most well-known field trials. Biarritz in France is one example; Higashi-Ikoma in Japan is another. They serve as show-cases for their respective national industries. Whether they succeed or fail, qua field trials, may not be so important. Through their media publicity, their guided tours, and their symbol-value, they will have paid off anyway.

Another well-known example is the field trial with two-way communicating cable television in Colombus, Ohio. In the end it failed, at least in some ways. It did not demonstrate a market for new two-way services. Yet this is only part of the story. To Warner Brothers, the main purpose may have been to demonstrate that they were able to build advanced cable networks. In the US, cable development has been regulated through franchising arrangements. Local government has decided which of several applicants should get the franchising contract, and one of the criteria has been how technically advanced the offers were.

THE INNOVATIVE FUNCTION

A third kind of result from field trials, adding to the agenda-setting function and the learning-processes, should be the development of new ideas. The traditional strict "experiment" or "evaluation" design may actually inhibit this development. If, for example, one wants to evaluate the use of videoconferencing as a substitute for travel for businessmen, this narrows the focus to one particular static application of the new technology. The chances are that this presupposed application will turn out to be fruitless.

An alternative design is to give the participants video communication possibilities, and let them decide on their own how to use them, and for what purpose. Though this approach too has its own problems, as there will always be a need for guidance and support to get things going. The ideal should be somewhere in between, with the researcher giving a helping hand, but not overdoing it. Realizing that the "social experiment" is a fiction, strictly speaking, should help us make more flexible arrangements that are open to new initiatives and directions during the field trial.

A field trial usually focuses on new technology. It is important that this should not overshadow the possibility of using already established technologies in new and better ways. The goodwill and interest that often surround a field trial could facilitate the analysis of the total communication needs in a user group, an organization, or a local community.

A preliminary study within the business sector at Jevnaker showed that most of the present communication problems could be defined as finding out the whereabouts of people, and being able to leave short messages (most businesses at Jevnaker are small, with no administrative staff). These problems may be solved by paging, mobile telephone, and centrex-solutions. The main obstacles seemed to be telecommunications tariffs, and lack of information about existing services. This fostered the idea (and the implementation) of a telematics center, where local business can share advanced terminals, and get user guidance. This is really based on an old concept (the telegraph station) and existing technology, but realized within a new context.

In the end, spin-offs like this may prove more important than the original idea behind a given field trial.

TURNING REAL RESULTS INTO THE RIGHT REASONS

The main proposition of this paper concerns the limitations and the possibilities of field trials, or "social experiments".

I think that some of the special merits that are claimed for field trials are false. The predictive value of the field trial - concerning markets, social concequences, and organizational forms - is low. I have given some sketchy evidence of this, by way of examples. A more systematic argument could be made with reference to the concepts of control, time, and scale. This argument essentially maintains that society is too complex to allow of any generalizations from a "social experiment". Other lines of reasoning might have been added to support the proposition; the most fundamental being rooted in the reflexive mode of society.

The field trial is, however, an active venture in a real life setting. This accounts for the actual results and advantages of the field trial: agenda setting, learning by doing, and the development of new ideas.

We should do field trials, but for the right reasons. Today, there is too often a gap between objectives and results. To exploit the real possibilities of the field trial, we have to raise consciousness about what we are actually doing and achieving in this kind of research.

When we have recognized the special characteristics of this mode of research, and consequently what its use might be, the next question is: of what use to whom? My short answer to this would be: the field trial is a method for people who want to shape the future, rather than predict it.

SOCIAL INVOLVEMENT IN PRODUCT DEVELOPMENT

Ole Nymann, P&T, and Malthe Jacobsen,
Mentor informatik

This lecture deals with how the activity of "orgware design" has become an important part of product development.

How this has led to involvement in "social experiments" understood as environments in which the man in the street can and will contribute to a creative process of finding new I.T. applications, is also discussed.

After this, experiences from the Danish "INFAA" project are presented. In this project, industries, unions, users and authorities have jointly established an environment for social and technological development. The philosophy behind it is to try to bring together as many potential development situations as possible within a limited geographical area, not as part of one big project, but as independent projects formulated, run, and controlled individually, but related to or modified in accordance with each other in such a way that they can support each other, and thus together form a kind of artificial future.

THE PRODUCT DEVELOPER'S POINT OF VIEW

In the foreword to the conference programme the organizers say:

> "that ... one ought to combine hardware and software production activities with the activity of orgware..."

and

> "that social experiments with information technology are important tools for orgware production."

Thus we can say that social experiments are important for all who develop information technology products. Those of us who do so must always bear in mind the social environment in which the technology is being developed.

That this subject is of interest to others than us who earn our daily bread by producing hardware and software, is because the problem is symmetrical: the development of information technology influences developments in society at large. The development of information technology today is important to all who want to understand the changes that our societies are going through at the present time.

In the first part of this article I will deal with the problem from the product developer's point of view. In my opinion, it is important for all who deal with these types of sociological problems to understand the industrial realities - as seen from the product developer's point of view. Just as we who produce the goods must face the spectre of sociological consequences facing the users of our technology.

In the second part of our article Ole Nymann will deal mainly with the symmetrical dimensions of our problem, presenting the Danish "INFAA" experiment, where considerations of this symmetry have formed the basis for the entire organisational structure.

Both Ole Nymann and I have our backgrounds in practical product development, and we have both been involved in the initiation of INFAA.

The objective behind all product development is to adapt a technology that the product developer masters to suit a market where it can be used. Therefore, work both with technology and with an analysis of market, its character, demands and spending power is always a necessary basis for product development.

The tricky thing about developing information technological products is thus related to two facts.

Firstly - as you know - technology develops fast. That means that I.T. products continuously penetrate into new fields. When you want to launch a new product you can't base this on an analysis of the existing edp-market - because this merely consists of the population of present edp-users. It tells us very little about the market for new products. But it is often precisely in these new markets, that the most promising developments take place.

We can thus say that market research in the traditional and professional way is often insufficient. The basis for our decisions must include visions, creativity and - simply - guesses. Terms that are difficult to handle in professional business management. We therefore often see that big and professional companies fall behind in this trade, and new financially weaker pirates take the lead. A few of these companies will later become big and professional. Most of them will most likely sink into obscurity. If they betted on the wrong horse or are not able to follow up their success, they will soon be forgotten.

The second fact I would like to point out in this connection is the changes which take place in new fields of application. The new technology contains possibilities for supercession of existing familiar problem solutions. For not only will the new technology be used to solve known problems with better tools. The job situation will change and the new technology will be used to solve new problems.

We often meet this phenomenon in a very precise guise. When we are asked to participate in development work, we are often confronted with quite exact and explicit expectations as to its results. The aim might be stock reduction through faster stock turnover, faster invoicing or the like. But soon it turns out that these wishes pall beside the new visions that the users get along with their understanding of the new possibilities.

As you will imagine, this often creates problems in project administration and for our chosen methods. I shall, however, not go further into this matter now. To develop products for new, as yet unknown markets, where the technology is used in a way which the users in question have not realized at the outset - that is the interesting problem for the product developer.

If we take a look at the developments which we have experienced, we can see two ways of handling this problem. One way is to introduce the product for the solution of already known tasks in such a way that the simple rationalizing aspect is made interesting. Typical fields are book-keeping, calculation jobs and statistics.

Another way is to find fields where we have users who are motivated and competent enough to join in a close collaboration with the product developer. This is typically the case with scientifically and technically well-educated users, or users who have a special interest in investing considerable resources in getting ahead of others technologically - for instance, the military.

Recent developments have, however, caused a movement in the user environment away from these user groups. The potential user today is more or less anybody, which renders this method more difficult.

At the same time, time needed for developing the hardware and software component of the new product has been reduced compared with the time and costs tied up with determining the function wanted, and, in competitive terms, this fact makes the latter problem even bigger.

The product developer today must seek new ways and be interested in establishing environments where the man in the street can and will contribute to the creative process of finding new applications.

The emphasis in product development is thus moving out of the designer's laboratory into a social environment where it is not all that easy to be successful.

INFAA provides an example of how we in Denmark have tried to create such an environment. I would like to point out that it has certainly not been easy. It has been difficult - very difficult. But it is my considered opinion now that it has been worth it.

"AABENRAA PRØVECENTER": A HOTHOUSE FOR SOCIAL PRODUCT DEVELOPMENT

As was mentioned above, the interaction between the development of information technology and equipment, and the development of the utilization of the same equipment, must begin much earlier compared to what has been common practice in connection with conventional product and utilization development. Product lifetime is very short, and therefore matching equipment and utilization during a product's lifetime has become well-nigh impossible. Also, the fact that the time from the conception of an idea inside the head of an engineer to the actual marketing of the corresponding product is today so short means that the normal method of using market surveys as the basis for product definition is too troublesome and lengthy.

Consequently, a coordinated development both of equipment and of utilization has been a necessity. This development must be carried out in an adaptive environment, which guarantees a framework simulating the future in which the technology, the equipment, and the utilization under development are going to be integrated. Such an environment is, of course, a utopia. So the second best is, first of all, to be aware of the problem of developing something for the future, and, secondly, to acknowledge that you are not the only person who has the problem of establishing a futuristic environment in your sphere of development and testing. So why not try to use others in the same traumatic situation to provide you with an environment for your development, and suggest to them that your project could form part of their environment?

This is the simple philosophy behind the "Aabenraa Prøvecenter" - try to bring together as many development situations as possible within a limited geographical area, not as part of one big project, but as independent projects formulated, run, and controlled individually, but adapted to each other in such a way that they can support each other, and together form a kind of artificial future. This does not only include product development, but, to a very large extent, awareness and educational activities.

The "Aabenraa Prøvecenter for Information Technology", also called INFAA, is not a big, top down formulated project, but it has the very sophisticated overall goal (which we try to achieve by stimulating initiatives) to start as many small projects as possible. The secret behind what we think is a success is that it is built up on the basis of a great number of small, non-dangerous decisions. The overall goal and philosophy are known to all participants, but no individual decisions or financial risks are so big that an error in one project can harm the overall goal or be a total disaster for those who have taken the risk of joining or supporting it financially. This does not, of course, mean that we do not have, or will not have, very large single projects or investments, but it means for example, that we do not have to invest large amounts in a broad band infrastructural telecommunication network before we get anything at all off the ground.

INFAA is thus the umbrella for a number of projects and project initiatives. Each project must involve the development of

-   technology,
-   the utilization of technology,
-   the organization of work, and
-   education.

For a project to be accepted within INFAA, its initiators have to be willing to allow it to be subject to an independent evaluation with regard to any social or structural consequence arising from the introduction of the technology in question. Furthermore, all results coming from the assessment of the project have to be made accessible to all interested parties, both within the project and outside it. And, as regards the planning and the execution of any given project, it has to be based upon the mutual understanding and acceptance of all the parties involved.

In the course of 1985 a number of projects, within both the public and the private sectors, have been started up, or have been continued from the year before. A number of projects are in their planning stages, or in their initial phases.

ONGOING PROJECTS

The most important ongoing projects are SAVI, DSL-EDB; and KA-udvikling.

SAVI is an information and edp network project connecting:

-   30 small independent garages (car repair shops),
-   their principal spare parts dealer,
-   their supplier of technical information used in connection with the repair and maintenance of motors and motor vehicles, and
-   their banks and their accountants.

The project is organized as a private business enterprise, owned by the participants in the project, including a large Danish supplier of edp, terminal equipment, and software and including the Danish P&T. The project budget is currently in the order of 10 mill. DKr., of which approximately 2 mill. DKr. come from a public technology development foundation, and the rest from the participants in the project, including the 30 garages. The present project period will extend well into 1988, but plans for further extending the project both in scope and in time, are being made.

Seen from the viewpoint of most of the users, the project takes the concrete form of a communicating PC, connected to a number of databases. It is presently the plan to include within the project the development and testing of simple Local Area Networks, integrating voice and datacommunication both in the workshops and in their adjacent households. A small business run by a family, consisting of husband and wife and one to five employees, is very common both within the service sector and in the manufacturing sector in Denmark. For the future employment situation it is of great importance to support the development of information technology suited to this kind of operation.

DSL-EDB is an experiment being carried out within the library sector, which makes available to the public the same edp-tools normally used by trained librarians. Via terminals, the users have direct access to national bibliographic databases. The terminals are located at "Det sønderjydske Landsbibliotek" (the public library in Aabenraa), in the library of the local Business School, and in the library belonging to a training college for infant school teachers. Another party involved is "I/S Kommunedata", working with public databases and databases for public administration. Among other things, the project will be used for the evaluation of user interfaces and the development of improved man-machine interfaces.

"KA-Udvikling" deals with the implementation and development of office automation in the public sector, more precisely at the Town Hall in Aabenraa. The project includes aspects such as improving the personal influence of the individual in relation to the municipal administration, and increasing the flexibility of the administration in such a way that it is only necessary for the user to contact a single person, instead of having to contact different departments, which would normally have been the case.

FORTHCOMING PROJECTS

The main projects which are at present being planned or are in their initial stages are MOBIDAT, Folkeskolen, and Landbrug.

MOBIDAT is a project which involves the development of mobile data communication. Technically speaking, it includes experiments with radio communication protocols in a four-station prototype for a public radio packet-switched system. The experiments are to be carried out in a live traffic environment. A supplier of mobile radio terminal equipment, and a supplier of mobile data processing equipment, are thus involved in the planning of the project together with the Danish P&T, and various potential user groups from both the public and the private sector. It is expected that the experimental system will start to operate at the beginning of 1987. Knowledge about the relationship between the behaviour of the users and the system's architecture and protocols is expected to be of great importance for the development of the future public network for mobile data and voice communication.

Folkeskole is a complex of projects within the primary school in Aabenraa. It will, of course, include all the classical elements of edp-assisted education, but in addition to this it will include school administration and the development of the role of the teacher. At present, the plan is that the teachers participating in the project are to have access to the I.T. system both at the school and from their homes.

Landbrug deals with the development of information technology to be used in the agricultural sector. It envisages the establishment of a connection between the participating farms and some large databases and also contact to the farmers' service organization.

To conclude this review, it might be of interest to add that our annual turnover is around 10 mill. DKr., - if I may use money as a measure of activity in a social experiment. If INFAA continues to grow as it has done so far, we will have a turnover of more than 20 mill. DKr. in 1987.

PART IV: ANALYTICAL METHODS

How is the social researcher to evaluate social experiments? And what new challenges do they represent in the field of applied sociology? These two questions are answered by Harry Bouwman/George Muskens and Sylvie Craipeau/Francis Kretz, respectively. Bouwman/Muskens present an experimental research paradigm inspired by traditional experimental research and applied to the Ditzitel trial in the Netherlands. Craipeau/Kretz analyse the methods and the structural parameters in social experiments conducted in France since 1980, considering a number of practical problems in the field of social experimentation.

INFORMATION NEEDS, INFORMATION-SEEKING BEHAVIOUR AND DITZITEL

Harry Bouwman, University of Amsterdam, and George Muskens, IVA, Tilburg University, The Netherlands

Most research on experiments with information technology is insufficiently based on theoretical arguments and in-depth conceptual specifications. So it seems to be more or less accidental and empiricistic by its nature. In this paper we propose an experimental research design to study the uses of new information technologies by a model concerning information needs and information seeking behaviour. The subject of research is the introduction of a new consultation medium viz. Ditzitel. Ditzitel is a hybrid viewdata system using telephone lines to call up information and cable networks to provide it.

In this paper we also pay attention to factors which may disturb the Ditzitel-experiment and consequently the proposed research.

In this paper we deal with theories and concepts concerning active information seeking behaviour. We present a research model of Muskens and Van Oorschot which they developed on basis of Septrup's model of information-seeking behaviour. The model intends to fit active consumption behaviour and will be applied to new public consultation media like Viditel and Ditzitel.

Viditel is the viewdata service offered by the Dutch PTT since 1979. With, currently, 17,000 subscribers who consulted 9,000,000 pages of information of some 950 information suppliers in one recent month. (Media Info 5, 1 November 1985; Allen and Visser, pp. 23-27).

Ditzitel is an experimental concept. It is a hybrid viewdata system using telephone lines to call up information and cable networks to provide it. Ditzitel will operate on Amsterdam's local cable network, which has 300,000 subscribers.

Information displayed by Ditzitel will be gathered and distributed by the VNU publishing company which means it will be submitted to an editorial line. It will not follow the neutral formula of exploring viewdata possibilities. (Kappetijn; Media Info 5, 29 March 1985; Allen and Visser, pp. 27-30).

EXPERIMENTS WITH NEW MEDIA AND EXPERIMENTAL RESEARCH

Most Institutions involved in new media experiments such as publishers, cable companies, post companies, broadcasters and so on, are accustomed to make decisions on basis of an institutionalized kind of media research, market research. In the past decades media systems have been institutionalized on mass markets. About these markets a huge amount of data has been collected, on their account, by broad panel research and surveys.

However, this huge amount of data lacks everything which might predict success or failure os some new media. The data are rarely based on adequate theories; the data gathered describe profiles (of potential) media-users, products and product use, opinions on services offered, price conceptions and so on.

In the case of media and new media services a more scientific and experimental or panel approach is possible than the kind of institutionalized media research described. A basic feature of a media experiment or the introduction of new media and new services is that an identifiable actor tries to change some audience behaviour by manipulation of supply factors. Something new is offered and some group is to be expected to make use of this offer with some effects, whereas those excluded (for the time being) from the offer, should not change habits. So, basically, media experiments look like scientific experiments in which stimulus groups should change behaviour compared to nonstimulus or control groups. Therefore, in some way, the design of experimental research is to be applied to media experiments to predict and explain outcomes.

At the moment someone is going to introduce a new medium or service it is an advantage that users and non-users are different and can be compared on reasonable grounds. Users and non-users are different, not by themselves but on behalf of the reach of the new medium/service. The new media will be distributed experimentally in a certain area; not in comparable other areas. People in the experimental area are users; those in other areas non-users. It must be possible to find non-users who can be matched with users in the experimental areas for characteristics such as socio-economic status, education, sex, age, opinions, personality, media consumption, social participation and so on. That means that an experimental non-users-control-group can be found. After the broad introduction of a mass medium or a mass media service it is hardly possible to find non-users who can be matched with users. For instance: there are hardly any non-TV-viewers since the sixties and, if there are some, they are quite atypical outsiders (Jackson and Beeck, 1977).

An actor who is going to introduce a new medium or some new service has an interest in making success or failure predictable, or, at least in letting the (interim-)results be explained. It is a way to gather indispensable feedback. Therefore, he must order applied research and look for optimal conditions for experimental or panel research, together with researchers. So, it is a task for both experimental researchers and practitioners to define optimal experimental conditions and find ways to approach them. Optimal conditions can be realized while an actor, e.g. a publisher, is devising medium or a mass media service. That means: some time before even the experimental introduction in some local area. So, possibilities are created to define goals, build on controls for possible disturbing conditions, formulate testable hypotheses on the effects and consequences of the use of a new medium or a new service. The coming introduction of Ditzitel in the Netherlands can be such an ideal case of experimental or panel research. From our side, a theory is needed about the functions of this medium. On the basis of this theory we may contribute to the design of the experimental research we plead for. The next parts of this paper deals with a theory on the use of public consultation media and on possible disturbing factors. We conclude with some preliminary remarks on the design of an experimental research project.

The theory on the use of public consultation media deals with concepts like information-needs and information-seeking behaviour. The factors which possibly disturb the use of public consultation media are directly connected with Ditzitel and Viditel.

THE USE OF PUBLIC CONSULTATION MEDIA

Viewdata systems like Viditel and Ditzitel are, generally speaking, public consultation media. Their key feature is that the audience is able to find information by seeking through public databanks by way of (value added) telephone line or (two-way) cable networks or both. One might see the idea of uses-and-gratifications approaches from the field of academic communication research realized in practice. So, the active audience, its information need and its information seeking behaviour, have to be the key concepts in a theory on the use of public consultation media. We shall treat relevant literature in the following sections.

Information needs

Relevant literature does not directly offer a neat conceptual framework to describe actual information needs and actual information-seeking behaviour. The different authors are mainly interested in answering why people in general have rather different information needs. The answers offered differ. Festinger (1964) claims that people aim at a situation of cognitive consonance, or, at least, a reduction of felt dissonance, e.g. by using information. Donohew and Tipton (1973) concentrate on the adoption of the 'image of reality' of an individual to environmental stimuli. Atkin (1973) seeks the information needs in the reduction of insecurity in the case of problemsolving. Moschis (1980) sees the information needs motivated by the endeavour to acquire a satisfactory social position and a satisfactory level of interaction. The list of theories about information needs can be enlarged endlessly, but they do not offer a framework to analyse actual information needs and information-seeking behaviour.

In general we talk about a need if a gap exists between an existing situation and a wanted one. If this gap can be closed by using information one can speak of a need for information. The size of the information gap defines the information need. The nature of the information need depends on the nature of the topic or the problem for which information is needed, the importance of the information and so on.

It is not realistic to assume that the information gap can be assessed in an objective way. The person who states that he has an information need speaks rather about his personal perception of his existing and wanted situation. In other words, it concerns his definition of the situation (Muskens and Van Oorschot). A definition of the situation by a person is the result of the interaction of personal and situational factors. Personal factors involved are cognitions, values and norms. Involved situational factors are dependent on structural and cultural environment, as they are: levels of education in society, the actual division of labour, power, material means, and so on.

We speak about an information need if:

- persons define their situation as being problematic;
- if these persons have an image of the situation they wish;
- and if they realize for themselves that information is a clue to the realization of the desired situation

Figure 1

Factors which influence the size and nature of information needs.

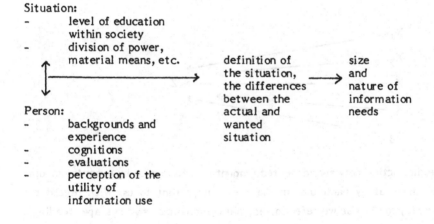

Situation:
- level of education within society
- division of power, material means, etc.

Person:
- backgrounds and experience
- cognitions
- evaluations
- perception of the utility of information use

definition of the situation, the differences between the actual and wanted situation

size and nature of information needs

Information-seeking

The factors which influence the decision to seek information are best described in Sepstrup's model (1980). This model (the most practical) describes the actual information seeking process. Others are mostly restricted to the psychological level and are based on interpersonal decision making processes (Donohew and Tipton 1973; Atkin 1973; Bettman 1979).

Sepstrup is not interested in the decision making process itself, but in the variables which explain the decision making process and the resulting decision, e.g. the decision to seek information.

Sepstrup expects five more general variables which may explain the decision to seek information. He intends to measure the concept of information seeking by the measurable probability of information consumption in relation to a certain need for information. We prefer to replace this variable based on probability by the variable based on the decision to start actually the process of information seeking. The five explaining variables are:

1. The size of the information need (X_1).
2. The importance of the issue (X_2).
3. Expected amount of information by everyday media use (X_3).
4. Expected amount of information by particular media use (X_4).
5. Expected costs of perceived information sources (X_5).

Figure 2

Sepstrup's information seeking model.

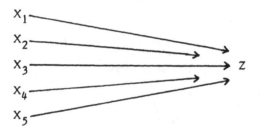

The distinction between 'expected amount of information by everyday media use' and that by particular media use is important to us. With regard to everyday media use we refer to personal communication, newspaper reading, television viewing and so on. With regard to particular media use we think about special interest magazines, but also new media, and especially those new media for which active information seeking is a key concept. That means: public consultation media like Viditel and Ditzitel.

Sepstrup distinguishes between the expected amount of information acquired by way of everyday or particular media use and the expected costs. Logically this distinction is correct. When Sepstrup elaborates his model he enumerates only items which indicate the expected amount of information. He does not relate these items to the expected costs of the information sources. In our view the consumers will make their decisions taking into account both the expected usefulness of the information and the expected costs. Therefore we wish to propose combining variables X_3 and X_4 with variable X_5 and to introduce two new variables:

1. Considering the expected costs and results of information seeking based on everyday media use; measured by the espected usefulness of the information acquired for everyday media use (Y_1).
2. Considering the expected costs and results of information seeking based on use of particular media; measured by the expected usefulness of the information acquired from particular media (Y_2).

These two variables intervene between the size and importance of information needs and thus the actual decision to start information seeking. We propose an adapted version of Sepstrup's model.

Figure 3

An adapted version of Sepstrup's model.

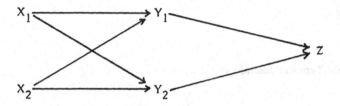

Some elaboration of the consultation model

At both levels the model needs elaboration. First we have to specify the items which indicate variable X_1 and X_2. Next we have to describe the items which indicate the constructs Y_1 and Y_2. Sepstrup already has offered some of these items especially where the expected amount of information and costs for everyday and particular media use are concerned.

He indicates the amount of information and costs of everyday media use by items like:

1. Experience.

The experience of the information value of media used daily gives people a certain opinion about quality and importance of the offered information.

2. Total consumption of information

The greater the total consumption the higher the expected amount of information will be and the lower the costs. Although it may be more realistic to start from the assumption that at a certain level the cost of more information in everyday media use does not pay-off. No new information is offered, or other (i.e. non-information) function of media might prevail.

3. Types of media use

The distribution of total information consumption on the use function of media and on the substantial heterogeneity of the content of these media may identify types of media use. Use functions of media are direct or indirect. Media are substantially (more) homogeneous or (more) heterogeneous. Direct media use means entertainment, and information seeking means, in that case, a way of pastime. Indirect media are used as a mean to reach a goal. Media content can be homogeneous: a lot of information on the same subject, or heterogeneous: information on a lot of different subjects. Muskens and Van Oorschot labelled these types of media use as follows:

Figure 4

Ideal Types of Media use.

		Nature of media use	
		direct	indirect
media content	homogeneous	addicted use	(proto-) professional
	heterogeneous	heavy use	ideal use

4. Other characteristics of media use

Media use may be described by many other dimensions, e.g. the distribution of the total media consumption (and topics), the suitability of the consumption situation (place, time and so on where the information consumption occurs).

Of course these variables can be related to other variables such as length of leisure time, other activities, tiredness, access to media, individual characteristics and so on.

The consultation of particular (new) media

Sepstrup enumerates the following three items to indicate the use of particular media:

1. The experience of a person with the information offered by particular media.
2. Physical and social factors influencing access to the relevant particular media.
3. Individual characteristics of information seekers.

The items which may indicate the expected costs of information are expressed in terms of time, money, revenues of postponement, alternative use of time, and physical and phychological strain. All these costs may be taken into account if a person decides to seek information by the consultation of a particular new medium. The relative importance of the different items remains to be established.

Until now we have assumed that these costs should be weighted by the expected profit from the information sought.

Choice and priority of information sources

Let us assume that some person starts to seek information. First of all a choice has to be made which source or sources might be consulted. Sepstrup claims that this particular choice is dependent on the expected usefulness of the sources (information value) known by the person who seeks information. A source with a high expected usefulness (information value) has a higher priority than a source with a low expected usefulness. The use of a particular source depends on the ratio of the information value and the expected costs.

The information value depends on the perceived importance of the information, the perceived comprehensibility and the perceived credibility. The information value of a source will be confronted with the perceived costs. These confrontation of values and costs for different sources will result in a choice between these sources or a priority list of the sources to be consulted.

This theoretical model briefly outlined so far needs to be tested to proof its validity.

FACTORS WHICH MAY DISTURB THE IDEALIZED USE OF PUBLIC CONSULTATION MEDIA

We stated earlier that optimal conditions for an experiment are not easily obtained. One might say that media experiments are vulnerable enterprises, even if they are based on sophisticated mediamarketing-concepts and broad media-experience as is the case with the publishers behind Ditzitel. We have discussed the users of information; those who might be ideal users of public consultation media. Their habits, their decisions, and the new ways to gather information may be described by the concepts developed. Information is a two-way process. It is produced as well as used. Some production factors may disturb possible effects of the introduction and use of Ditzitel. That means: success or failure is not only dependent on the information seeking behaviour of a consumer; it also depends on some production factors. We might discuss here shortly two of them, i.e. the dependence of public consultation media like Ditzitel on external information supply and sequentially unavoidable creative or editorial problems.

Dependency on information suppliers

Information suppliers will be forced to work with this concept by contract with the editor i.e. Home Information Service of VNU-Publishers. When a supplier fails the contract can be cancelled. At that moment (or earlier, from the moment that the supplier failed to supply new updated pages and information) the concept acquires lacunae and the public less information. Incidents on this level can be handled, but relatively frequent conflicts with information suppliers create major problems. Even if many people are going to use and pay for Ditzitel, it is not certain that the information suppliers will give sufficient priority to their Ditzitel information share. Corporate policy and policy research might look for strategies which make Ditzitel less dependent of external information supply, e.g. by making a real news and advertisement medium of it with its own and autonomous journalistic and commercial staff. The journalists should collect and edit information independently (within the limits of the information service concept of Ditzitel) while commercial staff edit commercial information such as advertising, teleshopping, and electronic banking.

Creative and editorial problems

A strategy aimed at an own and autonomous editorial staff will meet the following problems:
1. There is no established journalistic and creative tradition of editing teletex or viewdata pages in the Netherlands as has come into being in Great Britain.
2. Schools of Journalism, art and graphic schools in the Netherlands were not likely, at least until recently, to change their curricula to teletex or viewdata journalism and screen design.
3. So, there are hardly any skilled journalists, editors and designers to build up an own and autonomous editorial staff for Ditzitel.
4. The price of DF 2,50 a month will be insufficient to invest in journalistic and creative aspects of the medium, or pay a staff.

Investments in human capital, in-depth research into teletex and viewdata journalism and curriculum-development and the encouragement of initiatives by creative persons seem to be necessary conditions for a new medium-concept like Ditzitel. In the early seventies VNU was confronted with an analogous problem regarding journalism for mass periodical magazines: no schools, no curricula, no traditions, but a medium which needed a journalistic formula and graphic design of its own.

VNU started its own in-service training programmes for talented young (newspaper) journalists; it encouraged and participated in a foundation for the study of the mass periodical magazine press; marginal press happened to be, to a great extent, a periodical press in which new ideas of journalism and design were tried out. An analogous corporate policy, and the encouragement of applied research and of small-scale initiatives of screen freaks, video freaks and computer communicators may show the ways to functioning public consultation media.

Ditzitel is designed to be a public consultation medium for a general audience with quite heterogeneous interests. So solving such production problems seems to be the more necessary because we may foresee that the coming users of Ditzitel will not be idealized users of public consultation media as we identified them. They will not be only (and by majority) users of a heterogeneous supply of a particular new medium for indirect reasons. Many of them will be to some degree addicts, freaks, heavy users, snobs, so-called or real professionals. They will look for new fun in addition to magazines, TV, computer games, and other kinds of recreation. Some will discuss the concept of Ditzitel on professional standards which will not be approached.

Many will not learn the easy way to find the information sought. That means: the way people look for information from an information service is more complicated than even an experienced publisher or a researcher might imagine.

Bunt, a Tilburg colleague on informatics, told us, how difficult it is to implement automated information services for railway travellers. Quite a number of travellers, calling the information service, do not use necessary key words such as place and time, but say, for instance, that they want to visit their sick mother. They seem to exhibit a need for a personal recognition before they can interact correctly with an information service.

Unsolved anticipation problems like these may disturb the Ditzitel-experiment. As part of the introduction process they must be controlled and solved, step-by-step with research outcomes as an important kind of feedback.

GENERAL OUTLINES OF A RESEARCH DESIGN

This feedback can be based on experimental or panel research in which the following questions should be answered:

1. Which information needs of which information seeking persons may be satisfied by Ditzitel?
2. Does a new public consultation medium like Ditzitel change traditional patterns of information seeking behaviour and, if so, whose behaviour is changed and whose not?

The answers can be found by comparing different user groups and non-user groups. The comparisons should be made at different times beginning before Ditzitel is introduced experimentally, and with a final measurement after the broad integration of Ditzitel in the Amsterdam cable network (or after a possible decision of the publisher that the experiment has failed and that Ditzitel has to cease). We may approach the field situation by a before-after design for experimental research with several controls over different user groups and non-user groups. This design is fit to prove changes caused by 'the experimental factor', in our case, the experimental introduction of Ditzitel.

User groups should be gathered among persons with the following characteristics:

1. Professional users and non-professional users of consultation media.

   This difference is part of the typology elaborated on media users. Besides, practical experience shows that persons with professional, vocational and commercial roles in society are relatively heavy and early users of public consultation, i.e. viewdata media; whereas the general, non-professional public might be rather reluctant to accept the new ways of dealing with information, or, at least, less active than they promised to be in prospective market research for Ditzitel.

   In a broader context Flichy has shown that many new media of the last century were expected to have informational and educational functions for a general public, nevertheless, they were institutionalized by their mass entertainment functions (in our model: heavy or addict use functions) like going to the movies, listening music, staying home and watching TV, playing Packman, and so on.

2. Users with former viewdata experience and users without former viewdata experience.

   For the first group Ditzitel may be an extension of some kinds of media use which have grown into the everyday use; the second is going to use a new and, for them, a particular medium. So, we may control the difference between everyday media use and particular media use. Users with former viewdata experience might be subscribers of Viditel. (1)

The combination of the two criteria for user groups leads to four experimental user groups, as shown in the following diagram.

Figure 5

Experimental groups of Ditzitel-users.

	Viditel experience	Non-Viditel experience
professional information needs	1	2
non-professional information needs	3	4

For each experimental group of Ditzitel users a control group is needed consisting of matched persons who cannot fulfil their information needs by using Ditzitel. These controls are necessary to prove that differences between the experimental groups are caused by the experimental factor and not by some other factors like Zeitgeist, ongoing general changes of media consumption, publicity, and so forth. Effects have to take place in and between experimental groups only, and not in or between control groups.

The four control groups cannot be found under those Amsterdam cable network subscribers who will not subscribe to Ditzitel. They are able to use Ditzitel but decline that possibility (at the moment). So they are different on an essential and ucontrollable criterion. They must be found in some community which has no Ditzitel (or other hybrid viewdata) service at its disposal. The control community or communities must be equal to the Amsterdam community to exclude differences between experimental groups and control groups due to difference between Amsterdam and other communities. This requirement may be approached by the selection of one or, better, more large Dutch cities and their (prospective) local cable network, e.g. The Hague and Rotterdam, or larger cities abroad which have viewdata systems at their disposal comparable to Viditel (e.g. Prestel in larger British cities or Bildschirmtext in German cities with experimental cable TV).

In the selected cities (4) control groups of cable network subscribers must be compiled (i.e. professional viewdata-users, non-professional viewdata-users, professional non-viewdata-users, non-professional non-viewdata-users). They must be matched for education level, sex, age, wealth, etc. with the persons who compile the experimental groups.

We may find predicted differences caused by the introduction of Ditzitel by this experimental design, but, as we have discussed, the experimental introduction of a new medium is also an enterprise vulnerable by its production problems like external information supply and editorial standards. It is hardly possible to control these production factors experimentally. So, a serious and all-embracing evaluation of the introduction and growth (or failure) of Ditzitel cannot only depend on experimental research. Detailed observations and descriptions of the introduction process, policy analysis regarding VNU's strategies regarding external information suppliers and the development of editorial standards, and imaginative or critical interpretations of experimental results must accompany the experimental design and its intended hard proof.

So, the professional preference of many sociologists and communication researchers for the more qualitative approaches will also be met: and the identifiable actor introducing a new medium for public consultation will get an all-embracing evaluation of his cultural enterprise.

NOTE

1. The Ditzitel System is most attractive to those who have a teletex-TV apparatus at their disposal. So, almost all subscribers to Ditzitel in its first phase will have some rude experience with viewdata-possibilities, and especially with Teletext, a service provided by the Dutch broadcast institutions. This means the experience factor is not completely controllable.

LITERATURE

Allen, J.H. van, and M. Visser,
Social experiments with information technology in the Netherlands, Rotterdam (Erasmus University), September 1985.

Atkin, C.K.,
Anticipated communication and mass-media information seeking, in: Public Opinion Quaterly, 36, 1973, pp. 7-24.

Bettman, J.R.,
An information processing theory of consumer choice, Addison-Wesley Publ. Company, Reading, 1979.

Donohew, L., and L. Tipton,
A conceptual model of information seeking, avoiding and processing, in: P. Clarke (ed.), New models for mass-communication research, London, 1973.

Festinger, L.,
Conflict decision and dissonance, Stanford, 1964.

Flichy, P.,
La constitution des usages sociaux en matière de communication, paper Burgos, July 1979.

Jackson-Beeck, M.,
The Nonviewers: Who are they?, in: Journal of Communication, 1977 (27) 3, pag. 65-72.

Kappetijn, F.,
Lecture on VNU Home Information Services and Ditzitel, no place, no year.

Moschis, G.P.,
Consumer information use: individual vs. social predicts, in: Communication Research, 7, 2, 1980 (139-160).

Muskens, G., and W. van Oorschot,
Informatiebehoeften, informatiezoekgedrag, moeilijke doelgroepen (Information needs, information seeking behaviour, difficult target groups), Tilburg (IVA), October 1985.

Sepstrup, P.,
Consumption of Mass Communication, construction of a model on information seeking behaviour, in: Research in Marketing, 3, 1980, pp. 105-142.

Sepstrup, P.,

Consumption of Mass Communication, construction of a model on information consumption behaviour. Institut for Markeds Økonomi, Aarhus, 1977.

METHODOLOGICAL ANALYSIS OF EXPERIMENTS WITH COMMUNICATION SERVICES

Sylvie Craipeau, IDATE, Francis Kretz, CCETT, France

This study was embarked upon in mid-1982 with a view to analysing the methods and structural parameters of the social experiments devoted to communication services in France. The study applies more specifically to the "general public" services designed for use in households or public places rather than to institutional or professional services for use within organizations. The emphasis is laid on the practical, operational aspects of these experiments, even though the study started with a more conceptual approach in order to mark out the theoretical field within which the "social experimentation" took place.

The research has, amongst other things, enabled us to anatomize social experiments with telematics technology in terms sufficiently general to be (we hope) widely useful, and in terms sufficiently specific to be (we hope) of real value to any of the various participants engaged in such experiments who might wish to take stock of their situation, at any given moment in the experimental process.

INTRODUCTION: THE POSITION AND AIMS OF THE STUDY

Position of the Study

The study was carried out from the middle of 1982 until the beginning of 1984. At the same time the main experiments with videotex in France had started and were entering a phase of stocktaking, generalization and opening up for commercial operation.

The Electronic Directory service (2, 3, 4) designed in 1980 and 1981 was first tried out in practice from July 1980 onwards (in St Malo) and then in four communes with 1,000 users from July to December 1981. The official start of commercial use took place in the Département of Ille et Vilaine in February 1983. The service was subsequently opened region by region. By the end of 1985 a million Minitel terminals had been distributed. Users have access to the Télétel network, which at present offers them more than 1,500 applications, which are accessible according to three tariff scales. The service offered is expanding rapidly, and traffic is growing faster than the number of terminals.

The purpose of the experiment in Vélizy and the neighbouring communes (Télétel 3V) was to try out the widest possible range of applications. This experiment, designed in 1980 and 1981, became operational in July 1981 for 2,900 terminals, and was officially stopped in December 1982 in order to be extended as part of the Télétel network, which was gradually opened up at national level.

Other experiments (Claire, TELEM-Nantes, Gretel..., to mention only the best-known ones) were in progress, and by the middle of 1982 there were few fields of application or regions in France where experiments were not either planned or in progress. That was the ideal time for an investigation of the operational aspects of these experiments, despite their considerable differences.

And, although this period is now for the greater part past in France (various summings-up of the situation will be found in documents 5 to 8 in the references), other communication services especially for household use are being designed and have already led or are on the point of leading to experiments. Mention may be made of the development of videotex, in its graphic, photographic and sound- backed modes (9), and the memory card (10). But, above all, in November 1982, the Cable Plan was adopted by the French Government, and the period of designing the services which it makes possible (11) is now leading to experiments in its practical use with the commercial opening of the first ordered cable networks, scheduled to take place from December 1985 to 1987 in several French cities. At the same time, the Biarritz experimental network, with the very exceptional facilities which it offers, was opened in May 1984 and had reached a thousand users at the end of 1985.

We are therefore convinced of the future usefulness of our study. It seems to be sufficiently general to be applied to services other than videotex and to other institutional, political, regulatory or economic situations which may be encountered by new communication services in other countries, for instance.

1982 was in fact a fertile year in France as regards social experimentation. It was the subject of many speeches, IDATE devoted its IVth International Days (12) to it and the Minister for PTT himself made it a central point of his action (13). A CNET-CCETT working party (14) had discussed the question of its activity in the designing and evaluation of communication services. This working party defined social experimentation by centring it on social innovation in a participative dissemination process, as opposed to the product testing employed in marketing for quantitative purposes (we shall carry this approach further in the last Chapter). Social experimentation was, moreover, relocated in relation to the range of studies to be pursued generally in the field of communication services, comprising both more fundamental studies and operational studies. Lastly, the working party proposed, as a form of organization, a project team guided by a steering committee and based on a structure of concertation between the partners (we shall return to these aspects in the paragraph about modes of organization). Furthermore, another working party (15) took stock of the policy of social experimentation pursued in the 1970s (the power of the State and the monopolies, technocentric approaches and the virtual absence of evaluation) and proposed social experimentation as a method for the adaptation of social demand and technical supply, facilitating creativity and making possible rapid feedback to design.

Aims and Organization of the Study

It was therefore necessary at that time, in view of the great diversity and disparity in discussions and analyses, to re-examine the concept of social experimentation on a theoretical basis, to observe how the "experiments" and other "projects" which were taking place or in course of preparation before our eyes were organized, to see whether they were objectively entitled to be called social experiments and to endeavour to discern the structural parameters which would enable the concept and its ups and downs to be concretely understood.

With this aim, the study was organized in three sections:

- a theoretical and genealogical approach (16) of the concept of social experimentation, from the 17th century up to the present: the purpose was to define the various currents of thought around this subject, to describe the coming into being of the concept of experimentation in the "exact" sciences and then in the human and social sciences, and to arrive at an understanding of the concepts of change and social innovation;

- a practical approach (17) through an analysis of real "experimentation" situations: some ten experiments and projects in the telematics field were analysed;

- lastly - and it is on this last section that we shall concentrate in this paper - it was necessary, in the light of the two preceding approaches, to compile an organizational and methodological summary (18) of the various aspects, so as to enable social experimentation in the field of communication services to be described and pursued.

After having recalled the first two approaches via the lessons which we have drawn from them for our summary, we shall describe the various structural aspects of a social experiment within the three time sequences which we adopted for this paper: prelude, setting up and execution, and stocktaking (with a view to generalization).

THEORETICAL FOUNDATIONS OF SOCIAL EXPERIMENTATION

It would be vain to attempt here to summarize this phase of the study (16), which describes the evolution of experimental thinking, its comparison with social reality and then the use of social experimentation as a method of intervention of the political approach in the social aspect. Social experimentation cannot be a unified concept, and we shall deal here only with those dimensions of it which are most directly pertinent to the requirements of our methodological summary.

The Heterogeneity of the Idea of Social Experimentation

The Télétel 3V operation, the basic experiment with regard to telematics, was for some people a market survey, for others a technical trial and for still others a genuine social experiment. For our part, what is made clear via these attitudes and the experiments themselves is the relationship between technology and society, a relationship which had dominated the field of knowledge and of social practices since the 18th century. Experimentation is emerging, with the appearance of modern technologies and the social changes brought about by them, transforming the field of knowledge. Experimentation emerges afresh upon each appearance of a new technical rationale and a cultural and political crisis. We need not emphasize the different dimensions of the crises which help to promote social experimentation: a crisis of representation (19) in the social sciences, a crisis of justification (20) and of decision-making (21) in the social and political fields.

Social experimentation, fundamentally bound up with social change, essentially combines contradictory logics, those of scientific objectivity and of social action, and is always a project for the merging of ethical, political and economic factors.

The product of a changing society, the project of social experimentation is always centred on three poles, those of knowledge, of power and of the social aspect. From the knowledge component, social experimentation aims to retain the scientific model and the effort to achieve objectivity and neutrality; from the power aspect social experimentation derives its strategic objectives and its purpose of influencing society; its social object is to promote collective participation and the greatest possible support. It acquires its symbolic effectiveness from its ability to blend these three logics into a single event, embracing a combination of concrete social exchanges in - as it were - a spiral movement in order to incorporate them in a new code.

Methodological Procedure and Social Process

Social experimentation is, furthermore, both a procedure, as a method of administrating innovation, and a social process, as a place and dynamics enabling the strategies of the social actors, partners and users to be confronted.

This ambivalent form, always operating at the limits of the social, economic and legal organization, and going beyond them, is an instrument for recording a crisis and solving it, the defence of a threatened social identity and the promise of a new identity (22). When the extension of economic and technological rationality reaches the point of destroying the structure of both social exchanges and institutional frameworks of political representation, a project which springs both from the institutions (experimentation as a method of administration) and from the basic social groups (experimentation as a utopia converted into reality) is capable of establishing a consensus.

In the field of communication services, which is indeed the extension of technical rationality to the sphere of communication (the ultimate guarantee of social unity), this project acquires even greater strength. This form of dissemination of technological innovation is the one which accords best with its destabilizing nature. An up-to-date form of social experimentation must of necessity:

- propose flexible procedures;

- adopt the most varied and widest social groups as interlocutors, involving them in one way or another in decision-making and conducting of the experiments;

- include a phase giving full scope for breaking down existing structures.

It will be seen how this triple requirement affects different dimensions of the development of new telecommunication systems: technical, economic, legal and social dimensions. It limits the possibilities of predetermined experimentations.

Concretely, social experimentation must be the construction of a space for representation of all these challenges and for negotiation among the social actors which are vectors of it. This space for social experimentation greatly exceeds the territory within which the technical system employed is implemented. It must be a participative search making possible, at one and the same time, an analysis of social change, appropriation of the services which are being tried out and institutional negotiation.

EXAMPLES OF EXPERIMENTATION IN TELEMATICS

This part of the study (17) was carried out in 1983. Its analysis may be outdated and the facts which it describes are definitely no longer up to date. But their dynamics and the basic scale on which they were analysed remain valid. The actual experiments analysed were located in two regions, Picardie and the Midi-Pyrénées region. They can only be skimmed over in this article.

The Picardie Region

Picardie, a region which is in a state of crisis, was seeking a new identity. The regional authorities had launched a renewal programme, in which telematics was expected to be a primary asset. Several telematics projects emerged, and two were adopted: that for the agricultural sector and the scheme jointly produced by the regional newspaper, the departments of labour and employment and the Regional Council (Regional Assembly).

The agricultural project forms part of a strategy of making agriculture independent of the economic actors who, upstream or downstream, have a hold over farmers. Information is seen as an essential factor in this strategy. Its rationalization presupposes concerted action by organizations of different kinds. Here, videotex is the demultiplying technical element in the economic, institutional and technical project, which has already been embarked upon in other fields, bringing the partners together around a federating project.

The regional press sees videotex as an opportunity of coping with the crisis which it is going through. It is supporting its technical rationalization project and its multimedia strategy by an expanded programme of action. The technical project is becoming the vector of a consensus for remedying the regional crisis. The newspaper is joining forces with the Regional Council in a project, in which employment - the federating concept - is becoming the central component. The alliance entered into with its various partners is taking concrete form in the creation of an association, "Télématique en Picardie".

The regional newspaper is becoming the leader of a project which goes beyond its traditional activities. It is taking up a position as a national actor, has the ambition of acquiring a status as a data-bank service centre and publishing adviser and is proposing to develop know-how on writing for telematics applications.

It should be noted that the auxiliary partners, who became associated with the project after its conception, will transform it when it comes to making the transition from a service concept to the formulation of a content. An executive actor can thus impose its own rationality. In this case this actor is the ANPE (Agence Nationale Pour l'Emploi - National Employment Agency), which has imposed major limitations on access to the system by reserving it for its offices in order to maintain its pregoratives as an intermediary.

Midi-Pyrénées Region

This is a dynamic region, in favour of the new technologies, which is far from experiencing the industrial problems faced by Picardie. The Telecommunication Directorate is making a big contribution to this dynamism.

Among some twenty videotex projects developed in 1983 in this region, we have turned our attention here only to that of a bank (Crédit Agricole) and that of a regional daily newspaper, two powerful economic agents in the region.

For the press it was primarily a question of acquiring a footing and thus ensuring its hegemony in this new field. Videotex is part of a product diversification strategy. The press and the bank have joined forces within a structure in order to reinforce their respective projects. Institutional considerations take precedence over the definition of the services. This alliance actually conceals keen competition, in which the status of data-bank service centre accommodating the host computer is a crucial stake. These partners in fact neutralize each other at the very moment when they join forces.

Here, again, an auxiliary partner is creating a spin-off of the project. It is developing an original service which takes account of the end-users. It is when the experimentation goes beyond the directing bodies of the promoting organizations towards wider audiences that the project really begins to take shape.

Two Regions: Two Symmetrical Logics

These two cases are interesting owing to the symmetry of the logics which they display. In the one, the local partners are negotiating directly with the Central Administration and working out a federating strategy; in the other, private partners, the region's economic and institutional forces, are joining together with a view to excluding other possible partners.

Hence there are two forms of grouping: one which is dominated by a synergic logic and the other which aims at control. In both cases the regional daily press plays the part of leader.

The various projects are characterized by three types of experimental set-up, depending on the predominant aims:

- institutional aims: the project entails heavy investment and is carried by a co-ordinating project leader;

- commercial aims: the investment involved is small, built into the organization of each partner, and innovation is regarded as a supple-mentary element in their strategies;

- technical aims: the project is centred on the definition of an application and on the appropriation and institutional integration of the technique by the users.

In all the projects, however, the institutional and technical factors predominate over the definition of the service. This phenomenon is attributable to the historical stage of development of the technique: the initial moment of the innovation crystallizes these factors. But, now once again, at the moment when professional telematics services are being set up, the same phenomenon appears (23).

While videotex is indeed caught up in a rationality of development of the power of the actors which make it their own, it can also be a means of acquiring a dominant position for an actor who has hitherto been marginal. Nevertheless, while it can bring forth new leaders, videotex rather appears (for the time being) to be causing a redefinition of the roles of the dominant actors in the sector. These various strategies are crystallized around an essential trump card: the definition, location and ownership of the data-bank service centre.

The Role of the Telecommunications Administration

This role is essential in the various situations. In Picardie the dissemination of the Electronic Directory is imminent, and this is spurring the local partners into action and leading to the creation of operational services; in the Midi-Pyrénées region it is scheduled for later, leaving space for a purely strategic positioning.

The Telecommunications Administration is seen to be a central actor. At the cross-roads of local strategies, it is at one and the same time a regional authority and a national government department. It intervenes on the technical level by the distribution of terminals in connection with the opening of the Electronic Directory service and, institutionally, by influencing the regrouping of local actors and the evaluation of applications.

As the manager of the networks the Telecommunications Administration must in fact look after the dissemination of the innovation and therefore play an organizing role. This role is based on an ambivalent representation in which everything connected with the technical aspect, being surrounded by an aura of neutrality, consensus and the general public interest, makes it possible to go beyond the political aspect, which expresses the irrational factors and private interests.

GENERAL STRUCTURE OF SOCIAL EXPERIMENTATION

Social Experimentation as a Dynamic Process of Comparison of Design and Uses

Social experiments with a communication service can be analysed as being a process of social solving of a problem made up of three components corresponding to a three-fold uncertainty:

- uncertainty with regard to the subject of the experiment: this is the entire difficulty of the designing of services, from their definition to the implementation of applications. From the designer to the user there is a fundamental time-lag which experimentation will be able to overcome.

- uncertainty concerning the social impact of the subject of the experiment: observation, analysis, evaluation of uses, indeed the creation of new uses by users will make it possible to answer the fundamental question concerning the impact;

- lastly, uncertainty regarding the aims of the experiment: this uncertainty is perhaps at a different level from the other two, but it looms very large in the experiments. Experimentation is the place of competition between the aims, strategies or merely tactics of the actors, promoters or opponents, who give it its life.

This endeavour to find a solution to the uncertainties, which forms the basis of social experimentation, is founded on a structural parameter which is the determining factor in the evolution of the actors, the analyses and the users, namely time. And social experimentation can be looked upon as a dynamic process of interaction of the various times of the parties involved. Technical time or rather, designer's time, for whom everything is simple, inevitable to the natural inertia of previously existing uses. The user's time, which is that for appropriation in reaction to the natural inertia of previously existing uses. The investigator's time, that of the "neutral" or "external" (or would-like-to-be neutral) analyst, which is not that of the chronicler. These various times are intermingled, because they do not have the same trajectory, the same rhytm or the same significant events.

Social experimentation can thus be seen as a dual process:

- one process, a socio-institutional one, is a <u>negotiation between the social actors</u>, promoters or opponents;

- the other, a socio-technical process, is a <u>interaction between the design and the use</u>, each applied to the subject of the experimentation, that is, the communication service in question or one of its applications.

This second process can be schematically represented as shown in Figure 1.

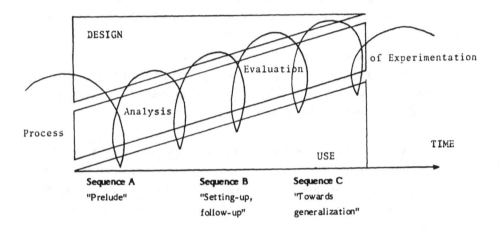

Figure 1: Social experimentation as a dynamic process of interaction between design and use by means of analyses and evaluations carried out throughout the three time sequences shown.

This solving process is based on one of the key aspects of social experimentation: the more or less formalized combination of the <u>analyses and evaluations</u> carried out on the subject of the experiment, on its uses, on its production processes, on the actors in the experiment and their aims. It is this analysis, introspective or conducted from outside, which is the driving force behind experimentation.

The Three Sequences of an Experimentation and Their Main Parameters

As we have just emphasized, the time involved in an experimentation is probably the most directly decisive factor for its analysis. For the purpose of this description we have adopted, schematically, three successive time sequences. This segmentation is, admittedly, outside the continuity of the dynamic process which characterizes an experimentation, and very often no specific event corresponds to the passage from one sequence to another. For each of them we shall present, further on, the aspects of the experimental procedure which it underlies and the main lines of the analysis of the experimentation. These are summarized in Tabulation 1.

First of all, the prelude contains the definition of the context, the aims and actors of the experimentation. This gives the experimentation its status. The services are precisely defined in terms of their technical components and the applications being tried out. The evaluation is programmed here, or disregarded.

In the central sequence of setting-up and execution the experimentation is concretely organized and then executed, simultaneously with the production of the service and the applications which are being tried out. The actors become partners in the experimentation or are eliminated from it. Lastly, the users are more or less actively involved in the process of designing the service.

This sequence leads into the phase of stocktaking, towards generalization, in which, in a more or less formalized manner, the uses, and indeed the course of the experimentation and its actual organization, are evaluated and analysed. The results are compared with the aims of the experimentation. The decision whether or not to generalize is made, and the mode of generalization is worked out.

The aspects which will be specified further on may overlap from one sequence to another: our choice is to try to be, if anything, exhaustive by presenting the same aspect, where appropriate, in various different lights depending on the subject or on the sequence in which we describe it.

SEQUENCE A: THE PRELUDE

- Context of the experimentation
- Definition of the service being tried out (technical components, applications)
- Aims and potential implications
- Actors involved
- Status of the evaluation

SEQUENCE B: SETTING UP AND EXECUTION

- Participants
- Organization
- Production of the service
- Users

SEQUENCE C: STOCKTAKING; TOWARDS GENERALIZATION

- Evaluation of the organization, of the execution
- Evaluation of uses
- Comparison between results and aims
- Generalization decision
- Modes of generalization

Tabulation 1: Aspects and main lines of the analysis of a social experiment on communication services according to the three main sequences in its process.

THE PRELUDE SEQUENCE OF AN EXPERIMENTATION

This sequence is quite obviously a key factor, the basis of the coming experimentation. It represents the initiation of the setting up and also of the analyses. The latter will in fact often refer back to it during the subsequent sequences. The experimental framework, simultaneously representing the local space of actors, services and applications implemented, and of users, is devised before being given concrete form in the next sequence. The decision regarding the setting up of the experimentation can be prepared by the conducting of experiments. These refer to events of limited scope in comparison with the experimentation proper, which presupposes sufficient duration and social space for its development.

The Context of the Experimentation

Two aspects can be dealt with under this head:

- on the one hand, the local organization of the location and of the content to be tried out (local actors and their relationships, available local resources, existing uses of related applications ...)

- on the other hand, the local/national relationship, both through the local function of national actors and through the position of the experimentation in question in relation to any similar or related applications at other locations.

The Definition of the Service(s) and Application(s)

We shall use the term "service" (communication service) in its technical sense. It is the medium used, defined by all its technical components:

- tools for the production of the elementary messages - pages, in videotex - and for their logical structurering - dialogue, in videotex;

- data-bank service centre or "server" - at one and the same time, both the storage of the messages and the executing power for the dialogue;

- communication network(s);

- user terminals.

A service may offer several applications (or "contents") and even several types of applications (e.g.: consultation, transaction, "letter box" messaging service, "dialogue" messaging service, for the videotex).

The definition of the service(s) and application(s) to be tried out represents the very foundation, the raison d'être, of the experimentation. Several dimensions are necessary in order to grasp it:

- technical aspects (configuration of the various components of the services, their geographical distribution, their dimensions) and industrial aspects (degree of technical innovation, extent of investments, industrial strategy);

- socio-economic aspects (applications, targeted user types, production and operating costs, institutional relationships between actors);

- the extent to which the choice of services or application is closed or open (whether evolutivity and adaptivity, or, inversely, a product test is offered);

- the degree of technical flexibility which, in relation to the preceding parameter, may be in respect of only one specific application.

The Aims and Potential Implications of the Experimentation

(see also the section below concerning the status of the experimentation)

a. The aim are expressed to a greater or lesser extent depending on the case in question. They are furthermore very diverse depending on whether the implicit or explicit "aim" of the experimentation arises from the symbolic nature, the "what is to be seen", from the occupation of the ground, or is a carefully prepared stage of a strategy. The aim may differ depending on the actors, and may develop in time.

b. The strategies can be classified schematically, firstly as either basically local strategies as opposed to strategies which are national but are locally applied owing to the need to carry out experiments initially on a modest scale. This distinction is due to the location of the initiative which forms the basis of the experimentation. All the intermediate situations will exist in reality depending on the degree of intervention by the national actors, as being instigators or called in to support a local initiative, and depending on the motivation of the local actors.

Secondly, the strategies can also be classified according to another main line, that of the degree of (social) innovation of the experimentation: continuity strategies, break strategies.

c. Lastly, an element which sheds light on aims and strategies is the definition of the criteria for evaluation of the experimentation (we shall give details of these further on). As these may differ or even be opposed to each other depending on the actors, they are a major source of conflict, and this is in fact so whether they are formalized or latent.

Identification of Actors

a) Here it will be necessary to describe each of the social actors which, closely or remotely, favourably or in opposition, affect the planned experimentation, depending on:

- their economic, political and strategic weight;
- their field of activity in relation to the content(s) to be tried out;
- Their membership of a national group and the effect of this membership on their action.

b) The relationship between the actors must be analysed: solidarities, dependencies, competitive situations, etc., and also the role of the individuals (inter-person exchanges) in relation to that of the organizations (institutional relationships).

c) The attitudes of these actors towards the experimentation will be of decisive importance for their degree of subsequent participation in it: promotors, actors who are favourably inclined to the experimentation, sympathetic, neutral or opposed to it.

Among the future partners in the experimentation, several attitudes or aims will become evident: an intra-organization aim (to improve its activity), the aim of extending or assuring its audience, the aim of, improvement or maintenance of an institutional position. Also, depending on the actors, there will be attitudes or aims which are either local or rather national in scope.

Status of the Experimentation

Asking the "why" of an experimentation, investigating its origin and describing the history which caused a given social space to focus initially on the idea of experimentation and then gradually to organize itself with a view to the operational setting up of the experimentation are essential in order to establish the framework, the environment, of the experiment. Does it occupy a larger space than that which it presupposes, and also the degree or degrees of uncertainty (see above) which accompany it. Lastly, its local or national origin is a decisive feature for its subsequent operation.

Following A. Touraine (19), we shall distinguish between two "classes" of experimentation:

-   "Social reproduction", where the content tried out is relatively fixed (product test, defined target population) but where a certain degree of uncertainty, especially quantitative (commercial), necessitates an interaction with users. In this situation the local actors are more or less ignored; they tend to resent such an approach, which aims at neutralizing them, while on the other hand they are sensitive to more local and value-enhancing actions;

-   "social production", which, on the contrary, endeavours to create the conditions for a demand and gives priority to local social dynamism by mobilizing the actors, placing the emphasis on the intervention of the users in the actual design of the services and applications.

These are the two extremes, the product test and "social" experimentation in the proper sense of the term, used in order to mark out schematically the continuum of the types of experimentation of services (14), with on the one hand commercial market-survey aims and, on the other hand, aims of social design/creation of uses and contents. These extreme or intermediate forms will subsequently be the determinants for the decision and the modes of generalization.

A last aspect can be associated with the status of the experimentation, and this is the legal framework in which it operates. Very different situations are observable. Thus, in France, telematics tried out its legal framework at the same time as its market, whereas television in general and cable television in particular was regulated before the first developments to take place.

Evaluation Strategies, or Evaluation as an Analysis Strategy

The evaluations, either formalized according to the various methods which are customary in psycho-sociology, socio-economics and marketing, or more or less informal (analyses, thinking, etc.), are a central component of the experimentation, and this centrality was illustrated earlier in Figure 1. This dimension, at least in its concrete formalization, is, unfortunately, often curtailed or even omitted. We are convinced (see (24) concerning the connection between design/evaluation with regard to services and the user-service dialogues) that this is detrimental to the effectiveness or "productivity" of the experimentations.

Be that as it may, the evaluation phase is at the centre of the experimentation operation. It runs across the three time sequences of our analysis. It reveals the status and the mode of experimentation through the actors' aims and the degree of formalization which they give to it. We shall summarize later on the various aspects of the evaluation in a tabulation (No. 2).

The Aims of the Evaluation

We shall distinguish between two types of aims which are usually encounter-ed:

- the short-term operational aims lead to a prescriptive evaluation which is an aid to decision-making (for designing or redesigning the services tried out);

- the longer term, prospective aims correspond on the one hand to a need for interpretation of what is happening (an interpretation which requires a certain distance and a certain neutrality in relation to the field of experimentation) and, on the other hand, to the gradual, cumulative, preparation of the future stocktaking and of the decision as regards generalization (see the third sequence).

These two clearly differentiated types of aims are often the source of conflicts between certain actors in the experimentation, especially between the promotor-designers and the external investigators, or between local actors and national actors. A Danish analyst (25) also makes a distinction between operational evaluations and "neutral" evaluations, which are outside the action. He proposes that these should be co-ordinated but financed and managed independently. It seems to us rather unrealistic to go as far as that; we consider that one should instead aim at a close linking of the two lines of action, with each remaining autonomous with its own aims but supporting each other by their analyses and results.

The Subjects of the Evaluation

Four mains subjects can be discerned. They correspond to specific methods of evaluation but have to be dealt with as a whole in order to enable the experimentation to be comprehended in its main components:

- Technico-economic aspects: relevance of the choices of the techni-cal operational configuration of the services and applications tried out, associated operating costs;

- Aspects connected with the production of the services and applications: the production system, associated costs, the capacity for evolution or merely updating and maintenance of the applications;

- socio-institutional dynamics: actually, evaluation of the experimental process itself through the evolution of the relationships between the actors;

- use and "acceptability", preferably arrived at by a combination of qualitative and quantitative methods, in-depth interviews (uses, attitudes), observations (uses, behaviours), or questionnaires (socio-economic approaches, market studies).

Acceptability is a concept which can in fact be regarded as being more ambiguous than that of experimentation (26). The evaluation of acceptance refers on the one hand to the measuring of an acceptable level of quality of a service or application, in its present state. This level is poorly defined, since it is somewhere between good and bad, above a rejection "threshold". But the evaluation of acceptability, too, is also understood to be an estimate - this time with a forward-looking aim - of an acceptance potential.

The chronological ambiguity between what is acceptable at present and future acceptance, and its semantic ambiguity, between acceptable and potentially accepted, induce one to avoid this concept by distinguishing different methods (and aims) for the evaluation depending on the sequence in which it is applied. We then find that the evaluation is closely involved in the experimentation process: general studies and prior analyses in the prelude sequence, operational evaluations linked with design during the central sequence, explanatory and summing-up evaluations in the stocktaking sequence. This application of the type of evaluation to the three sequences adopted should be regarded as an indication, since overlappings are usual and desirable.

Methods of Evaluation

The various methods relate to the execution of the evaluation, the mode of dissemination of its results and its implementation:

- The actual dynamics of the evaluation (if any) may have two structures: one, permanent, throughout the experimentation; the other, final, only when stock has to be taken of its result. These two modes are not mutually exclusive: on the contrary, they benefit by being linked. The permanent evaluation may have operational aims just as much as forward-looking ones. The final evaluation is only meaningful if it is based on a permanent evaluation which has preceded it.

- Confidentiality of the results of the evaluation is another structuring element of the type of experimentation: exclusive confidentially indicates a high degree of uncertainty concerning the subject of the experimentation, its impact and also the very aims of the experimentation, which then forms part of a strategy of definition of the services and applications; on the other hand, open dissemination of the results denotes an experimentation strategy which is ready for rapid generalization.

- The execution of the evaluation, where it is formalized, can be carried out by an "internal" team (in relation to the main partners as a whole) or by an external team - which, a priori, gives it more weight and impartiality.

THE AIMS OF THE EVALUATION

- Short-term, operational: design aid
- Medium-term, explanatory or forward-looking: stocktaking aid

(desirable linking of the two types of evaluation)

THE SUBJECTS OF THE EVALUATION

- Technico-economic aspects: configuration of the service, operating costs
- Production of applications: system, costs
- Socio-institutional dynamism: interplay of actors and their strategies
- Uses: qualitative and quantitative methods

THE EVALUATION PHASES

(criticism of the concept of acceptability)

- General studies and prior analyses (prelude)
- Operational and explanatory evaluations (execution)
- Summing-up evaluation (stocktaking)

THE METHODS OF EVALUATION

- Continuous or final evaluation (or combination of these)
- Confidentiality of results/open dissemination
- Internal execution/execution by external team

Tabulation 2: Evaluation in the experimentation process (see its central position in Figure 1)

THE "SETTING-UP AND EXECUTION" SEQUENCE

The prelude sequence ends with the definition of the various components of the experimentation: the - at least initial - definition of the services and applications to be tried out, adjustment of the experimentation and evaluation strategies among those actors who are to become the partners in the experimentation and, lastly, the decision to carry out the experimentation and assign the necessary resources to it. The new sequence is devoted to setting up the experimentation and then to its execution; this is the central sequence, the heart of the experimentation, without this implying - in our opinion - that one must disregard the initial and concluding sequences between which it lies.

We shall centre our analysis of this second sequence around three main lines: the partners in the experimentation and their organization, the production of the services and applications, and the users and their status in relation to the experimentation.

The Partners, their Degree of Involvement, the Opposing Parties

The Actors in and around the Experimentation

A given experimentation means that the local and national actors must take up a position in relation to it. It will be necessary to follow, on the one hand, the evolution of the partners in the experimentation, but also that of its opponents (and their opposition may be more or less marked).

By "partners" we mean the social actors who participate directly in the experimentation, either dynamizing it or blocking it. Among these various types of partners the following can be distinguished:

- the main partners: promoters of the experimentation, principals or main contractors;

- the associated partners, who participate actively in the experimentation without being its leaders in the strict sense of the term;

- the auxiliary partners who intervene partially;

- the "blocking partners", who are present in order to block or at least impede the experimental process.

The Degree of Involvement of the Partners

This involvement, even integration, in the experimentation is revealed primarily by the financial resources or contributions in kind (staff made available, rendering of various services, etc.) provided by the partners. The type of service or management involved in the partner organization, the fact that the partner creates a specific internal team to participate in the experimentation or makes available some members of his staff for a multi-partner project team are concrete indications of his level of involvement. Another indication is the degree of rationalization of this involvement in the experimentation, through, for instance, its importance in relation to the partner's general activity.

Modes of Organization: Effectiveness of the Project Team Structure

Three modes of organization, of management of the experimentation, have been observed:

- board-type management: each partner involves himself while re-maining within his own organization, management of the experimen-tation being made possible by a more or less formal coordination. Experience shows that this is in fact a neutralizing structure;

- the project leader: he has a certain authority which has been delegated to him by each partner over his own teams;

- project team: around a project leader, each partner has made available some of his specialists in order to form a multi-partner team which is given a certain autonomy.

Experience has shown that the last-mentioned organizational mode is the most effective, making it possible to solve within the team, day by day, a large proportion of the decisions to be taken. The major orientations are worked out at the level of a steering committee, which meets at intervals of varying length.

The maximum efficiency of the project team depends on three factors:

-   its competence (basic knowledge, know-how);

-   its authority (autonomy, delegation of power);

-   the existence of a minimum consensus between partners in order to overcome conflicts.

Subject to these conditions, the project team performs the executive function for the experimentation by taking the place of the partners in it. This organization is the one which best foreshadows a generalization of the experimentation.

On the other hand, it is fragile if it is excessively external to each of the local partners, and especially if it consists of too many contributions which are outside the local sphere.

In the various modes of organization, attention should be drawn to an important factor for future generalization: the degree of openness of the partners to other local or national actors, which, although more complex to manage, is conducive to generalization, whereas a more exclusive relationship between the partners is, more often than not, neutralizing.

Production of the Services and Applications

The organization of the production for the actual content of the experimentation embraces a great variety of forms and aims.

It may be established temporarily for the experimentation period or, on the other hand, it may be designed with a view to permanence or even expansion within a strategy of local development of a form of know-how, subsequently attacking the national market.

These opposing approaches may, depending on the partners' initial authority, take concrete form either in a production system within the partners' organization, in which case these partners endeavour to acquire the production know-how themselves, or in an external - local or non-local - system entailing a sharing of the investment, with a view, from the outset, to commercial operation.

Mention should also be made of the role of operational evaluations concerning the design and execution of the applications. In rare instances the users themselves play a part in this designing.

Operation of the Services and Applications

Operations, like production, is one of the strategic functions. It is thus likewise the subject of interplays of power or even sharp conflicts between the partners: control of the data-bank service centre which carries the applications (telematics), control of production of the contents and the associated know-how.

The choice of tariff of charges, for its parts, is indicative of the experimentation strategy adopted: offering of the services free or virtually free of charge indicates that the priority aim is acceptance of the service, at the risk of subsequent rejection when a commercial scale of charges is applied; a more realistic supply approach having regard to the future market is to choose an experimental charging system of a forward-looking nature, that is, which represents what the cost of the service would be at a specific future date when it would have reached a reasonable stage of development.

The Users and their Status in the Experimentation

The choice of the sample of users (size, nature, location and spread) is also revealing of the experimentation strategy: the endeavour to find a representative, possibly segmented, population, if the primary aim is generalization of the experimentation (but very often the designers and promoters have only a vague "a priori" idea of their users, and representativeness is a difficult matter); the choice of place for the experimentation, which is symbolic and, in other cases, even political.

The evaluation will reveal the ways of appropriating the serice as an object and in terms of media, the quality of the contents as perceived by the users, the uses and reactions to the methods and levels of charging.

The relationships between the promoters/initiators of the experimentation and the users range from mere information (the user being just a passive consumer) to more or less direct participation by the users in the process of designing and executing the services and applications (extreme case: the user as creator). Between these two extremes there is recourse to various forms of action whereby the users are made aware of the service and involved in it (promotion of user groups, messaging, etc.).

Experimentation forms the basis of the interaction of a service project with uses (see Figure 1); hence the need both for a permanent evaluation analysis of the development of the users and for local promotion enabling this development to be stimulated.

"STOCKTAKING (TOWARDS GENERALIZATION)" SEQUENCE

Experimentation is not an end in itself; there will always come a time when the question of stocktaking arises, and sometimes the length of the experimentation period is in fact programmed from the outset. The "stocktaking" sequence prepares for the end of the experimentation, which in most cases is the actual commercial opening of the service. If the experimentation was carried out with the aim of foreshadowing economic operation, the transition from the pre-commercial (experimentation) phase to commercial opening will not be as clear-cut.

Two major lines are characteristic of this final sequence of an experimentation: the stocktaking (concluding evaluation) and the definition, where appropriate, of the nature and manner of generalization. Both cases involve both looking back to the premises of the experimentation, its initial aims, and a forward-looking approach guiding the sto. taking towards the generalization decision.

Taking Stock of the Experimentation

Even if the evaluation had not been formalized in the preceding sequences, it is unusual for it not to be so at the stocktaking sequence stage. The stocktaking will at least comprise the results of the experimentation but may also include an analysis of its execution.

The Results of the Experimentation

It is a question of summarizing the analyses and evaluations made during the preceding sequences of the experimentation and of supplementing them, where necessary, at this stage in the experimentation.

We shall not refer back here to the description of the strategies and subjects of the evaluation procedure (see pp. 209ff and the associated Tabulation 2). In the stocktaking, one of the essential points will be the choice of the most promising applications tried out, coupled with establishment of the optimum organization for their production and exploitation (technical and institutional aspects and profitability). This organization will initially be based on the partners in the experimentation, but the possibility of a partial change in the partners when the generalization phase is embarked upon should not be ruled out.

If, as is probable, a generalization is envisaged, it will be necessary to define among the partners the relevant criteria for such a decision and to interpret the results of the experimentation in the light of these criteria as an aid to reaching this decision.

The Relevance of the Experimental Process

The stocktaking stage is often a time for looking back at the premises and at the execution of the actual experimentation:

- analysing the appropriateness of the results to the initial aims of the experimentation;

- evaluation of the relevance and effectiveness of the experimental procedure employed (organization, relations among partners, etc.)

and of its follow-up (evaluation procedure) and also of the impact of the follow-up on the adaptation of the content of the experimentation.

- evaluation of the method by which the experimentation and its results are made known locally (users, political leaders, etc.) and nationality.

Methods and Determinants of Generalization

As we have just seen, the stocktaking operation cannot be a mere summary of the results of the experimentation, but is essentially directed towards the idea of generalization, this idea having existed even before the experimentation. We shall therefore try to discover the methods of generalization and the conditions which govern it.

Methods of Generalization

If the experimentation does not lead to a service or to clearly viable applications, or, in the extreme case, if it is a failure, this may be due to the actual content tried out, which does not appeal to the potential users. In this case the conclusion of the experimentation will be outright abandon-ment of the scheme. If this is due primarily to a stalemate in the relationships between the partners in the experimentation, the idea behind its content may be taken up again either locally in other circumstances or in another location, by other actors. This will then be a more or less partial reproduction.

It is regrettable that not many analyses are carried out in such cases of failures or abandonments. Any field of innovation inevitably leads to failures, and an analysis of these is often more fruitful than the examination of successful cases, which tends to conceal the difficulties and concentrate on the course of action which led to success. There may, admittedly, be some examples of the contrary, one of these having been the analysis of the failure of the Claire experiment in municipal telematics at Grenoble (27).

In other cases, the stocktaking having revealed at least a partial success, the experimentation can embark on an <u>extension</u>. A qualitative extension if it is the field of services or applications which is to be expanded from the local nucleus of the partners in the experimentation. A quantitative extension if it is a matter of moving on to a development of the contents tried out primarily - now - on a commercial bais, either just locally or together with a geographical extension of the areas of use.

Some Determinants of Generalization

The experimentation, having reached the stocktaking sequence, will probably not have cleared away all the uncertainties which existed when it was initiated. But its mobilizing effect, the creative impact which it will have had, may be sufficient to induce its partners to decide upon generalization, in the conviction that solutions to the problems which have not yet been completely solved can be found during that phase. At this level the economic and commercial aspects will be the most critical ones, and generalization, even if it is a quantitative extension as defined above, will inevitably include a certain mode of experimentation, as a given product can never remain unchanged for ever.

Another decisive aspect for the effectiveness of the generalization is the transfer of knowledge and know-how of the partners in the experimentation to the partners in the generalization. The latter, even locally, may differ from the former without necessarily including them. Making the public aware of the service, giving it information and even training it, will call for an appreciable effort on the part of the partners in the experimentation, especially in relation to the national actors, whose role will increase with the extent of the desired generalization.

ELEMENTS OF A SYNTHESIS AND SOME CONCLUDING QUESTIONS

Three Extreme Poles of Social Experimentation

The theoretical study of the concept and the practical analyses of social experimentations have amply demonstrated that it was vain to try to devise a single, "ideal" model of social experimentation. The field of social experimentation ought, rather, to be viewed as a continuum bounded by a number of extreme poles. Two of these poles have already been mentioned (14): on the one hand, social experimentation centred on innovation and social creativity, a pole characterized by a quasi-ethnographic qualitative approach, and, on the other hand, the product test centred on the quantitative evaluation of a market. It seems worthwhile defining also a third pole, that of symbolic experimentation motivated by political considerations of the power stakes involved.

To sum up, we propose to present the field of social experimentation schematically by a triangle defined by these three extreme - and inevitably over-simplifying - poles. These poles are characterized in Tabulation 3 by four criteria: the dominant aim, the significance of the contents, the type of methodological approach and the existence of a generalization project.

Analysis Planes

The analysis which we have carried out through the three time sequences (see Tabulation 1) is neither a model nor a method of experimentation, because, as we have just emphasized, there is such a great diversity of aims and lines of approach. Its purpose is rather to give a structured description of the many and varied parameters and facets of social experimentation and to put them into perspective. We hope that this will help the various parties involved in or around an experimentation project to analyse the situation at a given moment and also the course which led to it and then to decide on the direction of their future action. This analysis is intended, at one and the same time, for the research worker (observer), the project leader (promoter), the partners in the experimentation and, where appropriate, the representative of users or suppliers of applications.

I - PSYCHO-SOCIOLOGICAL OR ETHNOGRAPHIC EXPERIMENTATION

- centred on appropriation and acceptance
- social creativity and invention
- qualitative approach, with a view to "action research"
- generalization absent in aims

II - SOCIO-ECONOMIC EXPERIMENTATION

- centred on commercial uses, forward-looking tariff charges
- services and applications with little adaptability
- quantitative approach, representativeness
- generalization of aims at the envisaged future date

III - SYMBOLIC EXPERIMENTATION

- centred on the actors and the power factors at stake
- contents are non-essential
- political and strategical approach
- virtually no generalization in aims

(In all these cases the experimentation is both an innovation process and a methodological procedure for the management of the innovation.)

Tabulation 3: Three extreme types of social experiments with communication service. These types refer to theoretical structures and are actually closely intermingled, with the possible predominance of one pole.

For simplicity's sake we have divided the period of experimentation into three sequences. We shall resort here to a grouping of parameters on five transverse analysis planes in order to make it possible to summarize in a table (Tabulation 4) the developments described in detail in the sections pp. 205-221 above. The central plane is that of organization and procedure, framed between the user plane and the institution plane and, lastly, by those of the contents and of the supporting technique.

Some Questions

Is the term "social experimentation" suitable for the experiments which have been analysed? For some people the word "experimentation" is a strong term for describing a situation where the experimenter does not have any real control (28). Actually, this approach relates to the scientific dimension alone, the social aspect being regarded as an object which is to be checked and logged in an experiment record. This is the negation of social experimentation as an action exerted by society on itself.

Society is the place and the dynamic centre where the technical innovation is negotiated and where the social changes which this generates take place. And, furthermore, who is the experimenter? For us the experimenters are the project leader and, more generally, the partners, the subjects of the experimental process. The research worker may have a decisive role if he plays a part in a research programme, a method which is preferable to a mere request to act as an external observer.

The reasons which are often put forward to justify (28) experimentation (evaluation of economic viability and the social consequences, determination of the forms of organization and control) are largely illusory, as the results cannot fully answer these good questions. However, giving a partial answer to them and involving the partners in an analysis based on concrete facts are in themselves essential advances, although, by their very nature, they are never definitive.

A last question is about the pre-commercial socio-economic aims, which are - and rightly - increasingly becoming the main consideration governing such experiments in France. The present situation with regard to cable television is significant from this point of view, as compared with the telematics experiments carried out four years ago. We have in fact turned our present analysis in this direction by supplementing it with technico-economic and socio-economic criteria. These socio-economic experiments border on generalization. They consequently call for larger investment, and this may hamper creativity and innovation. Lastly, they raise, in a crucial manner, the problem of the tariff charges for the services in the "experimental" phase. These are current questions to which our study could not give any answers.

PLANES \ SEQUENCES	A PRELUDE	B SETTING UP→EXECUTION	C STOCKTAKING (towards GENERALIZATION)
1. SERVICES AND APPLICATIONS (CONTENT)	• definition of services and applications (socio-economic and technical aspects) • project for adaptability of services • plan for evaluation of contents and of the process for their production	• their implementation and adaptation during the sequence internal/external production • production strategy: short-term/long-term • evaluation of contents and method of production (follow-up)	• results of evaluations: choice of most viable applications • choice of most efficient method of production • adjustment of results to aims with regard to services and applications
2. USERS	• pre-existing uses for related contents • degree of information given to users on the experimentation project • plan for evaluation of attitudes, behaviour and uses	• sample of users: "representative"/specific, size, geography • status: from mere consumer to creative partner (degree of participation) • evaluations: appropriation, uses, sensitivity to rates of charge (follow-up)	• summary of follow-up of users and, where appropriate, final evaluation • giving information to users concerning results
3. ORGANIZATION AND PROCEDURE	• context of experimental location: actors, resources • context away from the location: other experiments • origin(s) of the initiative for the experiments • the aims of the experimentation (see Tabulation 3) • degree of innovation and uncertainty • evaluation strategy (see Tabulation 2) • choice of a tariff charges for the experimentation • degree of definition of the legal framework	• organization: board-type management/project leader/project team • degree of exclusiveness of partners • evaluation of the organization and execution of the experiments (follow-up)	• evaluation of the execution and effectiveness of the experiments • analysis with a view to a generalization decision • choice of a method of generalization: • qualitative or quantitative reproduction/extension • communication of results • remaining uncertainties: flexibility of generalization

Tabulation No. 4: The various aspects of social experimentation with communication services presented on five thematic planes and in three time sequences.

SEQUENCES / PLANES	A / PRELUDE	B / SETTING UP+EXECUTION	C (towards GENERALIZATION) / STOCKTAKING
4. INSTITUTIONS	.the actors' aims and strategies .their attitudes: positive/negative .relations between local and national actors, role of the Telecommunications .plan for following up socio-institutional developments	.partners (promoters, associates, neutral parties, blocking parties); opponents .degree of participation (resources, activities, internal organization) and of rationalization .follow-up of socio-institutional developments .origin(s) of financing; role of the Telecommunications	.reorientation (generalization) .new local or national partners .more critical economic and commercial constraints .mobilizing effect of experimentation for generalization
5. TECHNIQUE AND COST	.technical configuration definition (production, operation) .investment and operating costs .initial economic analysis	.technical configuration employed .degree of technical flexibility .ownership of equipment/ partners .evaluation of operating costs	.evaluation of operating costs .choice of a technical generalization configuration

Tabulation No. 4 (continued): The various aspects of social experimentation with communication services presented on five thematic planes and in three time sequences.

NOTES AND REFERENCES

1. This study was conducted by IDATE. under the responsibility of the C.C.E.T.T., thanks to financing by the C.N.E.T.'s Action Scientifique. A working party led by the two authors of this article made it possible to specify, define and discuss the various aspects of the study. It was composed of members of IDATE (Alain Briole, Martine Lacabane), C.C.E.T.T. (Bernard Marquet, Monique du Crest), S.P.E.S. (Claire Ancelin) and C.N.E.T. (Nicole Celle). Our thanks to them for their active cooperation.

2. D. Leclercq, "Une utilisation à grande échelle du vidéotex: L'Annuaire Electronique", Informatique et gestion, No. 150 bis, April 1984, pp. 45-57.

3. J. de Legge , B. Marquet, "L'Annuaire Electronique en Ille et Vilaine: une expérience paradoxale", IVth days of IDATE (Experiments in Telematics), IDATE Bull., No. 9, Oct. 1982, pp. 93-102.

4. M. Bardoux, B. Marquet, G. Poulain, "Aspects méthodologiques de l'évaluation du service Annuaire Electronique", IDATE Bull., No. 11, April 1983, pp. 165-182 (in English in Pr. of Human Factors in Telecommunications, HFT, Helsinki, June 1983).

5. M. Ponjaert, P. Georgiades, A. Magnier, "Communiquer par TELETEL: les acquis des expériences de T3V et le l'Annuaire Electronique", La Documentation Française, August 1983, 243 p.

6. °°°, "TELETEL aujourd'hui", Informatique et gestion, No. 150 bis, April 1984, 154 p.

7. °°° (coordinated by C. Ancelin and M. Marchand), "Le vidéotex, contribution aux débats sur la télématique", Masson, coll. CNET-ENST, Oct. 1984, 240 p.

8. °°° (under the direction of M. Marchand and C. Ancelin), "Télématique: Promenade dans les usages", La Documentation Française - Ministère des PTT, Nov. 1984, 207 p.

9. F. Colaitis, "L'adjonction d'un canal sonore au vidéotex: l'Audio-vidéotex", l'Echo des Recherches, No. 110, Oct, 1982, pp. 41-51.

10. H. Boulan, F. Kretz, M. Volle, "Les applications de la carte à mémoire et ses scénarios de développement", in course of preparation.

11. °°° (under the direction of P. Flichy and G. Pineau), "Images pour le câble: Programmes et services des réseaux de vidéocommunication", CNET-INA-Documentation Française, June 1983, 309 p.

12. °°°. "L'expérimentation sociale en télématique", Actes des IVe journées internationales, IDATE Bull., No. 9, Oct. 1982, 673 p.

13. L. Mexandeau, "Comment révéler les besoins", Le Monde, 17-18 Oct. 1982.

14. K. Crochart, F. Kretz, Y. Londechamp, "L'expérimentation sociale des services de télécommunications", IDATE Bull., No. 9, Oct. 1982; pp. 578-587.

15. P. Flichy, "Rapport du groupe Demande Sociale" in the Annexes to A. Mattelart and Y. Stourze, "Technologie, Culture et Communication", Documentation Française, 1982.

16. A. Briole, R. Lauraire, "Analyse théorique et pratique du concept d'expérimentation sociale I. Genèse de la notion", IDATE report, Dec. 1982, 92 p. (also A. Briole, S. Craipeau, "Généalogie du concept d'expérimentation sociale", in Ref. 12, pp. 18-33).

17. A. Briole, M. Lacabane, "Analyse théorique et pratique du concept d'expérimentation sociale II. Monographies et étude comparative d'expériences françaises" (2 volumes + Annexes), IDATE reports, March and June 1983.

18. A. Briole, S. Craipeau, "Analyse Théorique et pratique du concept d'expérimentation sociale III. Vers une méthode d'expérimentation des nouveaux moyens de communication", IDATE report, March 1984, 91 p.

19. A. Touraine, "Le retour de l'acteur", C.I.S. Col. LXXI, 1981.

20. F. Lyotard, "La condition post-moderne", Minuit, 1980.

21. L. Sfez, "Critique de la décision", Presses de la Fondation Nationale des Sciences Politiques, March 1981, 392 p.

22. J. Habermas, "La technique et la science comme idéologie", Gallimard, les Essais CLXXXIII, March 1978, 221 p.

23. S. Craipeau, "Audit de services télématiques professionnels", IDATE report, 1985.

24. F. Kretz, "Dialogue, service, interactivité et leurs composantes: aspects de conception et d'évaluation", IDATE Bull. No. 11, April 1983, pp. 77-103.

25. H. Mammen, "Research strategies for research applied to social experiments", FAST International conference on social experiments with information technology, Odense, Denmark, January 1986.

26. F. Kretz, "Etude, conception et expérimentation des services de communication", C.C.E.T.T. note ESA/T/006/85/FK, April 1985, 5 p. (also in "La provocation: homme et machines en société", CESTA, MAY 1985,

pp.188-190).

27. [ooo] "Les lueurs de CLAIRE (enquète sur un projet ambitieux et inter-
rompu)", GRESEC-INA report, Dec. 1983, 117 p.

28. K.O. Mathisen, "Field trials: what's the use?", Proceedings of the FAST
International Conference on social experiments with information technology, Odense, Denmark, January 1986, pp. 176-188.

PART V: CONCLUSIONS AND RECOMMENDATIONS

In this concluding round of papers, Peter Pop, François Pichault, and Jill Hartley give a general evaluation of social experiments with I.T. from the different points of view of technicians, initiators, and end-users respectively. Peter Pop focuses on the design problem. The biggest problem in the design process seems to be the problem of communication between social and technical scientists. Therefore social experiments must improve the interface between social and technical systems design. François Pichault in his paper analyses the shift of initiators from public authorities to private actors who are playing a still more important role in the experimental field. Jill Hartley emphasizes the complex interaction between technological innovation and the response of individual and collective users to the technology, suggesting that the key to the diffusion process is the mutual learning process involving both supplier and user. In the last paper, Lars Qvortrup presents a proposed working definition of social experiments and a number of recommendations for political action in relation to future social experimentation. He finally emphasizes the concept of "orgware" as an important field of social research devoted to the development of socially-advanced information systems and to end-users' participation in system development.

SOCIAL EXPERIMENTS WITH I.T. IN THE EUROPEAN COMMUNITY; THE TECHNOLOGICAL POINT OF VIEW

Peter Pop, Rotterdam School of Management, the Netherlands

In this article an analytical method to design information processing systems is recommended.

Referring to Boulding's classification of systems, it is argued that there exists a communication problem between sociologists and engineers, participating in the design of social experiments with information technology.

The orgware concept is put forward to resolve this problem.

In the last part of the article a few other technological aspects of the design of social experiments with I.T. are described shortly.

Most of the contributions in this volume have had a rather sociological orientation. The technological aspects of carrying out social experiments with I.T. have hardly been considered. Yet, in my opinion a technological point of view may contribute to the design of successful social experiments with I.T. In this contribution, I am therefore going to present to you an engineering approach to these kinds of experiments.

First of all, I want to introduce to you an analytical method used in any technical design process, but for our purposes a little bit adjusted to the design of information processing systems (see fig. 1).

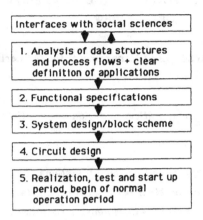

Fig. 1 Technical design and building
process, adjusted to I.T.
systems

In figure 1 the several steps of this process have been sketched. Let us first look at the steps 1 through 5 of this figure. After the analysis of the data structures and process flows and after the definition of the applications have been made, which should be as clear and precise as possible to avoid unnecessary work, the engineers have got the information they need to formulate the functional specification of the system to be designed. These are steps 1 and 2. This functional specification leads then to the system design, or speaking the language of electrical engineers, to the so-called block scheme; this is step 3. After the block scheme has been agreed upon, the stage of designing the required circuits begins; this is step 4. Then in step 5 the system is built together and tested. After the start up period the time of normal operations begins. This design and building process seems to be straight forward if we look only superficially. Great difficulties are hidden in the two arrows shown at the top of figure 1. Let me elaborate a little bit more on this issue (see fig. 2).

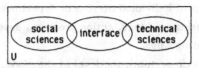

Fig.2 Universal set of all sciences

To be as precise as possible I use some elementary concepts from the mathematical theory of sets. In the figure we see U, the universal set of all science. Both the social sciences and the technical sciences are subsets of U. We see from this so-called Venn-diagram that the intersection of these two subsets is an empty set, or to say it less abstractly, the two fields of science have no overlaps, they have no elements in common. Even worse, they don't have a boundary in common! This fact means great difficulties in carrying out the first step in the design process we spoke about. The result of this is that it is very difficult to establish a well functioning and satisfying communication between sociologists and engineers, which is a necessary but by no means sufficient condition for cooperation. Nevertheless, cooperation between these two groups of professionals is essential to the design of useful information systems.

An explanation of the communication problem between sociologists and engineers can be given by referring to the classification of systems by Kenneth E. Boulding (1, 2). For better understanding, I will repeat this classification very briefly here.

Boulding describes nine levels of systems:

1. The statical structure, the level of a framework.
   Examples: organigrams, task descriptions, a network of traffic roads.
2. The simple dynamic system, the level of a clockwork.
   Examples: production techniques, administrative procedures, computer hardware.
3. Control mechanisms, cybernetic systems, the level of the thermostat.
   Examples: systems that compare performance with predetermined standards, budgetary systems, financial accounting systems.
4. Open systems with the ability to maintain themselves, the level of the

living cell.

Examples: actions of individual persons or departments in an organisation to prevent increasing workload, action programs developed by a company in case of decreasing sales.

5. Genetic and ecologic systems, the level of the plant.

Examples: functional specifications and division of work in case of increasing complexity. For other examples we can think of the processes that can be observed by looking at the design and the use of information systems. We could call these processes the phenomenology of social informatics.

6. Systems characterized by mobility, goal directed behavior and a limited degree of self awareness, the level of the animal.

Examples: measures to increase efficiency in production processes, long term planning and devising of strategies.

7. Systems characterized by extensive self consciousness, great complexity and the use of abstract concepts, the level of individual human beings.

8. Social systems, characterized by the interactions of human beings, that means interactions of systems at level 7.

9. Transcendental systems: now Boulding starts building Babel to the clouds, so we omit these kinds of systems.

If we look at the design of information systems from a general systems theory point of view, we conclude that the design process of I.T. systems in fact consists of adapting a level 2 system, computer hardware, to the needs of a system at level 8, a social system. The tools available to the designers to realize this adaptation are software and orgware. The orgware concept is described in some detail in Lars Qvortrup's paper. For the purpose of this paper it is sufficient to know that orgware deals with the mutual adjustment of social organisations and I.T. systems. By the same token, software is the tool to provide systems of level 2 with some of the characteristics of systems of higher levels.

Now, the reasons for the communication problem between sociologists and engineers are obvious. Sociologists deal mainly with systems at level 7 and 8, while engineers are engaged in systems at levels 2 and 3.

To solve this problem one has to define an interface, a grey area, between the social and the technical sciences, in order to have the communication between sociologists and engineers function in a satisfying and controllable way. Issues connected with this grey area deserve great attention and study; otherwise, there is only a tiny chance to carry out successful social experiments with I.T.

Now, I want to draw your attention to a few other technical aspects, which are important in designing social experiments with I.T. Because of time reasons we will have to treat those technical aspects a volo d'uccello, wit' . bird's eye view.

1. Reliable technologies

The first remark to be made is that we are dealing with <u>social</u> experiments; that implies that only reliable technologies should be used in order to avoid technical experiments. In this way the often made mistake is avoided that many experiments with I.T. in the past were supply- or technology-driven.

However, it should be noted that it is impossible to avoid any kind of technical experiment. Even in cases where 'old' technologies are applied in 'new' situations, an ergonomical fine-tuning will be necessary because of the absolutely needed userfriendliness of the system. The system should be designed in a way that a layman is able to use the system after an appropriate instruction and start-up period; if you need engineers to handle the system, it is no longer a <u>social</u> experiment, but a <u>technical</u> one with a part of society in use as a laboratory!

So, userfriendliness is a necessary condition for the acceptability of an I.T. system to the public in general.

Another, but related aspect is the recognition of the fact that the pace of the development and the acceptance of applications of new technologies is always slower than the pace of the technological developments itself. This time-lag implies that social experiments with I.T. are relatively time consuming. Therefore, an experiment should only be judged after a certain start-up period. This is an important point in the design and follow up of such experiments.

2. Standardization

In the design of information processing systems as well as in information technology in general, standardization is an important issue. Among a lot of reasons, some are very substantial for the subject of this conference. As financial resources are limited and recognizing the fact that carrying out social experiments with I.T. is all but a cheap activity, the huge possibilities of cost reduction by standardization of the technologies used become very important.

A second argument for standardization is that a transition from small scale experiments to big scale operation is much easier if standardized subsystems and components are used.

Another very important advantage of standardization to social experiments with I.T. is the fact that standardization facilitates greatly the so-called service compatibility. This means that a new I.T. system which provides a certain service is compatible with other infrastructural I.T. systems already in use and providing all kind of other services.

3. Security aspects

Nowadays, abuse of information is rather common. It is quite clear that prevention of abuse is very important if information of confidential or private nature is handled. Also the processing of financial data requires much attention in this respect as any banker will confirm! Regarding the evolving legislation in this area, security aspects are becoming an essential part of the design process of information handling systems. To avoid problems in case of boundary crossing information flows, the legislation in this area should be unified, at least in the countries of the European community.

4. Boundary conditions

In each design process the engineers are confronted with boundary conditions of different nature. Apart from the boundary conditions the employed technology imposes upon a specific design, there are in most cases boundary conditions imposed by the social and economic environment in which the system is going to be operated. Examples of social boundary conditions are the aforementioned ergonomical requirements a system has to come up to, the available degree of computer literacy of the users and the privacy aspects. As to economic boundary conditions we can think of the maximum allowed investment amounts, the maintenance costs of the system and the requirement of gaining economies of scale, for example by using standardized subsystems and components.

CONCLUSIONS

I now want to present some conclusions to you that are of course open to discussion:

a. No technical design should be made before detailed models of data structures and process flows of the application have been made.

This implies that the interface between the technical and social aspects of designing social experiments with I.T. should be studied very intensively. Anticipating Lars Qvortrup's presentation, system design in a technical sense is part of orgware design.

b. Network structures should be independent of the application. This facilitates greatly the so-called service compatibility of different systems; many services can then be provided by one single network.
(ISDN = Integrated Services Digital Network)

c. Application specific developments are necessary with respect to value added services, such as database management for agriculture, health care, education, traffic management, etc.
(VAN = Value Added Network)

To conclude this presentation, I want to formulate a recommendation for further research in the area of technical aspects of designing social experiments with I.T.

The experiments so far have been carried out in the following areas:

. Environment, ecology and agriculture, rural area applications;
. Health care;
. Social service on local community level;
. Education and training;
. Traffic management, domestic applications.

In my opinion it would be very interesting to investigate if each area of application requires its own technical approach in order to design optimum information processing systems.

NOTES

1. Kenneth E. Boulding, General Systems Theory - the skeleton of science, Management Science, Vol. 2 (1956) pp. 197-208.
2. Walter Buckley (editor), Modern Systems Research for the behavioral scientist, Aldine Publishing Company, Chicago, 1968.

SOCIAL EXPERIMENTS WITH I.T. FROM THE INITIATORS' POINT OF VIEW

François Pichault, University of Liège, Belgium

At the present time one can find powerful national telecommunications administrations conducting social experiments. But private actors (cable TV companies, newspaper organisations, banks, etc.) play a still more important role in the experimental field. Social experiments are increasingly aimed at professional users, and, in effect, at very limited categories of users. If one wants to retain the primary aim of socially beneficial and advanced social experiments, the intervention of public authorities, encouraging social initiatives deliberately oriented towards social aims, will require serious reconsideration. Only in this way will public authorities be able to define more specific goals for their intervention in this field.

Any attempt to distinguish, amid the multitude of social experiments in telematics launched in the various European countries, the specific features of their initiators is undoubtedly a hazardous task. The very modest aim of this paper is to "set the scene" for such initiatives by attempting to pick out certain general tendencies at the risk, thereby, of simplifying or even caricaturing reality.

The question of the "initiators" cannot in any case eliminate two basic and largely interrelated questions.

New Technologies?

The first is connected with the alleged "novelty" of telematics systems. The present fashionableness of this term is liable to make one overlook the fact that applications combining the potentialities of telecommunications and informatics have been exploited for many years in the professional fields (large firms and public departments). These are very specific applications accessible to highly qualified users: data transfer, computer-to-computer dialogue, pooling of programmes, etc.

The new aspect of telematics springs from the generalization of its possibilities of application. When the Nora- Minc Report appeared in France in 1978, this did not mean that telematics had just been born then, but that its services were becoming more and more accessible to non-specialist users, whether as a professional tool or even, still more widely, as a set of services available to households. Such services bear the names of videotex, tele-messaging services, teleconferencing, home-banking, teleshopping, videophoning, etc.

A Product in Search of a Market

The second important comment is a logical consequence of the first. The prospect of a generalization of the possibilities of application of telematics has considerable economic implications. The "general public" - so often referred to since the end of the 1970s - is a very attractive potential market for the heads of informatics and telecommunications firms desirous of promoting the products which they have just perfected. Telematics has therefore, since its official "birth", been a supply in search of a market. In this context the dominant actor is of course alle the manufacturing firms, which are endeavouring by every means to create a demand.

But in order to penetrate this market, the manufacturers need, for reasons of social acceptability, to operate via an intermediary whose social legitimacy is beyond doubt: the public actor. The latter's direct or indirect intervention in the economic sphere has in fact become a reality which, willingly or unwillingly, has been accepted by most of the partners involved. In order to capture the "general public" market, what better way is there than to resort to the institutions which are regarded as serving it and are not suspected of pursuing any commercial aims? Furthermore, as telematics presupposes recourse to one or other of the telecommunication networks - usually operated as a public monopoly - it requires, by the same token, the intervention of the State, represented by the Telecommunications Administration and the public broadcasting and TV organizations.

The public PTT Administrations will therefore play a decisive role in the promotion of the telematics tool by, in a way, concealing the powerful economic interests involved. The effect of this concealment of the economic stake and of the multifarious associated interests - which we shall analyse - is to maintain a veritable mythology concerning experimentation (which is assumed to reveal needs) and the technology itself (presented as a means of "improving the relationship between the administrations and those administered", of "democratizing access to information", "rationalizing the operation of the public service", "introducing (or re-establishing) the transparency of civil society", etc.).

Sometimes the public departments go so far as to regard telematics as a means of "testing their relationship with society". Wishing to present an image of modernity while at the same time increasing the justification for their own existence, some of them are seizing on the new tool as a veritable institutional issue.

In some cases, which are particularly illustrated by the example of France, public intervention is assuming the guise of a nationalistic campaign: all efforts must be mobilized around the promotion of the new tool in order to ensure that the country in question shall not lag behind internationally. This then triggers off a process of chain imitation, from country to country, in which each of them tries to present itself as a front-runner both technologically (mastery of the tool), socially (the "social experimentation" aspect) and culturally (the struggle against the Anglo-Saxon hegemony, etc.). Sometimes it is a matter of supporting the development of a rapidly expanding national industry (as in France or the United Kingdom).

The increasing multiplicity of these issues must not be allowed to obscure the essential issue, which is primarily and above all economic.

When we come to deal with the role of the initiators of social experimentation in the field of new information technologies, we must bear in mind these two points. By new information technologies we mean mainly the extension of the possibilities of application of the telematics tool which took place at the end of the 1970s. When we speak of actors, this is in the knowledge that their power relationships exist primarily and above all against a background of economic and industrial strategies.

We shall in fact see that the question of the profitability of the new tool, which has for a long time been left to one side, is today becoming the central question in the developments of telematics. The derived issues which we have just mentioned tend to fade into the background with the emergence of economic preoccupations which have hitherto lain below the surface. For the public authorities this development represents - or at least this is the hypothesis we are putting forward - an opportunity for rethinking the specific nature of their intervention.

The Concept of Social Experimentation

A last word about the concept of social experimentation in the field of new information technologies.

It should be noted that such a terminological borrowing from the field of science clearly has an authenticating function. The concept of experimentation presupposes the prior preparation of a model which represents the reality studied, the different variables constituting which are tested one after the other - which assumes that these have been fully mastered. Now in most cases no prior model of reality has been perfected, and no means have been employed in order to distinguish the specific influence of each of the variables to be taken into consideration.

PUBLIC INTERVENTION

The launching of such experiments by the public authorities is spread out over nearly ten years (the first experiments took place as early as 1976, and some of them are still being launched at present). We should emphasize that public intervention in this field is absolutely peculiar to Europe. The American situation is in sharp contrast from this point of view, in that new services are directly tried out on the market without passing through the stage of seeking an institutional guarantee such as that of the public PTT administrations. Despite this, however, there have been similar disappointments on both sides of the Atlantic (1).

The public authority's intervention in the launching of social experiments in telematics is therefore defined in terms of time (the time when the prospect of a "general public" market opens up) and of space (in most European countries).

But we shall see how this intervention also varies in time and space with, on the one hand, a tendency towards redefinition of the roles between public and private partners and, on the other hand, an extreme variability in form depending on the national socio-political contexts, ranging from laisser-faire to state centralism, via tax incentives, promotional initiatives etc.

Where Two Universes Meet

Some distinctions need to be made in order to define more closely the role of the public authority in the carrying out of various social experiments in telematics. The first separates the universe of telecommunications from that of the media.

As telematics brings together information media which had previously been clearly separated (the telephone, television and the press), it is not surprising to see a proliferation of initiatives emanating from these different universes and aimed at producing increasingly similar services.

Actually, in most of the countries concerned, the public authorities present in these two spheres have separately launched initiatives which are in fact being brought together by technological development.

The involvement of the Telecommunications Administrations is the most widespread case: Prestel was launched by British Telecom (still a public body at that time), the Teletel 3V experiment was conducted at the Vélizy location by the DGT; the Bildschirmtext system was offered to certain categories of users in Berlin and Düsseldorf by the Deutsche Bundespost; the Videotel experiment was conducted by the SIP in several Italian cities (Rome, Turin, Milan, Naples, etc.); the Teledata project was tried out by the Danish PTT in the province of Jutland (Silkeborg and Skanderborg), and in the suburbs of Copenhagen, the Viditel system was put into operation by the Dutch PTT, etc.

But the world of public media itself also became involved in such experimentations: thus, to mention only the best-known cases, there was Antenne

2 in France; the WDR in the Federal Republic of Germany; the BBC in the United Kingdom; the RAI in Italy, the NOS in the Netherlands; the RTBF and BRT in Belgium, etc.

Even though, technically, such experiments differ from the former in so far as they resort to unidirectional equipment (where the receiver of information cannot transmit information in turn), they bear witness to a similar desire on the part of the public authorities to expand the application possibilities of telematics. For that matter, as the equipment is becoming increasingly sophisticated, is it really still possible to distinguish between the selection of a page of information among many pages which are continuously broadcast over a distributed network and remote consultation of a database via the switched network? Not infrequently, virtually competing applications are to be found in the two types of media: that is the case in Italy, for instance, with similar services providing meteorological bulletins, stock exchange information and aircraft flight timetables offered by the RAI's teletext and the SIP's videotex; in Belgium the RTBF's Télétexte experiment broadcasts a magazine for farmers, most of the information of which is contained in the Agritel videotex system, etc.

One of the best examples of this gradual integration of the various information media is certainly provided by the Biarritz experiment (France) conducted by the DGT, based on the establishment of local optical fibre network. This network is capable of simultaneously offering distributed services (television, tele-video library) and switched services (videotex, videophone, interrogation of image banks). Now, the legal responsibility for the distributed services lies with the Sociétés Locales d'Exploitation Commerciale (SLEC), in which various public and private local partners are associated. On the other hand, the DGT is responsible for everything connected with switching. But the frontier between these two universes is not always very precise in the case of some services such as the tele-video library or the interrogation of image banks. The DGT, the prime contractor in both cases, frankly confesses its embarrassment about this situation, in which, for the first time, it has no direct contact with its clients. Even though the setting up of an SLEC was legally required only after the launching of the Biarritz experiment (2), this case illustrates the growing interpenetration of responsibilities of partners from the sphere of telecommunications and the world of the media.

From the National to the Local

Another way of presenting public intervention in the field of telematics experiments consists of distinguishing between national and local initiatives.

In most of the cases mentioned so far, the experiments conducted by the Telecommunications Administrations or the public broadcasting bodies are national in their scope. Even when situated on the local plane, initiatives such as those at Vélizy or Biarritz in France, those in Rome, Turin, Naples and Milan in Italy, in Berlin and Düsseldorf in the Federal Republic of Germany, in Silkeborg, Skanderborg and Copenhagen in Danmark, etc., form part of much more extensive national programmes. Furthermore, some of these experiments have already moved on to a commercial extension phase: that is the case with Minitel in France, Bildschirmtext in the Federal Republic of Germany and the Videotel system in Italy.

But, simultaneously, many initiatives emanating from local authorities are appearing on the scene, often in accordance with the policy pursued by the central Telecommunications Administration but sometimes in opposition to that policy. They are then rejecting an excessive centralism which causes preference to be given to what the French call "broadcasting" telematics (centralized general information with a low degree of updating, which, most of the time, the user can only select and consult with little possibility of interaction) at the expense of "proximity" telematics (precise and well-suited local information, frequently updated and involving the user to a greater extent by intensive exploitation of interactivity facilities).

Such experiments often pursue the aim of improving the relations between local administrations and citizens by means of databases concerning administrative rights and measures and local cultural facilities. This is the case with TELEM in Nantes, Claire in Grenoble, the rural experiments in the Alps of Haute Provence and in the Lot-et-Garonne region in France, the initiatives carried out in Italy in Milan, Turin and Genoa, those adopted by the municipal authorities of Odense in Denmark, etc.

PRIVATE INTERVENTION

Generally speaking, however, it can be said that after several years of operation of the experiments with a "general public" orientation, the tendency is if anything towards disenchantment. It was believed that these experiments, if not responding to a demand, were generating one. But in most cases the call rates are low, once the phase of curiosity about and discovery of the new tool has passed. Admittedly, there have been unexpected appropriations (the pirating of the messaging services in Strasbourg and the success of these services at Vélizy), but it must be admitted that these cannot serve as a genuine basis for the development of the profitable market which the manufacturers and the service-providing bodies are seeking to create, even if the success of such services seems to be very great on the Minitel system.

It was expected that telematics would involve an increasingly wide public, but the democratic effects of the new tool have proved very limited. The typical profile of the average user is still the young household with a high cultural and economic capital, often specializing in the technico-scientific field and already a large consumer of the other media. The establishment of a market which has extended to embrace all households therefore appears somewhat questionable for the time being.

Furthermore, most experiments evaded the problem of cost by providing the necessary equipment often free of charge and by offering access to the services at prices distinctly below the real operating cost of the system. This problem is in fact now showing itself to be of primary importance, especially as the demand even for a product offered on artificially advantageous terms is not very great.

Realization of the economic dimension of the telematics tool contrasts with the presence of substantial industrial commitments, which have always marked the development of new information technologies. Actually, as we emphasized earlier, these interests have been concealed by other commitments which, for a certain length of time, have caused the importance of the former to be forgotten. Today the economic consideration has become the central question, as is evidenced by the recent IDATE symposia at Montpellier devoted to the price of the new media and the establishment of a European communications market.

It is the solving of this problem that forms the centre of a new wave of experiments observable since 1982-1983. After the euphoria of the beginnings of telematics, this fiction of the "general public" whose needs are, it is claimed, being met by information systems to which access is offered on artificially advantageous terms is at last being abandoned. True, the aim is still to promote the use of new information systems, but this is now being done by getting down to developing specific functional applications clearly aimed at covering both initial investments and operating costs by sufficiently high fees. Applications of this kind are intended primarily for the professional or in any case institutional sector, in which there is a solvent demand and the users are prepared to pay for their recourse to such services.

This development of the aims pursued is concretely reflected in a gradual privatization of the actors involved in the launching of the various experiments. Admittedly the private actors had already been present since the beginnings of "general public" telematics, but their role is now becoming increasingly explicit. Only France is continuing, in the face of all opposition, to pursue the course of arbitrary government action. In the present proliferation of private initiatives we shall emphasize in particular the role of two important actors: the press groups, whose investment in the telematics field is all the more significant in view of the fact that they had for a long time confined themselves to adopting a defensive attitude to the new media, and the banks, which occupy a key position in this connection as regards both their internal operation and their relations with their clients.

The Role of Press Groups

At first the press groups adopted a wait-and-see attitude to contemporary technological developments. Now their involvement in the universe of the new media is very pronounced. This applies, for instance, to the videotex project called "Ditzitel" in the Netherland, which originates from a publicity agency and employs an approach inherited from marketing (low initial investment taking advantage, at one and the same time, of the opportunities offered by heavily cabled areas and the switched telephone network;

targeted and functional services). In Belgium there is a similar movement with the proliferation of initiatives from press groups (V.U.M., Concentra, "Het Belang van Limburg", Mediatel, etc.) which, making use of the public-access switched telephone network, offer videotex services for limited categories of professional users (foreign exchange dealers, members of the press, businessmen, shipping companies, etc.) or institutional users (promoters of private local radio stations).

In Italy, the press agency "Italia" offers a videotex information service on national and international economic, financial and political events for politicians, businessmen and industrialists.

In France, the press groups have been present in this sector a good deal longer. What is worthy of note is the veritable explosion which is taking place now: whether at national level (with groups such as "Le Monde", "Libération", etc.) or at regional level ("Dernières Nouvelles d'Alsace", "Ouest France", "Parisien Libéré", etc...), the present proliferation of initiatives in the telematics field and, more broadly, in the audio-visual sphere as a whole is an indisputable fact. The majority of daily newspapers have embarked upon videotex systems, in some cases investing very substantial sums in them. In view of France's special situation (with massive state interventionism leading to the installation of more than 2 million videotex terminals, most of them in households), the press groups offer both services designed for the "general public" (witness the success of the telemessaging services offered by the "Parisien Libéré or "Libération", which brought in an estimated FF 10 to 20 million each in 1985) and services for professional use (stock exchange, scientific and political information, etc.).

But, as is noted by J.M. Charon in a study entitled "La Politique des Etats et son poids sur le choix des entreprises de presse", it must be admitted that, in the telematics field, the newspaper companies do not have real control of the development of these new tools and often remain confined by the lines of action adopted by the Telecommunications Administrations. Thus, the choice made by the French DGT to leave responsibility for the running of the system (host computer, software, etc.) to the bodies providing the services, while at the same time imposing certain technical guidelines, naturally caused most press groups to offer services of this type, thus becoming the first groups in Europe, or even in the world, to place videotex in the forefront of their diversification strategies. On the other hand, in other countries (the United Kingdom or Italy), in view of the guidelines laid down by the public authorities, the involvement of the press groups is confined to supplying the content of the service, while the operation and management of the system is looked after by the Telecommunications Administration.

The involvement of press groups in the telematics field has been clearly demonstrated in the United States since the beginning of the 1980s by the initiatives taken by the Times-Mirror, Knight-Ridder, Reader's Digest and other groups. This involvement in fact lies within the more general framework of the transnational multimedia strategies which most of the major press groups are nowadays endeavouring to develop.

The Bank Networks

Apart from the establishment of interbank data communication network, the banks' involvement in the telematics field is primarily reflected in the telebanking applications for their clients (cashpoints, point-of-sale termi-nals), which are increasingly blurring the boundary between systems de-signed for the "general public" and professional systems. Belgium occupies a prominent position in this sector, with over two million cards in circulation in 1985.

In Italy, too, bank telematics are flourishing. In only two years the number of cards in circulation has gone up to over three million. Furthermore, several Italian banks - including the Banca Popolare, Milan - have developed home-banking systems and the Italian Bank Association is considering the establishment of an overall system embracing the various banks, in co-operation with the SIP.

In France, likewise, various experiments have been tried out in this field by Crédit Agricole, GIE Carte Bleue and CREG, the latter in co-operation with the "Carrefour" hypermarkets. Only one bank, in each case, is involved in these systems, but the public authorities have encouraged the development of systems in which several different banks are associated. Furthermore, over 200,000 households equipped with Minitel are subscribers to a home-banking service, making France the world leader for this type of application. Most of the banks offer their customers the possibility of checking the balance of their accounts together with the previous entries going back 15 or 30 days, showing the dates of the operations and even, for firms, the value dates. Other frequently offered services are: searching for movements in the account corresponding to a certain sum; operations on internal accounts (transfers from current account to savings book or vice versa); teletransfers within the same bank and even between different banking institutions, etc. It should be noted that such services, some of which are offered only to business clients, are subject to charging principles which vary very widely from bank to bank.

In the Federal Republic of Germany, banking services and services offered by insurance companies were a driving force behind the development of Bildschirmtext. In the United Kingdom too, the establishment of a telebanking service (Homelink) is one of the factors which explain the recent progress made by the Prestel system.

The press groups and the banks are two private actors which are particularly active in what could be called the "new wave" of telematics experiments. As can be seen, such initiatives are aimed more at identifying the most profitable applications based on a given technique (videotex) than at stimulating the development of the technical systems which are most suitable for meeting social needs.

REDEFINITION OF PUBLIC INITIATIVES

The general evolution which we have just described likewise applies to public initiatives, which find themselves obliged to redefine their aims owing to the poor performance of the first "general public" experiments. This reorientation is taking place along two major lines: the first aims at a certain degree of economic profitability of the systems developed by the public authorities; the second endeavours, rather, to optimize the "social" aims of these systems.

Towards Greater Profitability of Public Investment

The redefinition of aims is observable both in the initiatives for which the public authorities remain solely responsible ("pure" public initiatives) and in the ever-increasing association of private partners in the implementation of public projects.

"Pure" Public Initiatives

A number of experiments embarked upon by the public authorities are at present being directed towards narrowly targeted categories of users who are prepared to pay for the use of the services offered. This applies, for instance, to the Viditel project in the Netherlands, which, after the relative failure of its "general public" phase, is now being increasingly opened up to connection with private videotex systems, concentrating on professional and/or commercial applications.

In Belgium the RTT's videotex system has undergone a similar development: initially designed as an experiment of the "general public" type with terminals installed in homes, the project has been shifted year by year and is now beginning since March 1986 with an exclusively professional orientation.

In the United Kingdom the Prestel system redefined its aims as early as 1981, shifting its orientation towards a professional-type clientele prepared to pay for the use of interactive services. This redefinition took place at a time when the system was still a government-operated undertaking. But this does not mean that the prospect of "general public" applications has been abandoned. An intensive policy of concentration on the most profitable features of the new tool (a result of the privatization of British Telecom?) has caused this system to offer, on the domestic plane, functional applications such as telebanking (Homelink), teleshopping (Club 403) and telesoftware (Micronet), etc.

In France, as is pointed out by Claire Ancelin (3), all the initiatives adopted by the DGT in the telematics field moved into a commercial phase some time ago. From this point of view the period of experimentation in the strict sense of the term appears to have ended (closing of the Vélizy Télétel Test

Centre in July 1984, etc.), while the search for profitable applications is being intensified. Where the experimental character of the initiative is maintained, an increasingly marked orientation towards professional applications is likewise observable. Thus, in the case of the Biarritz experiment, the tendency is towards the development of business in-house video communication services and of the use of such services in commercial operations.

In Italy, the Videotel experiment launched in 1983 was able to incorporate the lessons learned from foreign experiments and was directed from the outset towards predominantly professional users. Videotel is one of the few public initiatives to have been directly developed on the basis of real prices: the user in fact has to pay SIP a rental for the terminal, the charge for the telephone call and a charge for access to the service.

The problem of profitability is likewise taken into account in more specific applications, such as the system developed by the Electronics Centre of the Italian Supreme Court of Appeal. This system is designed for use by, on the one hand, the various sections of the Department of Justice and, on the other hand, various categories of professional users (lawyers, firms, other government departments). The latter now have to pay a subscription for the purpose of enabling the system, recourse to which was originally free of charge, to pay its way to a certain extent.

Associations between Public and Private Partners

In a fair number of cases the change of course is also reflected in the proliferation of initatives in which public and private partners are closely associated. Initiatives of this type are characterized by a very pragmatic approach concentrated on the development of profitable applications. On the plane of infrastructures, hybrid solutions (distribution cables and telephone lines), which are less expensive in terms of the initial investment involved, are often preferred to the development of technical systems which are more sophisticated (optical fibres, wideband networks) but also very expensive.

In the Netherlands, the Agro-Business, Rotterdam Teleport or CATV projects (the latter in South Limburg) are operated jointly by public participants (the PTT, the Ministry of Economic Affairs, municipalities) and private participants (industrialists, banks, shipping companies, etc.).

In Belgium, the Bistel system, which interconnects the various ministerial offices and the Prime Minister's departments via a network through which information and telemessaging services can be continuously exchanged, has the participation of the Belga press agency as the main private supplier of information.

In the United Kingdom, mention may be made in particular of Club 403, in which the Department of Trade and Industry has obtained the co-operation of British Telecom and various manufacturers of data-processing and television equipment and also of various service-providi:.g bodies in order to develop information and transaction services (teleshopping, telebanking, telemessaging service, etc.) of a commercial nature.

In France, the situation is obviously special in that the DGT is continuing to pursue a policy of massive investment in "general public" telematics.

At the end of 1986, the DGT has invested more than $ 1,000 million in the Minitel programme (source: Le nouvel Economist 18.04.86). This substantial public investment is, however, coupled with a very close association with a large number of private partners, as regards both equipment and services offered. Thus, orders worth over FF 3,000 million were placed over a three-year period with manufacturers and service companies for the terminals, equipment and software for the Télétel network and the Electronic Directory. The French telematics policy makes the DGT responsible for the transmission of information, while the operation of the actual service is left to the private sector. The charge structure of the "Kiosk" function, which redistributes part of the fee received to the body providing the service without requiring the latter to keep an account of the calls, is a concrete reflection of this close co-operation between the public and privat sectors. Such a co-operation - while advantageous in the short run for the private sector - is, however, a way of binding this sector in the longer run to the lines of action adopted by the public authorities.

Moreover, many European Telecommunications Administrations are studying the possibility of developing home-banking systems in co-operation with the banking associations. Several systems are already operating.

The teletext experiments are not unaffected by this general trend. This is the case, for instance, with the Italian Televideo system: the RAI's aim is, if possible, to cover the system's operating costs or even to enable it to make a certain profit, while still pursuing its "general public" objective. Recourse to sponsorship of the information distributed or the imposition of sufficiently high rates of charge for occupation of the databank by the service-providing bodies are good illustrations of this type of association directed towards diversification of the financing sources.

Towards the Pursuit of Social Aims

However, within this general context of privatization of the actors and commercialization of the aims, there is still room for another type of intervention by the public authority, probably more normative but also perhaps more in accordance with the traditional function of a public service. It is no longer a question of trying to achieve immediate economic profitability but rather of encouraging greater social mastery of the new communication tools. Thus the public authorities in several countries have launched - or collaborated in the introduction of - a set of experiments access to which is deliberately confined to user categories which are traditionally excluded from the information circuits or the use of advanced technologies: handicapped persons, women, ethnic or cultural minorities, young unskilled unemployed persons, etc. In many cases these are initiatives originating from the community sector, supported by public subsidies.

The situation in the United Kingdom is an exemplary case from this point of view; although other countries too are adopting initiatives in the same direction.

A short time ago the Greater London Council (GLC), and also several local authorities, launched a set of experiments, which sometimes proved extremely effective, placing the accent more on this social dimension. Mention may be made of the case of the LNTN, mainly financed by the GLC. Apart from its function of making people aware of the new information technologies and giving them training in their use, its primary aim, in co-operation with several local enterprises in particular, is centred on the creation of small industrial or commercial companies involving workers who are in a social minority situation. In other cases (Sheffield, Newcastle) there are projects aimed at training young unemployed persons or giving data-processing assistance to various community associations. The community sector appears to be very lively in the United Kingdom, right from the local committee up to the powerful nation-wide organizations: its involvement in the field of the new information technologies may relate to internal projects (automation of management, establishment of a documentation network, etc.) or external projects (programme for data-processing training, consultancy and assistance and for the creation of awareness of this technology among the members of, or the persons attending, the association, etc.).

But the United Kingdom is not the only country in which such experiments have been launched. There is also the "Aspasie" experiment conducted in Marne-la-Vallée, in the suburbs of Paris, which aims at a take-over of the tool by the users themselves (the creation of committees for each type of application, the establishment of training facilities for the new technologies, etc.). Other examples, in Denmark this time: the initiative of the municipal authorities at Odense endeavouring to stimulate local production of information and to exploit the results of the new information technologies in the field of training; mention should also be made of the case of the community centres at Egvad and Lemvig, where an attempt is being made to lift several rural areas out of their economic and cultural isolation by encouraging a participative attitude to the new information technologies. In Italy, mention may be made of the Prato project, designed to stimulate, via a telematics network, the exchange of information between the various companies in a small industrial town, whose major activity is in the textiles sector.

Admittedly, these experiments are nowadays subject to increasingly restrictive budgetary constraints, whether owing to the actual abolition of the body which provides subsidies (the abolition of the GLC, which finally took place in 1986, is the result of a long-standing opposition between the Conservative central government and the Labour-dominated government of Greater London) or to the automatic application of accounting scales which those responsible for the various experiments agree are unsuited to the aims which they are pursuing. In both cases those responsible for the experiments are beginning to come to terms with these budgetary constraints and have been trying for some time now to diversify their financing sources. Some have no qualms about resorting to the provision of information services against payment (for instance, the LNTN or Community Computing Network, another initiative mainly financed by the GLC and designed for London community associations), to training courses, against payment, for businesses or other institutional partners (for instance Aspasie, the Biarritz Communication Nouvelle association, the LNTN, etc.). Recourse to advertising or to sponsorship of the services is also very frequent. Thus the Aspasie experiment is developing a project for a local professional directory on a telematics data medium, in which information added to the standard list (in the form of advertising or in any other form) has to be paid for.

This diversification of financing sources - a sign of growing budgetary pressure - confirms the general trend in all telematics experiments which we were pointing out earlier. It is incidentally liable, in several cases, to lead to a latent - and sometimes open - opposition between the social aims initially pursued and the commercial strategies which these experiments are being obliged to develop, precisely in order to maintain these aims.

Nevertheless, the fact remains that the initiatives which we have just described are the sign of another form of public intervention, more normative and perhaps more directly political. It is a question of giving priority to certain quasi-philosophical conceptions of life in society (equality of access to information, training of the most impoverished, self-expression of minorities etc.).

As we have seen, it is the private bodies concerned, attracted by the possibilities of immediate profit, that are primarily engaged in seeking economically viable applications. In this context, if the public authority is content to be just one economic actor among others, seeking to expand one kind of profitable market or another, what now remains of the specific character and raison d'être of its intervention? On the other hand, if, within this framework, it gives priority to the aims which are social and cultural in nature rather than economic, is not this precisely a way in which it can affirm this specific character? All the more so because, despite the decisive importance of the economic strategies of the private actors in this field, the public authority still has a wide potential field of action. This can be seen from the strong reactions nowadays aroused by the question of the public monopoly in telecommunications.

The way in which the political authority views public intervention obviously plays a fundamental role here. Cases where some form of arbitrary state action prevails (the French Minitel, the German Bildschirmtext or the Italian Videotel) are clearly different from those where the State confines itself to intervening by means of changes in regulations (privatization of the Prestel experiment in the United Kingdom following the privatization of British Telecom, the opening up of the Dutch videotex experiments to private initiative in view of the anticipated privatization of that country's PTT, etc.).

The first form - that of arbitrary state action - was, in a way, the starting point in most European countries at the end of the 1970s. It can range from the giving of incentives - tax reliefs, experiments, various forms of aid - to the assumption of virtually sole responsibility for the development of the medium via various types of promotion (see in this connection J.M. Charon, op.cit.). Despite the vicissitudes of political life characteristic of each country, there is found to be a gradual evolution from this first form of intervention towards the second, with a general trend towards privatization. However, even in cases where the public initiatives are privatized, their original initiators retain a very considerable possibility of intervention via the regulations. Privatization is too often assumed to be synonymous with a complete absence of rules.

A suitable legal framework can encourage the development and proliferation of original experiments, even conducted by private partners. Countries such as France, the Federal Republic of Germany and Italy have provided themselves with specific sets of regulations embracing telematics experiments (In France: the "Commission du suivi des expériences télématiques", followed by the Loi sur la Communication Audiovisuelle of 29 July 1982, Article 77 of which covers the present development of videotex; in the Federal Republic of Germany and Italy, rules establishing the framework and aims of experiments, etc.). It is a striking point that other countries which are less well provided in this respect rarely occupy a leading position in the field of socially advanced experiments with new information technologies.

All this shows us how the future in this field is undoubtedly bound up more with economic choices - those made by the manufacturers and by the bodies providing services - and social choices - those made by the public authorities - than with technical refinements. While certainly not denying the importance of the former, we wish to stress the most inconsiderable role which can be played by the latter, in - if not guiding - at least channelling the interventions of the various partners on the basis of criteria which are more in accordance with the democratic ideals of western societies.

This is therefore a priority field of action for local, national and European public authorities. While at the same time promoting the formulation of suitable industrial policies, what they need to do is to encourage the creation of the tools necessary for the appropriation and mastery of the new information technologies - the major role to be played by which does not need to be further stressed - in accordance with aims which are more social than immediately economic. Initiatives of this kind have already been taken in several European countries.

NOTES

1. According to a recent article in Business Week (which, incidentally, refers to European telematics as a "State business", 14.10.85), the forecasts for the United States predicted for 1988 a videotex market of around US$ 1750 million. When updated in 1984 these forecasts put the market at only just under $ 100 million. A consultancy company which originally estimated that 1.9 million videotex terminals would have been installed by 1988 now puts the number at less than 100,000 ...
2. Which explains why there are still none at present.
3. See the national report on France: Claire Ancelin: "Les Nouveaux Medias en France: Experimentation, Acculturation et Developpement Economique". In: Lars Qvortrup (ed.): Social Experiments with Information Technology in E.E.C. Countries. Telematics Project and FAST Programme, December 1985.

SOCIAL EXPERIMENTS AND THE ROLE OF END-USERS

Jill Hartley, PREST, University of Manchester, United Kingdom

It would be misguided to view technological developments as the one and only determinant of new forms of social and economic organisation and behaviour. Rather there is a complex interaction between technological innovation and the response of individual and collective users of the technology. Thus the key to the diffusion process is the mutual learning process involving supplier and user and their consequent mutual adaptation. The responses of the users provide indications for the development of new technological applications; but these new applications in turn often modify the users' behaviour, thus giving rise to what might aptly be termed "social inventions". Thus it is important to recognise, to encourage, and to promote the crucial role of the end-users.

INTRODUCTION

It is often thought that information technology will constitute the basis of a new technological revolution and bring in its wake substantial changes in our economic life. It is already obvious that IT has potential or actual applications in a very wide range of activities: manufacturing, design, management, commerce, health services, education, household activities, and it would be very difficult to identify activities where it could be said that IT has no relevance whatsoever. Numerous examples also illustrate how the introduction of IT can alter existing practices and habits, eg the operation of financial markets.

But it would be misguided to view technological developments as the determinant of new forms of social and economic organisation and behaviour. Rather there is a complex interaction between technological innovation and the response of individual and collective users of the technology. Thus, the process of diffusion of a new technology is not one in which the characteristics of the technology are given, but one which is characterised by continuing innovation on the part of suppliers in response to the needs indicated by users. Just as suppliers (designers, technologists, entrepreneurs) cannot accurately forecast the recipe of successful innovation, neither can end-users generally anticipate innovations which will be of value to them. The key to the diffusion process is thus one of supplier and user <u>learning</u>, each learning from the other and responding to this information. While suppliers respond by modifying or developing the technology or service, the response of users may also extend to that of innovation in two senses; first, users may indicate, or even develop, novel applications of the technology and secondly users may modify their behaviour as a result of using the technology. The latter activity could be called "social innovation", for example, the social innovations of the super and hyper-market would not have emerged without new forms of motor transport. Innovations on a similar scale are to be expected over time with the application and diffusion of information technology.

Indeed in a recent paper (1) Ian Miles suggests that the more wide reaching a technological innovation is, the more dependent it will be on appropriate social innovation for its successful adoption.

The process of experimentation may be undertaken in a variety of different institutional circumstances. Experiments organised by governments and other public institutions are obvious examples, especially where uncertainty and the costs of learning are high. But experimentation also proceeds in the marketplace when novel, immature products/services are launched commercially. The process of continuing innovation in the face of market responses is in principle the same as innovation in response to the reaction of "monitors" in a trial.

It would be hazardous to attempt to categorise experiments in terms of the role played by end-users. Indeed it is important to appreciate the fact that - as experiments generally operate with a range of participants - different objectives, different approaches and different concerns vis-a-vis end users may be pursued by the various experimentors. In her paper (2) Claire Ancelin makes this point with respect to the Teletel trial in France - the project team from the Direction Generale des Telecommunications viewed the experiment largely as a technical one, the service providers, on the other hand, were concerned with product and market development and were thus more attuned to the responses of end-users.

What I attempt to do here is to make some generalisations about the role of end-users in experiments, to comment on the categories of end-users targetted by the social experiments discussed in the national reviews (3) prepared by members of the FAST 10 + 1 network and to make a few observations about trends.

The experiments reported upon in the national reviews, and spoken about at this conference are extremely diverse in nature, and it should be no surprise that it is possible to discern not one, but a number of roles played by end-users. I would like to mention four major roles, remembering that more than one role may be played within a single experiment.

Before proceeding a point should be made about those IT projects where end-users are not assigned a role at all but rather, to borrow an expression used by Robert Jungk on the first day of the conference, are treated like "bits of lego" and simply expected to fit into, or comply with the project. For example, when the Danish telephone companies first announced their plans for a national hybrid cable network they were met with widespread public dissent. Little if any consideration had been given to the potential community of users, and, crucially, to those communities which would have been denied participation in the proposed "national" network. In this case public dissent forced the telephone companies to take on board some of the criticisms levelled at their plan and subsequently a different, more acceptable proposal was produced.

Although the telephone companies were forced to learn from potential end-users, this was not an objective of their initial plan, and it is a debatable point whether or not one should classify this example as a social experiment. However it does serve to illustrate the presence of the phenomenon of "technology push" well known in the technological areas such as aircraft, nuclear power and fifth generation computing.

END-USER ROLES

Where end-users do have an active role to play their function may be one or more of the following (and there are probably others):

1. to act as "guinea-pigs"
2. to perform R & D and undertake innovation
3. to become informed about IT
4. to be the primary subject(s) under study.

To Act as "Guinea-pig"

I have used this expression deliberately to convey an approach which has much in common with scientific experiments in a laboratory. Thus a new drug is tried out on laboratory animals and their responses are used to judge the effectiveness or safety of the drug. Unsatisfactory results lead to modifications of the drug's composition and so on. The experiment is "top-down", all expertise is invested in the experiment's designers and operators. Typical examples from the realm of social experiments are most interactive videotex experiments where services are offered and usage rates are recorded. If a service is not popular the experts will attempt to devise new services to put in its place. The optical fibre wired-city experiment being undertaken in Biarritz is another example of this type.

I would estimate that the majority of social experiments follow this approach, and employ end-users as "guinea-pigs".

To Perform R & D and Undertake Innovation

Secondly, in this much more active role end-users are recognised as innovators and R & D personnel in a social context. Given the opportunity, end-users in such a role may indicate or even devise alternative or additional uses of the technology in question. Both uses intended by the experiment's organisers and spontaneous uses may also involve the development of new forms of social organisation and behaviour, already referred to above as "social innovation". An example which may already be becoming a classic judging by its frequency of citation at this conference, is the tele-messaging innovation by end-users involved in the videotex experiment in Strasbourg. Users of the videotex system "hacked" their way into a private tele-messaging system and began using the service. Responding to this unexpected revelation of consumer preference, a local newspaper acting as a service provider agreed to make such a facility part of the experiment. A similar, unanticipated demand for the communications capability of videotex has been experienced in the UK by Prestel. Its service for home computer owners "Micronet 800" offered a bulletin board service, although little demand was perceived for it. The service proved so popular that Micronet eventually returned it to Prestel for ease of management.

It is significant that very few examples are known of experiments where end-users display their talents as innovators. Even if "end-user as innovator" is seen to be important it is no small problem to devise an experiment to foster such behaviour. One wonders if such outcomes are more likely to arise as a result of serendipity than as a result of experiment design.

To Become Informed About IT

The third function end-users may fulfil is that of becoming informed about information technology. As a result end-users may become better able to assess new technologies and services and thus to be more discriminating as consumers, to be better able to act as innovators, and possibly to play a greater political role as citizens with respect to government policies in the IT area.

Good examples of this end-user role are awareness campaigns, such as "IT Year" in the UK in 1982, and resource centres where people can have "hands-on" experience with information technology. In the UK the community based ITECs perform this open access function amongst others (4), as do the X2000 centres in France. In Paris a new centre is planned to be opened in 1988 called the International Communications Crossroads Centre. This centre will have IT familiarisation for the public as its major objective (5).

To be the Primary Subjects Under Study

In this role end-users generate information for researchers on the consequences and implications of the use of IT systems for life style, behaviour patterns, social interaction, methods of working etc. In other words the focus of interest is on the end-users and the social implications of the technology, rather than on the technology itself. Thus roles "1" and "4" are distinct: "end-users as guinea-pigs" test out new technologies and services whilst "end-users as primary subjects" test out reactions to and implications of new technologies and services. An experiment designed with these intentions was undertaken by the Canadian Federal Department of Communications and the University of Montreal in 1984, to examine the effects of the introduction of office automation on work relationships, morale, methods of working and so on. The organisers hoped to obtain information to guide them as to how office automation could be implemented most effectively. Similar office automation projects are being undertaken at the local municipal level in South Jutland in Denmark (6).

The way in which social experiments are organised, and the specific objectives of the initiators and other participants will largely determine the extent to which end-users fulfil one or more of the roles identified here. Obviously a great many factors are involved in experiment design, but a critical factor for end-users to play an active role is that organisers explicitly recognise that end-users have a major contribution to make, indeed, to quote from Lars Qvortrup's review (6) that end-users are "the real experts on their projects".

END-USER TARGETTING

The social experiments reported upon by members of the FAST 10 + 1 network demonstrate much variety in this respect. Experiments range from minimal targetting, eg "the general public" or "households", to the quite specific identification of groups with common characteristics or needs eg "the farming community" and "home computer owners".

Although it is difficult to discern trends, and we are examining a period of less than 10 years, it is probably true to say that increasingly social experiments are aimed at specific, rather than general, groups of end-user.

This could be at least partly to do with the disappointing outcome of those experiments aimed at "the public" and other general groups, of which interactive public videotex trials eg Prestel in the UK, are examples. In response to this a different approach was adopted - that of attempting to meet specific needs of particular groups. Although several videotex trials in other countries have followed the early Prestel model, despite its lack of success in terms of consumer acceptance (Bildschirmtext for example), there are recent exceptions. In Belgium RTT's plans to adopt a similar model for a videotex service were dropped recently in favour of a strategy to target professional users only.

Another reason for more specific targetting may be due to an increased awareness of potential applications of IT, and conditions of easier access to IT systems as a result of factors such as:

- more widespread IT skills
- lower thresholds of investment
- cheaper running costs
- the existence of IT infrastructure (eg packet switching networks, public videotex systems etc).

Thus people and organisations in diverse fields, not only in telecommunications organisations, have begun to ask "What could IT do for us?" and have initiated social experiments as a result eg health sector institutions, press groups, voluntary groups and public services.

Two propositions could be made here: first as end-users have been more closely targetted, the range of initiators has increased and secondly closer targetting has drawn together initiators and end-users in some cases, such that end-users are, in fact, the initiators as well.

One aspect of "easier access" is the existence of certain infrastructural elements, and I think that the issue of infrastructural provision and experiments aimed at general publics are related. Infrastructural investment in such systems as public videotex systems and interactive cable TV networks can only be legitimised if a critical mass of potential users can be identified. For high cost developments implying substantial overhead investment, such as cable TV, this critical mass is a very large one indeed. Thus in these cases there may be a tendency to approach experiments in terms of very large, and therefore general markets eg the household sector.

CONCLUSION

In conclusion a couple of observations about possible trends in the role of end-users, particularly in the context of the change in official jargon and public policy attitudes referred to by Alain Briole in his paper (7). He commented that the notion of "experiment" has been superceded by the notion of "acceptability", terms which convey quite different connotations. Concern has been voiced that experimentation is no longer seen as being necessary, rather the major problems are seen to relate to the pace of acceptance and irrational resistance to IT. Thus, are we witnessing a trend towards the rejection of experimentation and the discounting of end-user roles?

Certainly there are an increasing number of experiments involving routine rather than very novel innovations, particularly the substitution of IT methods of working for conventional methods eg the projects being under-taken in Eire by the Department of Health to develop a computerised information system for hospitals (8).

Even if the idea is not novel, such projects involve considerable social and organisational innovation, and are likely to also produce incremental technical innovations. Ventures of this kind may not be perceived as "experiments" but nevertheless "learning" is a crucial element in their implementation.

In addition, two developments in recent years provide some reasons for optimism: First, there has been a growing emphasis on informing the public about IT through awareness campaigns, resource centres and through the education system. This could be interpreted as a (belated) recognition of the importance of the end-user link in the chain of technological development and diffusion, whilst one result may be an enhancement of citizens' ability to question and influence the nature of technological options with which they are faced.

Secondly, there appears to have been a growth in the number of projects where end-users define for themselves the uses to which IT could be put where they are recognised as innovators. Such projects tend to be small, run on tight budgets and local in nature, and probably the majority are initiated by the voluntary, community and municipal sectors. For those who fear that opportunities for experimentation and social innovation in IT are being stifled, these projects are welcome developments.

REFERENCES

1. Miles, Ian (1985) "Social Innovation and Information Technology", SPRU, University of Sussex, paper prepared for Nordic Summer School seminar on social innovation, Stockholm, December 1985.
2. Ancelin, Claire (1987) "The Dissemination of the New Information and Communication Technologies", this volume pp.45.
3. Qvortrup, Lars (Ed) (1985) Social Experiments with Information Technology in EEC Countries, Telematics Project, Odense University, CEC FAST Programme.
4. Hartley, Jill (1985) "An Overview of Social Experiments with Information Technology in the United Kingdom" in L. Qvortrup (Ed) (1985) op. cit. and Mothobi, Conway (1986) "The Experience of IT Centre 6502" ITEC 6502, Manchester, paper circulated at Odense, 13-15 January 1986.
5. Ancelin, Claire (1985) "Les Nouveaux Medias en France: Experimentation, Acculturation et Developpement Economique", in L. Qvortrup (Ed) (1985) op. cit.
6. Qvortrup, Lars (1985) "Social Experiments with Information Technology in Denmark", in L. Qvortrup (Ed) (1985) op. cit.
7. Briole, Alain (1987) "A Moment in the History of the New Communication Techniques: Social Experimentation 1980/1985", this volume pp. 53.
8. Frawley, Jim (1985) "Social Experiments with Information Technology in the Republic of Ireland" in L. Qvortrup (Ed) (1985) op. cit.

SOCIAL EXPERIMENTS WITH I.T.: SOCIAL BASIS, PILOT DEFINITION, FUTURE PERSPECTIVES

Lars Qvortrup, Telematics Project, Denmark

In this final article a number of concluding hypotheses, based on the above articles, are elaborated:

- *Even though many field trials with new information technology have been conducted in Europe under the designation of "Social Experiments with Information Technology" the concept is not well defined. A general classification is presented.*
- *In a historical perspective social experimentation is a reaction "from below" rather than the result of some plan imposed from above.*
- *Despite the current diversity, a pilote definition is relevant, emphasizing that social experimentation should be an action exerted by society on itself.*

Based upon an evaluation of future perspectives for social experiments the article argues for the further elaboration of "orgware architecture". Finally, seven recommendations for action are presented.

CURRENT STATUS OF SOCIAL EXPERIMENTS WITH INFORMATION TECHNOLOGY IN EUROPE

A General Classification of Social Experiments with I.T.

Since the beginning of the 1980s the concept of social experiments with I.T. has lent its name to a wide variety of social and commercial strategies, and even though the name has been the same, the various specific strategies have reflected very different societal interests and trends. A more precise analytical classification of current experiments with I.T. may be made on the basis of the fundamental distinctions among these societal interests which are outlined below.

Social Experiments: Governmental Planning Instruments

Social experiments with I.T. have been used by governments as tools for the planning of I.T. systems. The background has been a political will to strengthen the capacity of the society concerned for the development and full utilisation of the latent potential of new I.T. in a socially acceptable way.

On these terms, social experiments with I.T. have thus been considered as pilot projects, or, if you will, as model activities. If one selects a specific "social territory" and defines it as a "social laboratory", one can carry out very detailed research projects assessing the positive and negative consequences of the specific I.T. system and subsequently modify the model until it can be extended to the whole nation. This has been the philosophy behind a number of experiments in The Federal Republic of Germany, such as Bildschirmtext. Between 1980 and 1983 two pilot projects, with some 2,000 private and 1,000 commercial users each, were conducted in Berlin and Düsseldorf. These videotex projects gave rise to many scientific research projects whose object was to predict the consequences of - and the necessary regulations for - a nationwide application of the system under consideration.

The same general philosophy can be found in social experiments in, for example, France and Italy. In France a number of different videotex experiments have taken place since 1979, preparing the way for the present development of the Electronic Directory Service with the target of three million Minitel videotex terminals to be installed by the end of 1986; the well-known Biarritz experiment is a corresponding two-way broadband experiment, launched in preparation for the ambitious national cable plans in France. In Italy, several experiments within the National Public Health Service sector have been conducted with the aim of planning a national Health Information System.

Social Experiments: Instruments for Popular Social Movements

Social experiments with I.T. have also been used as tools for popular social movements. To some extent they are in fact a reaction to Nora and Minc's warning that the unregulated development of I.T. wil result in highly centralized networks and databases. It is, at all events, often pointed out that one cannot count on national governments to entrust unions, grassroots movements, new political parties and the like with the power that new I.T. gives them. Consequently, grassroots movements have considered themselves obliged to start computer organisations themselves in order to meet specific needs for information exchange and dissemination at the grassroots level. One such example in Denmark is "Folkedata", the People's Data Processing Organisation, and several comparable examples are to be found in the U.K., including the Community Information Project which was established in 1982 as a national resource centre for advisory and information organisations, and the Community Computing Network, whose membership is open to individual and non-profit-making organisations who provide computer services or advice to community associations, and voluntary and trade union groups. Another example in the U.K. might be the CODA project in Nottingham, which provides computer-based services for the trade unions, community groups and unemployed in the urban district concerned. In France, the Aspasie community project is a local resource centre aimed at providing I.T. services for citizens, local associations, educational groups, etc.

Social Experiments: A Service for Private Companies

Finally, social experiments with I.T. have been used as tools in private companies' interests. Many experiments have been initiated by - or for - suppliers of I.T. systems in order to test the efficiency of the technology or the demands for specific services under "realistic" social conditions, with a view to its eventual modification and refinement. The English Club 403 experiment provides us with one such example. Club 403 offers two main categories of services. The first provides traditional information; the second provides information which can lead to customer-response and mail-order shopping, banking, electronic mail facilities, etc. This trial is commercially oriented and represents a concerted effort by the government, through the Department of Trade and Industry, to enable TV equipment manufacturers and distributors, information providers, and British Telecom to investigate the residential market for interactive videotex services on the Prestel system.

Similar examples can be found in most European countries. In the Netherlands, for example, the VNU publishing company (supported by the
government) has launched the Ditzitel videotex experiment which is
designed to test new services with regard to their market value. In Belgium,
press groups and financial groups have been implicated in social
experiments. The press groups have taken a number of experimental
initiatives (in the fields of videotex and pay-TV), often involving local
private radio stations or R.T.L., the private broadcasting station in
Luxembourg. Strong financial interest groups have launched two competitive
telebanking experiments, "Bancontact" and the "Mister Cash" network.

The Current Diversity of Social Experiments

In France, social experimentation with telematics has been part of the
"official" national policy for five years. Still, it has never been satisfactorily
defined: the concept has been used to designate a vast number of heterogeneous activities. It has been used for practical tests of new information
technologies, and for the development of new services based on older
technologies; it has been used to cover activities with quite different actors:
national and local public institutions, national and local private organisations, etc.; the users involved in all these so-called social experiments
have played different roles, from "guinea pigs" to active and authoritative
participants, and they have represented different social categories - local
citizens, specific user-groups, professional users, etc.; furthermore, activities going under the name of social experiments have been organised in
many different ways; and finally the objectives of the various field trials
labelled as social experiments have been very heterogeneous: some have
tested some specific technology, others have mapped potential needs or
tested new services. This heterogeneity - which represents the situation in
other European countries as well - has led to much confusion both in relation
to public policy, and with regard to the exchanging of experiences within
national and international research fora, and as far as the pooling of
experimental qualifications has been concerned, as well. A more precise and
generally accepted pilot definition of the concept of social experiments
would thus be of considerable practical relevance.

THE SOCIAL BASIS OF SOCIAL EXPERIMENTS

In recent years we have been confronted with an astonishing variety of utopian theoretical writing, where Daniel Bell's The Coming of Post-Industrial Society, from 1973, and Alvin Toffler's The Third Wave, from 1980, are only two of the more popular examples. And similarly, as we have seen, we have been confronted with a corresponding variety of practical social experimentation, with different subjects, aims, modes of organisation, etc. In effect, however, what we have been confronted with is no more than a continuation of a long tradition of utopian thinking and experimentation in Europe which stretches back to the earliest days of modern history, and includes such projects as those described in Henri Saint-Simon's De la réorganisation de la société européenne (1814) and Charles Fourier's Le nouveau monde industriel et sociétaire (1829) - not to mention the utopian experiment made by Robert Owen at the turn of the 19th C., with his "New Lanark Community".

Positive utopian thinking and accompanying social experimentation are, indeed, recurrent features of modern European history - but the astonishing variety which has characterised such thinking and experimentation from the outset is indicative of the fact that social experimentation and its attendant utopian theory, are first and foremost reactions "from below", as it were, to specific phenomena in modern society, rather than the results of some abstract and centrally-coordinated plan imposed from above. The length and variety of the historical tradition suggests, in effect, that there are certain contradictions inherent in modern society which pose insoluble problems - problems which represent a recurrent challenge to human technological and organisational ingenuity, but which defy solution since they are of the very nature of modern society itself.

Rooted, thus, in societal phenomena, social experimentation - with or without I.T. - has to be defined from below, in terms of its societal roots, rather than from above, in terms of some initiating and regulating central body. For the purpose of definition the question of who initiates a social experiment is far less relevant than the question of why it was initiated; the question, in other words, of which specific existing societal contradictions gave rise to the need for a specific solution, which, in our time, may well involve the use of some highly developed technology. This in turn means, though, that an adequate pilot definition of social experiments with I.T. has to be sufficiently broadly based to be able to do justice both to the full variety of contemporary social experimentation and to its historical perspective.

The Scandinavian Telehouses: Realism and Anticipation

In our search for an adequate foundation on which to base a pilot definition of social experiments with information technology, the Scandinavian tele-houses would seem to be a good place to start. The material about them in this volume clearly illustrates that they are essentially ambivalent pheno-mena. On the one hand, they are reactive, in the sense that they are intended to avert certain socio-historically determined threats to sparsely populated rural districts in Scandinavia: they are to reduce above-average unemployment levels, mitigate the lack of public services, etc., etc. But, on the other hand, some of these telehouses are also proactive, in that they constitute attempts to realise "global village" scenario goals; they demon-strate that new information technology is not necessarily synonymous with private cultural consumption in affluent individual homes; and they demon-strate the possibility of distance work as a collective local community enterprise rather than an isolated private enterprise. In the most promising-ly innovative social experiments with Information and Community Services in Scandinavia, sober reactive realism goes hand in hand with anticipatory enthusiasm.

In effect, the experiments with these telehouses reflect the age-old pastoral opposition between "authenticity" and "progress", between what is considered "traditional", "natural" and "unsullied", and what is considered "rational" and more highly "civilised". On the one hand, homage is paid to "authenticity", in that the purpose of the telehouses is to "save" the villagers in sparsely populated rural districts from becoming what they would inevitably otherwise become - the victims of ruthless modernization and urbanization. In this sense the telehouses are based on a respect for the traditionally-rooted virtues of village life: the sense of community fellow-ship, of personal participative influence, security, and parochial pride, which stems from long familiarity with a bounded and readily comprehensible physical and sociocultural environment and its history. But, on the other hand, the telehouse experiments in themselves are the expressions of a strong belief in the ability of the newest and most highly-developed technology to ward off the worst threats to the continued existence of the isolated villages: jobs and public services are to be saved and furnished by means of highly sophisticated information technology.

Finally, too, the ambivalence of these telehouses extends to the fact that they endeavour to bridge the gap between the local microcosm and the national macrocosm, between what is of particular and what is of general relevance. Ongoing telehouse activities are essentially local community activities, sustained by local organizations and local interests. But these activities simultaneously have national, and international, interest in that they seek to demonstrate on an experimental basis the very general relevance of the solutions which telehouses could represent.

Social Experiments with I.T. in France

Continuing our quest for the societal roots of recent social experimentation with I.T. at a more general level, we could most profitably, in my view, turn our attention to the history of the present decade's social experimentation with I.T. in France. The early 'eighties saw a renaissance of the whole concept of social experimentation per se in France in the guise of "expérimentation social en télématique". At that time the designation referred to such R. and D. activities as the interactive videotex programmes known as Télétel 3V around Paris, CLAIRE in Grenoble, and TELEM-Nantes, as well as the integrated broadband network project in Biarritz. And at that time, not least in connection with the mobilisation of public opinion responsible for the Socialists' electoral victory on May 10th 1981, social experiments with I.T. aroused very high expectations. As Alain Briole's paper indicates, they were regarded by not a few people as potentially catalytic for a greater degree of openness and, in themselves, as being instruments of no little anticipative and generalizable significance. In themselves they were supposed to constitute open research fora, in which everything was openly said and understood by all the participants; in which future scenarios could be realised anticipatively; and whose local significance was potentially of national importance, since their results might become generally applied. Such expectations were clearly in line with late 20th C. utopian thought: one recalls, for instance, Jürgen Habermas' normative definition of communicative activity as "the kind of interaction in which all the participants bring their own individual proposed activity into harmony with that of all the others, in order thereafter to pursue their own illocutionary goals without further reservation" with the production of social rationality as the inevitable result (Jürgen Habermas 1981: 395). For a time, at the beginning of the present decade in France, social experiments with N.I.T. by some people were regarded as small, isolated, but realised utopias.

Expectations about the results of these experiments were equally high. In March 1982, the then Minister of Research and Technology, J.P. Chévènement, commissioned two researchers, Armand Mattelart and Yves Stourdzé, to draw up a report on the economic and industrial, and, above all, social and cultural issues related to the challenge of the information technological transformation of French society. The report, which was completed in September the same year, emphasized the importance of social experimentation. Quite rightly, in many places the authors were careful to modify the claim that social experiments with I.T. were some kind of patent remedy for all the problems arising from the introduction and assimilation of information technology within French society, but their generally undeniably optimistic expectations about social experiments clearly emerge in Mattelart's introduction to the English edition of the report:

"To carry out experiments on the socio-cultural acceptability of new technologies is to adapt technological supply to public demand, attempting to escape from "the logic of economic production" and promote democratic control over communications systems..." (Mattelart/Stourdzé 1985: 25)

Such expectations about the democratizing effect of social experimentation with I.T. soon gave way, however, to less exalted expectations. Mattelart himself went on to write that social experiments could also help to "avoid rejections and delays in the socialization of innovations by the market" (ibid), and this point was certainly not lost on those who were responsible for the ambitious programme for the modernization of the French telecommunications network, with their plans for a nationwide broadband cable network, for interactive videotex services, and for the universal introduction of the electronic telephone directory. Only a month after the appearance of the report, Louis Mexandeau, then France's P.T.T. Minister, emphasized the economic advantages of social experiments for launching new I.T. products onto the market, rather than any potentially democratizing effect the experiments might have. Social experiments should redress the deficiencies of traditional market surveys for the technology, he wrote, and they should permit easier supervision, control and analysis, thus reducing investment risks (see Louis Mexandeau: "Comment révéler les besoins" in Le Monde Oct. 17th, 1982).

Increasingly, since then, social experiments in France have unashamedly become mere market promotional tools furthering the centrally-planned "modernization" of French society. The development of new forms of social intercourse within local communities has been given low priority beside the desire to test new technology under purportedly "realistic" social conditions, with a view to legitimating it, and thus rapidly being able to sell more and more "hard" and "soft" technological products to potential users.

The tendency has brought social experiments in France into disrepute, and, in some cases, has even led to their termination or outright rejection. But it is, of course, not the experiments themselves which ought to be criticized, but political developments in France in recent years which have determined the content of a number of these experiments from above, as it were, in accordance with aims which are entirely incommensurate with the funda- mental essence of social experimentation per se. For true social experi- ments can never be ready-made solutions imposed from above, intended to solve essentially insoluble problems in contemporary society. On the contra- ry, true social experiments are rooted in such insoluble dilemmas and reflect them in themselves, just as the remaining but threatened social experiments so clearly do in France, and the essentially ambivalent telehouse experi- ments do in Scandinavia, and just as many other experiments do in other countries - as our entire body of material indicates. These essential conflicts - between democratization and efficiency, between traditional "authenticity" and modernization - can never be magically solved by social experiments; on the contrary, they constitute the social basis of social experiments, which thus serve as yet another arena for their familiar struggle.

Social Anticipation and Experimentation

"If we are to continue to exist, our task must be defined as the careful consideration, the anticipatory consideration of human beings as they are now in relation to their immediate, let alone their distant, future (...) This, however, is what makes it immeasurably pleasurable, and indeed something quite extraordinary, for human beings, who are constitutionally anticipative, to live in this present age". (Bloch 1982: 28)

True social experimentation is essentially anticipative, in a Blochian sense, and any definition of social anticipation has to start with a recognition of the fact that, in materialistic terms, anticipation is rooted in the need for something other than that which is already available. To lack something means that one feels a need for something, one wants a change, as it were. Yet, if this need is to be defined in concrete terms, and is to be persistently imagined and expressed, a necessary precondition must be satisfied: in principle, that which is so vividly and generally and persistently imagined must actually be attainable, at a given moment in history. Only when the feeling of lacking something has become a consequence of the prevalent modes of production at any given moment in history, instead of being a direct consequence of Nature's niggardliness, only then will human need be connected with anticipative social action; social experimentation is one such "anticipative action".

Social experiments, then, understood broadly as the agents of consciously and collectively-willed change, are socio-historically determined human needs for "something else", for some qualitatively new and alternative historical reality. In Bloch's terms, they constitute "heuristic models": "Every heuristic model is methodologically a 'thesis', and every thesis involving concrete anticipation refers to a concrete experimental model which participates in the creation of the world itself and its creatures" (Bloch 1977 [1965] : 88).

This explains how closely social experiments are bound up with the inherent and essentially insoluble value conflicts within modern society. For the desire for "authenticity", for instance, which often informs the ideology of rural social experiments with distance working, etc., has not arisen because the countryside has suddenly become prettier, or because parochial community-life has suddenly become less parochial. On the contrary, it has arisen because the modernization of our societies has become more and more urgent. Similarly, the growing interest in local community living, which is reflected in many social experiments with I.T., is the direct result of more and more centralized social planning, administration and control.

Such fundamental societal conflicts provide the parameters within which all true social experiments are situated, and the most realistic and self-aware experimenters know better than to opt for one or the other of the equally attractive, but potentially mutually exclusively, conflicting social values. For the luxury of "authenticity" is actually only enjoyable because our societies have been sufficiently modernized to render it desirable - just as increased political participation by our entire populations is only possible because our productive and administrative capabilities have become so efficient. Social experiments, as I pointed out in my previous section, cannot and will not resolve these essentially irreconcilable societal conflicts, but they can and do mitigate the worst disadvantages attendant on the blind pursuit of one apparently desirable goal at the expense of another which may be in direct conflict with it.

TOWARDS A PILOT DEFINITION OF THE CONCEPT OF SOCIAL EXPERIMENTS WITH INFORMATION TECHNOLOGY

In the preceding section I have sought to clarify the claim which I made at the outset of this paper that social experiments, in the truest sense of the term, are reactions "from below" to specific subjectively perceived deficiencies within the fabric of modern social life, rather than the results of some abstract and centrally-coordinated plan imposed from above. Yet the fact that social experiments are essentially rooted in specific societal phenomena does not preclude the possibility of a general definition, and in effect, as I mentioned earlier, the current diversity of social experiments with I.T. is so great that a generally accepted pilot definition of the concept would be of considerable practical relevance. Clearly however, such a definition must comprehensively embrace the social basis of these experiments if it is to be correct.

Social Experiments and Social and Technological Innovation: the Desirability of Normative Guide-lines

The practical relevance of a general definition of social experiments with I.T. in classificatory terms is readily appreciable if it is to be used retrospectively - i.e. if it is merely to be used as a tool for systematically organizing the wealth of material about specific social experiments which has become available to us in recent years, so that we may be able to make a comprehensive analysis and evaluation of it. The desirability of a normative or pilot definition is, however, less immediately comprehensible, but the following is intended to clarify the issue.

To start with, it is important fully to comprehend the vital intermediary role which social experiments with information technology play at the core of the interrelationship between social and information-technological innovation.

In his summary of the "Information Technology, Households and Communities" project under the E.E.C.'s FAST-programme, Ian Miles concluded that "I.T. is a revolutionary technology which is liable to be associated with significant changes in many areas of social life. The application of I.T. (...) will demand reactive changes in behaviour (...). (But) I.T. offers the potential for reorganisation of many established practices in a proactive way, too...". But Miles added a word of warning: "...without appropriate strategies for social innovation which take account of these proactive possibilities, new technologies will be posing serious questions for social justice and economic progress...". The "appropriate strategies" Miles referred to here could, of course, cover a variety of different traditional political strategies, but, in my opinion, social experimentation is one, very relevant, strategy for social innovation which can realise the proactive possibilities of new technology in ways that are equally compatible with the demands of social justice and (national) economic growth.

In essence, social experiments with information technology constitute an enactment at the micro-level of the ongoing dialectical relationship between social and information-technological innovation, with a view to influencing the society at large. Their declared aims may vary substantially. On the one hand, the aim may be a fairly modest and passive one, where trial services may be introduced within a statistically representative and scientifically observed local community so that "bugs" may be removed and guide-lines worked out for the planning and regulation of similar services on a larger (nation-wide) scale. The experiments with "Bildschirmtext" in West Germany provide a typical example of this. More ambitiously, the aim may be to involve socially-representative users more actively in the development of hardware, software and orgware, such that their influence is institutionalized, and they participate both in the technological R. and D. carried out in their midst within their own so-called "realistic social laboratory", and/or contribute to the realisation of the proactive potential of the technology for social innovation, with a view - in either or both cases - to the subsequent more general diffusion of the refined hardware or software and/or organizatorial experience. Some of our material on small-scale health sector experiments, undertaken with a view to the reorganization of health sector organizations generally, provides a very clear illustration of the latter. And finally, at the other end of the scale, the aim may be that the social experiment itself, rather than any "results" it may come up with, is intended to influence the surrounding society. One thinks of the show-case type of experiment, which allows the public at large to make the acquaintance of new technology; or the demonstration-type experiment which allows a number of users in a realistic, but carefully monitored, social context to "learn by doing"; or the experiment which is quite simply intended to legitimate the introduction of new I.T. or telematics services over the heads of potential users.

Yet, whatever the declared purpose of the social experiment with I.T. - whether the aim is passively to observe the social effects of the introduction of new technology, or, more actively, to influence various technological or social processes, it would appear that, as I said earlier, social experiments with information technology constitute a microcosmic enactment of the ongoing dialectical relationship between social and information-technological innovation, with a view to influencing the society at large. I choose the word "enactment" advisedly, since what seems to be happening in these experiments is clearly a consciously initiated, observed, and influenced - though essentially creative and improvised - exploration, on a miniature scale, of something which is unreflectedly taking place more and more often on a larger scale.

Since this is the case, the desirability of a normative pilot definition of social experiments with I.T. becomes all the more apparent if we apply a linguistic metaphor, and regard the social experiment with I.T. as a particular kind of "speech act", which, if it is successful, must satisfy the following two requirements:

1. Syntactic rules must obtain for the participants; - in relation to the social experiment with I.T., one thinks in particular of the ways in which a dialogue between social and technological innovation factors must be established.

2. For the speech act to be demonstrative, certain rules must obtain regarding its relationship to its illocutionary context; in terms of the social experiment with I.T., certain requirements would have to be met which would institutionalize the influence of the experiment on the society at large.

The FAST Programme's project on social experiments has worked out an operational definition of social experiments with information technology which is normative in precisely the same way as syntactic rules are normative for successful speech acts: in itself, the definition seeks to define the conditions whose fulfilment is necessary a) if technological innovation is to be the catalyst of democratic social innovation on a microcosmic scale, and b) if the resultant technological and social improvements are to be extended to the surrounding society at large.

In linguistic terms, conditions whose fulfilment is necessary if a speech act is to be felicitous are traditionally referred to as "rules". But with regard to our normative definition of social experiments with I.T. we have preferred to use the term "guidelines", since we have no desire to stifle the creative and independent growth of specific social experiments. We do, however, hope very much that our guidelines will become generally operational, since they will facilitate research cooperation between the various different researchers and coordinators, so that experience may more easily be exchanged with regard to comparable aspects of the different experiments, with obvious advantages for comparative research and to the exclusion of unproductive confusion and misunderstandings, which the abundance of disparate material today may so easily give rise to.

An Operational Definition of Social Experiments with I.T.

Social experiments may usefully be defined if we start with a conception of them as specific forms of implementation of new information technology.

Generally speaking, any implementation of new I.T. is a kind of transformation process involving two variables: human users, on the one hand, and the specific I.T. system under consideration, on the other. The human users will undergo a change (be it positive or negative) effected by changes in their employment or general social conditions - changes involving a demand for new qualifications, necessitating educational and re-training activities, awareness and acceptance campaigns, etc. And the I.T. systems will undergo changes effected by the demands placed on them for modified hardware (demands for improved telecommunications networks, improved display units, keyboards, etc.), and for modified software (demands for improved accessible information, improved search structures, file organisation, format, etc.).

The really decisive question then becomes: what is the primary aim of the implementation process? Is it the production of new technology or is it the production of new forms of social organisation? In the former case, it would clearly be a misconception to describe the experiment as a "social" one, in any immediate or generally accepted sense of the word.

A further decisive question is: who is the primary subject in the implementation process concerned? Is it a hardware or software manufacturer (representing the "interests" of the information technology under consideration)? Is it a third party (for example an organisation or public authority offering information services)? Or is it the users involved in, or affected by, the development of the I.T. system concerned? Depending on the answer to this question, it becomes neccessary to distinguish strictly between two types of social experiments with I.T.: "participatory workshops" (in which the users are the primary subjects), and "social laboratories" (in which manufacturers or third parties are the primary subjects).

The proposed normative definition of the concept of social experiments with information technology thus becomes the following:

Social experiments with information technology are specific forms of implementation of I.T.

- in which the primary aim is to establish new forms of social organisation using information technology;
- in which the activities and the resulting socio-technical products can be used as models for a more widespread - though necessarily contextually-modified - implementation of similar I.T. systems;
- and in which, to this latter end, independent researchers describe and evaluate the implementation process concerned and its results.

Social experiments qualify as "participatory workshops" if all the parties involved in, or influenced by, the development of the I.T. system concerned, participate on an equal footing in decision-making with regard to the social organisation and application of the I.T. system in question. If not - that is if the main subject is a hardware or software manufacturer or a third party - the social experiment may more appropriately be designated a "social laboratory".

FUTURE PERSPECTIVES FOR SOCIAL EXPERIMENTS WITH INFORMATION TECHNOLOGY

The Myth of Information Technology

As I made clear in the earlier sections of this paper, the normative definition of social experiments with I.T. is a synthesis constructed on the basis of a vast number of individual analyses of social experiments with I.T. in relation to their socio-historical contexts. If the driving-force behind the socio-political development of modern society derives from ongoing conflicts between irreconcilable but essentially mutually dependent social ideals - progress/authenticity; efficient, centrally-coordinated administration/personal political influence; the cynical pursuit of profit/concern for the individual; etc. - social experiments have derived their own developmental energy from the same source, and they allow the conflicts full rein within their own limited spheres: they represent, in effect, miniature political battlegrounds - arenas within which political ideas are tested in practice.

The renaissance of social experimentation at the beginning of the present decade was naturally not unconnected with the general upsurge of grassroots movements which were born out of opposition to the increasingly blatantly economic concerns which characterized the political leadership of a Europe plagued by recession. But social experiments specifically with information technology were to a large extent also fuelled by the specific characteristics of the technology itself. While much of modern technology otherwise seems to be unambiguously in the service of materialistic progress, information technology, by contrast, seemed to hold out the promise of reconciling ideals of economic growth and bureaucratic efficiency with the other - more appealingly humane - side of the coin. The "global village" concept, or the concept of "ingenious and infinitely flexible technology", were essentially paradoxical: they seemed to reconcile, through the special "magical" properties of the technology itself, such antinomial oppositions as that between the local and the global, or between individual concern and social efficiency, etc. Alvin Toffler's Third Wave provided the clarion call to usher us into the new global utopia of "information societies", while social experiments with I.T. seemed to constitute corresponding utopias at the local level, areas where communication was free and untrammelled by considerations of political economy.

The Need for "Future Workshops"

Not many of these illusions remain, but there is still a need for "future workshops" with I.T. - for processes and institutions within which potential suppliers and users of I.T. can exchange views and explore the potentially useful and felicitous options which the technology comprises. For it is in this sense that social experiments with I.T. constitute strategies for mediating the dialectical interrelationship between social and technological innovation. Generally, still, social experiments with I.T. exhibit a tendency to alter the balance of traditional power relationships in the direction of decreased influence for suppliers, technicians and armchair planners, and increased influence for potential users, social researchers and ordinary citizens. Thus, social experiments are clearly distinct from the traditional political and economic new-technology-strategies of the market, or central government, which tend to be out of touch with the subjectively perceived needs and interests of the man in the street, insofar as these are not based on any comparable fully-participative experimental activity.

The success of social experiments with I.T. is, however, dependent on two essential factors. In the first place, there must be wide scope for non-technologically-determined social experimentation. Many studies - and our own body of material - have indicated that a simple cause-effect relationship between the introduction of new technology and social change is impossible to uphold. The technological determinist fallacy is, for example, clearly apparent in studies on office automation, where the introduction of new information technology has certainly led to a rationalization of traditional work processes, but other results have included entirely unforeseeable qualitative changes in the nature and organization of the information work undertaken by the office itself. In this respect, Ian Miles very aptly concludes his report on the FAST-programme project which investigated the relationship between social and technological innovation by saying that "to some extent the balance between the two may be influenced by prior technological developments (eg. the establishment of a new infrastructure), but there is always more than an element of strategic choice available". (Ian Miles, p.14 - my emphasis).

The second essential precondition for the success of social experiments with I.T. on the national or international level is a large degree of political respect and goodwill on the part of central governments and their advisory bodies. Without a national and/or international political commitment to respect, and abide by, the results of social experiments with I.T., their valuable demonstrative function will be betrayed, and, at worst, they may become mere tools for legitimating the socially inexpedient introduction of new technology over the heads of its potential victims.

The Contradictory European Context for Social Experiments

The large body of evidence which has been made available to the project on social experiments with I.T. corroborates the hypothesis that Europe, with its advanced social structures, constitutes a very promising environment for the development of socially advanced information systems and for hosting social experiments.

The succesful development of socially-advanced I.T. systems presupposes a societal context consisting of purposively democratic political and cultural institutions, together with widespread public expectations about the desirability of the existence of such institutions. This is because the technological development of any social system involving information technology is inseparably bound up with the social attitudes and expectations surrounding the project concerned. Thus, as we have defined them, 'socially-advanced' I.T. systems, facilitating democratic exchange and dissemination of information among the citizens of any modern society, will be much more readily attainable on the basis of an already well-established tradition for the democratic exchange and dissemination of information. Obviously, for instance, socially advanced I.T. systems enhancing the efficiency of public libraries are inconceivable without the prior existence of a comprehensive network of well-stocked public libraries throughout the society concerned, as well as an already very high degree of literacy among the population concerned. And if we take videotex systems, as another example, valuable prerequisites for the development of socially-advanced systems include, on the one hand, the prior existence of a large number of potential, and already efficiently functioning, information suppliers, and, on the other hand, a population which already has a high degree of education and experience in information searching and retrieval, as well as having general expectations about the desirability of the provision of such services.

On the other hand the development in Europe of socially-advanced I.T. systems has - in a number of glaring instances - been aborted because political institutions and suppliers, marketers, and buyers of I.T. products have accepted or even invested in I.T. systems without seriously informed concern as to the specific nature of their social potential. For it is an undeniable, though regrettable, fact that I.T. products and systems which are currently available are, from a psychological and sociological point of view, frequently very primitive, requiring substantial and imaginative modification if they are ever to become in reality the truly socially advanced instruments of information processing and communication which they are mistakenly supposed already to be.

All too often in our material we have been confronted with instances in which the introduction of I.T. systems in Europe has been purely 'supply-driven', as it were. Statements such as - 'We can't afford not to buy what's on offer', or - 'It will come anyway, so we might as well invest in it now' - are paraphases of all-too-common attitudes towards the new technology, indicative of wide-spread defeatism. Statements such as - 'What can we as citizens use this technology for?', or - 'How can we civilise this technology, so that it may enhance rather than diminish our existing democracies?' - are political and cultural, rather than primitively economic, considerations, which are much more in harmony with our democratic tradition, and which can - if we are sufficiently far-sighted - be strengthened, by the coordinated modification and refinement of I.T. and telematics systems.

Three Specific Aims for Social Experiments with I.T.

Generally speaking, the aim of social experiments with information technology is to establish processes (social laboratories or social workshops) in which society as a whole (and not just directly involved hardware, software, and marketing companies) can benefit from the potentialities of new information technology.

More specifically, there are three overriding reasons which make social experiments urgently desirable at the present time.

The first relates to the necessity for the democratization of decision-making in the realm of I.T. An unfortunate syndrome - an 'expert-syndrome' - has been developing in this area, with software and hardware consultants and engineers visiting various organisations to offer them patent remedies long before the users concerned - or even the so-called 'experts' themselves, for that matter - have managed to identify the problems which really need to be remedied. If, on the other hand, one starts with an analysis of the network of relationships which constitutes the various organisations, one is in a position to identify problems and needs before suggesting any (possibly very costly) remedies. In this way, the needs, the experience, and the visions, of the users involved become the basis for any remedial proposals - irrespective of whether they actually involve some form of I.T. or not. And, in this way, decision-making relating to I.T. may be democratized.

The second reason concerns the necessity for sound rational planning. An approach offering ready-made solutions before any problems have been identified will almost always turn out to be synonymous with bad planning. In some cases, for example, a solution involving I.T. is chosen for problems which might be much better solved without I.T. This is true, for example, in the teaching field, where the real problems are frequently of a pedagogical or organisational nature (badly prepared teaching materials, projects and presentations, or too few teachers, for instance), and where the most which any CAT or CAL equipment can achieve is often no more than a temporary distraction of pupils' and teachers' attention from the real problems involved. At the present time, state education in Denmark abounds with disheartening examples of seriously mistaken I.T. investment of this kind.

The third reason concerns the real content and quality of organisational solutions. In their book Zukunftswerkstätten, Wege zur Wiederbelebung der Demokratie, Robert Jungk and Norbert Müllert claim that our age is characterised by the fact that the number of technological inventions greatly exceeds the number of social inventions. Multifarious ways and means of producing technical products have been developed, but the number of innovations concerning human intercourse and societal institutions is incredibly small. We lack 'social inventions'.

Inventions, however, of whatever kind, have never simply been a matter of purely accidental insight. And today, far from being abandoned to chance, truly productive insights are carefully incubated and nurtured. The decisive question becomes, then, the question of how best one can incubate and foster an increasing number of social inventions. It is a question which is precisely what social experiments with I.T. are intended to answer, in that they provide us with the necessary institutional framework - the necessary ways and means for making 'social inventions', or, more precisely, 'organisational products', within a realm whose new forms are on the brink of creation - entailing far-reaching changes to the status quo - under the impact of, and through the mediation of new information technology.

THE CONCEPT OF ORGWARE

Perhaps the most important results of social experiments with information technology to date have been the contributions they have made to our growing understanding of what exactly information technology is, and the ways in which they have enhanced our insights into the relationship between social and information-technological innovation. Practical experience from a large number of social experiments with I.T. has indicated that the connection between social and technological invention and innovation is much closer than traditionally supposed, and changes in social organization have direct influence on the nature of appropriate technical systems and structures. Such empirical observations have given rise to much fruitful speculation about what, in principle, are the specific properties or distinctive features of I.T. as a practical tool.

I.T. as a Social Tool

A tool may be defined as an instrument which influences a chosen object in accordance with some particular human will. In order to be able to influence the chosen object, the tool must in itself transform the human will into a mode which is "understood" by the object - in linguistic terms, one might say that the tool is a translation of human will into the language of the chosen object.

Most tools are designed for working on natural objects, whether animate or inanimate. Such tools speak, as it were, the language of physical, chemical or biological nature, and their creation is premissed on the entire historical project of the natural sciences, which have to date so successfully discovered the inmost languages of so many animate and inanimate objects, from atomic structure to the structure of D.N.A. But information-technological tools are not used for working on natural objects, but on symbols, which they store, or manipulate, or transfer from place to place: their objects, in other words, are human products and human relations. Thus, where traditional tools have been essentially physical tools, information-technological tools might more appropriately be designated social tools. And one consequence of this essential difference - which is perhaps the most significant consequence of all - is that the humanities and the social sciences, rather than the natural sciences, are by far the most important bodies of knowledge when it comes to forging such tools.

The Relationship between I.T. and Society

The above realisation has, in turn, a large number of other fundamental consequences for the production and evaluation of information-techno-logical tools: one thinks, for example, of the ways in which traditional research boundaries have to be redefined - of the ways in which electronics engineers and mathematicians have to work closely with sociologists and linguists - if I.T. products are ever to become successfully marketable on the widest possible scale. Suffice it to say here, within the present context, that the most far-reaching consequence for Europe generally is the fact that our entire notion of the relationship between technology and society is called into question and has to be redefined.

Traditionally, it has notionally been possible to operate on the assumption of a clear distinction between technology, on the one hand, and society, on the other. With information technology this is no longer possible. If, for example, we take the case of a library, we can ask ourselves whether it is a social institution or a system of information-technological tools, for the storage, retrieval and distribution of information. In some senses, of course, there can be no doubt that a library is a social institution: it is at once the incarnation of a specific society's mode of monopolizing and/or distributing information, and it constitutes a microcosmic network of hierarchical social relationships. But the way in which these institutional features are incarnat-ed involves information-technological tools: the institutionalized human will becomes manifest, as it were, in and through the "language" in accordance with which these specific information-technological tools have been con-structed - and this fact becomes all the more obvious when traditional information-technological tools are supplanted by new information-techno-logical tools (the file system, and the helpful librarian, by the computer terminal with the "helpful" search procedures, etc.). The library as a system of information-technological tools thus consists of a large number of individual information-technological tools, ancient and modern, which to-gether constitute a "translation" of the library itself as a social institution.

Orgware

Potentially valuable consequential insights of this kind have been derived

from recent years' intensive work on the production of systems of information-technological tools - not least as the result of social experiments with
I.T., which have actually functioned in many cases as practical workshops
for the production and development of such I.T. socio-systems. For future
purposes, I would like to recommend that such systems be denoted by the
term "orgware", so that the creation of such socially advanced systems of
information-technological tools, on the basis of a dialogue between sociological and technological expertise, would be denoted by the term "orgware
architecture".

Hardware, Software - and Orgware

Metaphorically speaking, the majority of I.T. projects resemble an iceberg
with three different layers. The topmost layer, visible above the water-line,
consists of machines and cables: computers of various different makes and
kinds, interlinked with coil upon controversial coil of optical or coaxial
cable. This, in other words, is the hardware layer.

Lower down, on the next layer, are located the invisible archives known as
'databases' and 'memories'; the invisible flows of data; and the invisible
instructions controlling such flows. This, in other words, is the software
layer.

And at the bottom we have the weightiest, the most extensive, the most
intractable layer - the organisational layer. Today it remains the most
invisible, the least accounted layer of all. Anybody can give you a selection
of 'big' names in hardware. Many people are familiar with the details of
high-definition VDUs, of RAM capacities, of different kinds of floppies,
etc., etc. And many more people are capable of discussing the advantages
and disadvantages of the various word-processing, accountancy, CAL or
CAT or computer games programmes available on the market. But in
contrast to all this, they know remarkably little about the organisation of
I.T. systems, either on the theoretical or the practical level. The lowest, the
most covert, and yet the most significant layer of the I.T. system's 'iceberg'
is constituted by the social organisation of the system: this, in other words,
is the 'orgware' layer.

Orgware Architecture

When one wants to build a modestly sized, modestly priced, and unpretentious dwelling, or even just make alterations to, or repair, an existing building, one calls upon the services of a brick-layer. The latter knows how to build walls so that they stay up. The brick-layer is familiar with the physics of the individual components in the building process.

If one's project is a bit larger, one will probably have to get hold of an engineer - someone who is familiar with the physics of buildings in toto. The engineer knows what spans are permissible, and which materials one must use.

But, if the building is as large as this, one usually calls in the services of an architect, too. An architect is familiar first and foremost with the functions of buildings. What is the building to be used for, and what are the wishes and desires of its users? Questions like these form the necessary basis for designing buildings which are pleasing and appropriate to their users. So the architect's qualifications include a not inconsiderable amount of knowledge about the æsthetics of architecture and the behaviour of the users of the various kinds of buildings, as well as sufficient knowledge about structural physics and the physics of individual building materials to ensure that the drawings are realistic and the demands made on both the brick-layer and the engineer are feasible.

Precisely the same situation obtains - or ought to obtain - within the realm of information technology.

At the top of our pyramid - or iceberg, as we have called it - we have the engineers; those who know something about the technicalities of computers and data transmitting equipment. Beneath them we have the systems planners, the programmers and the software consultants; those who know how databases can be constructed, and how the processing and flows of data may be regulated.

At the bottom (at the most fundamental level) we have - or ought to have - orgware architects.

Orgware architecture can formally be defined as a field of scientific sociology. Its objects of study are the ways in which electronic systems and social organisations are (or might desirably become) interlaced, together with the art itself of such rational and socially beneficial interlacement - the generation, in other words, of what we have called advanced orgware systems. It is concerned with applying the methods and models of sociology to the design and implementation of electronic systems for use by human beings.

More broadly speaking, orgware architects are the ones who can analyse forms of social organisation and, together with potential users, can define desirable future functions for the organisations concerned, and can plan with them the necessary organisational changes to be effected in accordance with these proposed new functions. In other words, orgware architects know a lot about information processing and exchange as processes taking place within and between the minds of human beings; they know, that is, about the human faculties of perception, cognition and interaction. They know, too, a lot about social organisations as the more or less makeshift institutionalisations of these human faculties. And they know enough about hardware and software too, of course, to be thoroughly familiar with their different capabilities, so that they can elaborate plans for proposed systems with sufficient precision to enable the hardware and software experts to get on with the job.

RECOMMENDATIONS FOR ACTION

Based upon the experiences, the analyses and the evaluations of social experiments with information technology in the European community, and in accordance with the proposed, normative definition of social experiments the project on social experiments with I.T. has proposed the following recommendations for action. They relate to three different areas: recommendations regarding the specific organisation of social experiments with I.T.; recommendations regarding national or international action in relation to social experiments; and recommendations regarding research and development activities in relation to social experiments with I.T.

**Recommendations Regarding the Specific Organisation of
Social Experiments with I.T.**

1. The concept of social experiments presupposes a dialectical relationship between technology and society, as we saw in the section on 'orgware' above. Therefore a close collaboration between social and technological expertise is very much to be recommended. In addition to this, the relative allocation of priority between social and technological expertise in social experiments should be changed in regard to today's situation, where technicians design the systems and sociologists assess the consequences. When building a house the architect comes before the engineer. Correspondingly, in social experiments, when building information and communications systems, the social design should precede the technical design.

2. Social experiments should be organised as mutual learning processes, ensuring that the needs of society and the specific individuals concerned influence directly, and at an early stage, developments in new information technology. With regard to the practical use and organisation of new technology, the end-users are very often experts, as they possess a vast amount of everyday experience related to the opportunities bound up with - and the possible consequences of - the new technology concerned. This means that social experiments should be organised as mutual learning processes, thus enabling the end-users to use them as tools for generating social inventions.

**Recommendations Regarding National or International
Action in Relation to Social Experiments with I.T.**

3. We have seen in a number of cases that parties involved in social experiments all too often fail to exchange experiences; for instance, our accounts of experiments with interactive videotex illustrate the fact that the same faults have been repeated in almost every European country. One positive example, on the other hand, is the dissemination of so-called Information and Community Service Centres in Scandinavian countries, or ITEC centres in the U.K. For these reasons, we recommend that a European documentary network should be established, permitting participants in social experiments with I.T. to pool their multifarious knowledge and experience.

The basic elements might be a documentary data-base, and a number of informal newsletters within specific fields of experimentation, concerning rural-area experiments, health-care sector experiments, social sector experiments, etc.

4. Many of the potentially most socially beneficial experiments are informal experiments at the grass-roots level. However, they often suffer from financial problems. This means that it is important to give such experiments public support - with no strings attached, of course.

5. Quite often, social experiments have been activities isolated from the general public planning process. This means that their immediate influence has been limited, and they may even have functioned as token activities, legitimating laisser faire government policy. A number of the videotex experiments have exemplified this problem. We therefore recommend that social experiments be integrated into general public planning concerning the adoption of new I.T. - partly as a pioneer element in the planning of informational infrastructures, and partly as a means of determining minimum standards of service for potential users of I.T. systems. To strengthen the influence of social experiments we recommend

- that social experiments be evaluated by independent researchers employed by public research institutions or national research councils
- that social experiments be promoted by public bodies (for example technology assessment bodies)
- that European institutions set up a mission promoting social experiments on a bi- and multinational basis within the Community in fields likely to be most profoundly affected by new information technology.

Recommendations Regarding Research and Development Activities in Relation to Social Experiments with I.T.

6. In the field of new information technology the European Community has in many cases arrived too late on the scene to take the lead. However, high quality with regard to integration of the human and social factors in electronic information and communications systems is becoming still more important both for the internal dissemination of this new technology, and for external market competitiveness. Furthermore, a social context of

already-existing, high-quality social institutions, and a research context of high-quality social science are two preconditions both to be found in Europe. We therefore recommend that research should be stimulated in the areas of social experimentation and of the social design of information systems.

7. One of the most important results of the various social experiments with I.T. is that they have expressed a growing awareness of the social-design aspect of I.T. systems. The imaginative exploration and the potential modification of socio-organisational systems forming the basis for I.T. systems are of great importance. It is thus an important future task to further develop and refine the theoretical and methodological competence arising from all the ongoing social experiments with I.T., which is the reason for our elaboration of the concept of 'orgware' above. We therefore recommend that a permanent interdisciplinary orgware workshop be established, permitting researchers in Europe to analyse and elaborate the concept of orgware architecture, and to evaluate the potential social and economic relevance of orgware architecture activity and of social experiments with information technology generally. Its aim should be to provide the Commission of the European Economic Communities with a sound and comprehensive basis for evaluating the potential usefulness of stimulating orgware research generally. Furthermore, the workshop should consider the desirability of eventually establishing a European Centre for systematic interdisciplinary pure and applied research in orgware architecture.

LITERATURE

This concluding article has been based upon the large body of evidence and the articles made available to the FAST Programme's project on social experiments with I.T. In addition, the article reproduces sections and arguments from the so-called "Executive Summary" on social experiments which I have written together with Claire Ancelin, Jim Frawley, Jill Hartley, François Pichault and Peter Pop.

Bloch, Ernst (1977), Tübinger Einleitung in die Philosophie. Gesamtausgabe vol. 13, Frankfurt a.M. Original version: 1965.
Bloch, Ernst (1982), " Anticiperet realitet - hvad er utopisk tænkning, og

hvad kan den?" In: J.E. Andersen et al. (eds.): Ernst Bloch - en introduktion. Aarhus.

Habermas, Jürgen (1981), Theorie des kommunikativen Handelns, Band I-II, Frankfurt a.M.

Jungk, Robert und Norbert Müllert (1981), Zukunftswerkstätten, Wege zur Wiederbelebung der Demokratie, Hamburg.

Mattelart, Armand et Yves Stourdzé (1982), Mission technologie, diffusion de la culture et communication: Note de synthese, Paris. English translation, 1985.

Miles, Ian (1985), "Social Innovation and Information Technology". Paper presented for the Nordic Summer University.

Name Index

Subject Index